$15.
'3

Hostile Action: The KGB and Secret Soviet Operations in Britain

By the same author

Revolutionaries in Modern Britain
Editor, *The Guardian Directory of Pressure Groups* and *The Directory
    of Pressure Groups*, 2nd Edition
The Militant Tendency: Trotskyism in the Labour Party

HOSTILE ACTION

The KGB and Secret Soviet Operations in Britain

Peter Shipley

PINTER PUBLISHERS, LONDON
in association with John Spiers

First published in Great Britain by
Pinter Publishers Limited
in association with John Spiers
25 Floral Street, London WC2E 9DS

British Library Cataloguing in Publication Data

A CIP catalogue record for this book is available
from the British Library

ISBN 0-87187-007-7

First published 1989

Photoset in North Wales by
Derek Doyle & Associates, Mold, Clwyd.
Printed and bound in Great Britain by
Billing and Sons Ltd, Worcester

Contents

Preface

This book sets out to draw a new map across some familiar territory and to explore some hidden and forgotten quarters. The shelves are bulging with all manner of books about spies and spying: investigative, biographical and historical. Most are about people who spied for Russia, or the people who were supposed to catch them. Increasingly, there is greater emphasis on case studies, or on particular topics or periods. This is inevitable as more material is discovered and the field becomes more specialised. But in the process the sight of some wider themes is lost.

It is my intention to address one of those themes: the use and development by the Soviet Union over the past seventy years of covert measures directed against Britain. Soviet persistence in deploying its secret services inside Britain has been remarkable. But, for a number of reasons, there have been few attempts to form an appreciation of the totality of clandestine Soviet activity in a general, historical survey. Some writers appear to take it for granted and leave it there. There are many practical difficulties in undertaking such a study: there is a shortage of source material from the Soviet side, and it is easier for an Englishman to indulge in his national obsession by writing about the idiosyncrasies of his own social system and the incompetence of his own goverments.

The examples which break through the fogs of secrecy and deception often appear as isolated fragments in a private game. My aim has been to reconstruct those fragments and to set them in a broader context. This entails asking some basic questions about the Soviet Union's aims and objectives, the place of clandestine methods in Soviet strategy, how these methods have been put into effect, their extent and variety – what they comprise besides espionage – and how they have evolved and what results they have achieved.

With these questions, and the limitations, in mind I have explored two secondary themes: first to consider British experiences and British perceptions of secret Soviet activity, mainly through official papers and government archives. The Public Record Office contains scatterings of valuable historical material in this respect, mostly in Cabinet papers and Foreign Office files, among which are items from the Special Branch, MI5 and the wartime Security Executive. These items add to the existing knowledge of the character and scale of Soviet operations, and give an indication of what the British government knew at any particular time and what it did about it. The actions of the British authorities are relevant to the main theme in the effect they had on the Soviet Union's capacity to mount certain types of activity; each British countermove has itself been countered by a new phase of Soviet action.

Secondly, I have consulted the secondary literature about espionage matters, to look at it in the light of my main interest in the aims and methods of the KGB and its predecessors. This literature is vast and still expanding, and some of it is pioneering and indispensable. I have made reference throughout to works which give the historical background, and especially to those which provide fuller material on individual cases than I have been able to or indeed wished to include in such a brief survey.

There is a good deal in books which are primarily concerned with British intelligence or British subjects, about Soviet spy controllers and how they carried out their operations. There are, however, many differences of fact and interpretation between them. This is particularly true of the 1930s. Who, for example, of a dozen people whose names appear in various books, recruited and controlled Kim Philby before the war? The lack of a consensus among specialists on some fundamental aspects of covert Soviet activity convinced me more than anything that a different approach, beginning by asking questions about Soviet objectives rather than British responses, was worthwhile and would open up new avenues of enquiry. The results of this approach also give a fresh perspective on some well-known cases: many of the spy trials which usually feature as British scandals of the 1960s, have their roots in Soviet initiatives of the 1950s and in a history of Soviet intelligence, belong in the circumstances of the earlier period rather than the later one.

Some of the numerous problems which exist in this field have been further complicated – rather than solved – in a number of books which were published towards the end of 1988. I regret that as my own manuscript was at an advanced state of preparation I was unable to take them into account. There is for example, in John Costello's substantial work, *The Mask of Treachery*, a new name for the 'mole' in MI5: Guy Liddell, Deputy Director-General of the Security Service from 1947–52. Mr Costello itemises twenty reasons why he believes Liddell was a Soviet spy. Ten of them correspond to the explanations offered by Chapman Pincher as to why Roger Hollis was a traitor. Both writers use some of the same material and make similar allegations to reach different conclusions. This is perhaps unavoidable when two experienced investigators cover the same ground. The additional 'charges' which are relevant only to one or the other do not in my view clinch either case. It is my belief that we do not yet know, and may never know, the truth. Perhaps one man who could tell us, Mr Gorbachev, might open this corner of the Kremlin's files in the interests of historical truth and glasnost.

The bulk of Mr Costello's new documentation comes from MI5 papers in American archives. There are, however, in these pages some examples of Liddell's work which are openly available in Britain. These and other documents show that British awareness of secret Soviet cells before the war, including those at Cambridge, reached more widely and further back than had previously been supposed.

I would like to thank John Spiers for all the help and encouragement he has given me. I am also grateful to Clive Rose, Bill Gutteridge, Hugh Thomas and former members of the security and secret intelligence services for their advice; my thanks to Pieter van Nek, Barbara Rochester and Jayne Cahill for their help with foreign material, to Sir William van Straubenzee and to friends and colleagues who lent me books or drew articles to my attention. I am also grateful to the staffs of the the Public Record Office, Kew, the British Library, Guildhall Library, Westminster Central Library, the United States Information Service Library, the Institute for the Study of Conflict and the Institute for the Study of Terrorism. I should further like to thank the Controller of Her Majesty's Stationery Office for permission to reproduce Crown copyright material in the Public Record Office. Above all I would like to thank my wife, whose patience and support enabled me to complete the research and writing.

All the products of research, the conclusions, the views expressed, and any errors, are entirely my own responsibility.

Peter Shipley
January 1989

1 A 'Swarm of Intriguers'

'A PUSH ON THE WEST'

In the earliest days of the Soviet regime the leaders of the Bolshevik revolution viewed Britain with a mixture of fear, suspicion, and hope. As the birthplace of modern capitalism and the heartland of a colonial Empire, Britain and her bourgeois institutions represented everything they loathed. But behind the façade of imperial splendour the Bolsheviks detected signs of rottenness and decline. British industrial pre-eminence was already a thing of the past and the war had exacted a further toll in men and morale. The social unrest which had engulfed Russia to remove the Tsar in March 1917 was now sweeping across the whole of a war-weary continent. The Bolsheviks believed Britain, too, might not escape the wrath of the discontented masses. In January 1918, two months after they had seized power in Russia, Georgi Chicerin told the All-Russian Congress of Soviets that 'the cause of English imperialism is near to bankruptcy', and added that 'in the very nearest future the fire of revolution will seize the English people also'.[1]

Chicerin, a nephew of a former Mayor of Moscow, who until 1904 had worked in the tsarist Foreign Ministry, spoke with bitter feeling: just three weeks earlier he had been released from an English gaol, where he had been interned since the end of the summer with another Russian revolutionary, Peter Petrov, for anti-war activity. His extravagant prediction did his standing in the Bolshevik hierarchy no harm, for within two months he succeeded Trotsky as the People's Commissar for Foreign Affairs.

His words summed up the expectations of the early rulers of Soviet Russia for Britain as for the whole of Europe. But first the war must come to an end. On the day after the Bolshevik coup of November 1917 Lenin announced the proclamation of a decree on peace. In the name of the Workers' and Peasants' government it appealed 'to all the belligerent peoples and to their governments to begin immediately negotiations for a just and democratic peace.'[2] The decree proposed an immediate armistice leading in three months' time to a settlement without annexations or indemnities, a conclusion which would be guaranteed by the abolition of secret diplomacy.

Hand in hand with the cry for peace went a call for revolt. The decree was directed towards the factories and the trenches as much as the chancelleries of Europe. Lenin hailed the historical achievements of the workers of France. England and Germany were lauded as 'models of proletarian heroism', and he hoped revolution would soon break out in all the belligerent countries.[3] In those early days of revolutionary enthusiasm Trotsky, the first People's Commissar for Foreign Affairs, obligingly explained that the 'plan of our universal policy is to give a push to the revolution in the centre and on the west of Europe'.[4] The rest of the world was not, however, to be neglected in Bolshevik designs. In December 1917 the Council of People's Commissars appealed to the peoples of the east to overthrow the 'robbers and enslavers' of their countries, with a particular mention for the subjects of British India.[5]

Thus, from the outset Lenin, Trotsky, Chicerin and their co-revolutionaries attached a special importance to destroying British power and British interests. The notion of covert activity towards these goals was implicit from the start. What could not be approached openly would have to be achieved by stealth, employing all the arts of subterfuge in which the Bolsheviks had become so expert during their long years in exile and underground. In the case of Britain, the pre-revolutionary years had taught them much about their enemy.

For generations London had provided a place of refuge for Russian exiles of many beliefs, liberals and anarchists as well as socialists. Among the more celebrated, the radical thinker Alexander Herzen came to settle in England in 1852. And in London in 1886 Prince Peter Kropotkin founded the anarchist journal, *Freedom*, which exists to this day. Following in their footsteps, many of the early Bolsheviks came to London before 1917 to attend meetings or confer in relative safety with their comrades, and in some cases to adopt it as a temporary home. In the early years of this century the exiled Russian community numbered many thousands, congregated in the anonymous back-streets of areas like the East End of London. The careers of various of these exiles figure prominently in the early history of covert Soviet activity in Britain. They were able first to advance the Bolshevik cause as revolutionaries-in-waiting, and then after November 1917 several managed to put what time they had remaining in England to the service of the Soviet state.

For a year from April 1902 Lenin and his wife, Krupskaya, lived near King's Cross while Lenin worked with Martov and Zasulich on the journal *Iskra* (*The Spark*) and studied in the British Museum. It was in London that Lenin and Trotsky first met. Though not close they sometimes attended socialist meetings together, where they formed their first impressions of the weakness of revolutionary socialism in England.[6]

Three of the early congresses of the future Communist Party of the Soviet Union were held in London. In August 1903, the fateful Second Congress of the then Russian Social Democratic Workers' Party was transferred from Brussels when the Belgian police took action against it. On arrival in London the delegates were 'pelted with wet papers and other missiles by a gang of street urchins' and were given police protection.[7] At the congress the party split into two factions – Lenin's majority Bolsheviks and the minority Mensheviks – and the future shape of Soviet socialism was determined. The Third and Fifth Congresses also took place in London, in April 1905, at a time of revolutionary uprisings in Russia itself, and in August 1907. At the latter gathering, one of the delegates whose credentials were disputed by the Mensheviks was Koba-Ivanovitch, better known as Joseph Stalin. That congress, held in the premises of the Brotherhood Church, was also the occasion of another first encounter between two giants of Soviet history – Stalin and his future adversary, Trotsky.[8]

Between these major gatherings the resident Bolsheviks made what they could of their lives. Some, like Maxim Litvinov who was to be appointed the first official Soviet representative in England, flourished. He fled to London in 1908 from Paris, found work in several major publishing houses under the name of Harrison, and married a well-connected writer, Ivy Low.[9] He also became deeply involved in the various political clubs and committees formed by socialist *émigré* groups. By 1917 these included the Russian Delegates Committee, the Russian Political Prisoners and Exiles Relief Committee, the Communist Club, which met in Soho, and the Russian Socialist Group. In these obscure bodies the exiles plotted and conspired, ever mindful of the eyes and ears of the British Special Branch and the threat, even in London, from the agents of the Ochrana, the tsarist secret police.

Sometimes their activities went disastrously wrong. One of the most notorious events of pre-war England occurred in December 1910 when three London policemen were murdered in Houndsditch by a group of Latvian anarchists. One of those arrested was a 24-year-old tailor's presser called Jacob Peters. He was a member of the Latvian Social Democratic Party and had lived in England for just over a year. At his trial in May 1911 Peters stated that his identity had been confused with that of his cousin, Fritz Svaars, who had died in the associated Siege of Sidney Street in January, and he was acquitted.

Peters remained in England for a further five years, until he left his English wife, the former Miss May Freeman of Worcester, to return to Russia. He quickly became embroiled in the preparations for the coup of November 1917 and was a member of the Petrograd Military Revolutionary Committee under Trotsky. After the revolution he became a deputy chairman of the Cheka, the original political police force of the Soviet Union, and held a variety of senior party posts until his arrest at the end of 1937 and disappearance the next year, a victim of the Stalinist purges.[10]

After the overthrow of the Tsar numerous other Bolshevik sympathisers followed Peters in the trek eastwards. Among those who made the sea journey to Russia from Aberdeen in the summer of 1917 was Ivan Maisky, who was to serve in the Soviet Embassy in London from 1925–7 and was Ambassador from 1932 to 1943. Before the revolution Maisky had spent nearly five years in England, during which time he had met Litvinov and befriended Labour Party politicians such as Ramsay MacDonald, Philip Snowden – Chancellor of the Exchequer in the first Labour government of 1924 – and Arthur Henderson, wartime party leader and Foreign Secretary in the second Labour administration.[11] A few, such as Joe Fineberg, Litvinov's secretary, had no recollection of their homeland. He came to London with his parents in the late 1880s when he was 18 months old and lived there until June 1918.[12] Another son of an exile family, who was born in London in 1891, was D. V. Bogomolov. After his return to post-revolutionary Russia, he was sent back to London in 1924 as a First Secretary alongside Maisky at the newly established Soviet Embassy and in 1937 he was appointed Soviet Ambassador to China.[13] One of the most famous Soviet spies, Colonel Rudolf Abel, who operated in the USA in the 1950s, was born in Newcastle upon Tyne in July 1903 as William Fisher, the son of a Russian exile, Genrikh Fisher. The Fishers stayed in England until 1921, and six years later William joined the Soviet secret police to begin his underground career.[14]

Not all the long-term exiles left after the revolution. The Lithuanian-born Zelda Cahan married a Communist, W. P. Coates and remained in Britain. Andrew Rothstein, the undergraduate son of Theodore Rothstein, a TASS correspondent and Comintern courier in London and in 1921 Soviet representative in Persia, became a leading member of the British Communist Party.

Other Bolsheviks in London who had become involved in domestic politics before 1917 were also able to exploit their connnections on the British scene after the revolution. One of their favoured organisations was the British Socialist Party. The BSP was formed in 1911 as a successor to the Socialist Democratic Federation which was founded thirty years earlier by H. M. Hyndman. In 1920 its 2,500 members made it the largest of the organisations which formed the Communist Party of Great Britain. And as industrial unrest spread in the later years of the war and after, leading members of the BSP, such as Willie Gallacher and John Maclean on Clydeside, stood in the forefront of agitation. The Russian members of the BSP included Joe Fineberg who was a member of its executive committee. Theodore Rothstein contributed pro-Bolshevik articles in the BSP's press under the name of John Bryan. A courier between the Russian Bolsheviks and their supporters in England in 1917, named Holtzmann, was a member of the BSP's Central Hackney branch, while Chicerin had been a member of the BSP branch a few miles away in Kentish Town.[15]

Chicerin and his fellow internee, Petrov, had extended their activities dangerously wide. Both had links with prominent British revolutionaries – Chicerin with the *Workers' Dreadnought* magazine, run by Sylvia Pankhurst, the sister of the suffragette, Christabel, and Petrov, another BSP member, with the Clydeside schoolteacher Maclean. Chicerin was also secretary of the Russian Socialist Group in London and the Russian Political Prisoners and Exiles' Relief Committee and was a member of the Communist Club.[16] During 1917 he approached trade unions and wrote articles which described alleged atrocities committed by the tsarist government against political prisoners. The articles were reprinted as pamphlets and circulated among trade unionists. Aided by anarchist groups he was also alleged to have addressed meetings in the East End at which he 'violently denounced' the war and preached the doctrine of international revolution. This 'anti-Ally and pro-German activity'[17] led to his detention with Petrov under wartime regulations.

One of Trotsky's earliest actions as Commissar for Foreign Affairs was to write to Sir George Buchanan, the British Ambassador to Russia, to protest about the arrest of these two 'stainless, self-sacrificing men of high ideals'.[18] At first, even under the threat of reprisals against British subjects in Russia, the British Cabinet declined to take any notice of the request for the release of the two agitators.[19] But the matter threatened to complicate an already delicate situation in relations between Britain and the new Russian regime. Early in December 1917 the Foreign Secretary, Balfour, came to the conclusion that they should be returned to Russia where 'judged by local standards, their opinions will probably appear sane and moderate'.[20] On 3 January 1918 the government accepted his advice, which was echoed by Buchanan, and Chicerin and Petrov were set free. Petrov applied for readmission the following month but was refused, in the words of an official of the British Home Office, because he had been 'actively engaged in encouraging strikes among workmen engaged in work essential to the war'.[21]

Chicerin's and Petrov's release opened the way for the Bolsheviks to appoint their first representative in an allied country. On the day they were freed *The Times* reported that Maxim Litvinov, believed to be the president of the London Committee of Russian Delegates, had been appointed provisional Plenipotentiary of the People's Commissariat for Foreign Affairs.[22]

As defined by his superiors in Petrograd, Litvinov's duties were as unorthodox as his formal status. Trotsky took a relaxed view of his own responsibilities as Commissar for Foreign Affairs. Within a month of the revolution he had dismissed most existing Russian ambassadors and their staffs, and appointed only three representatives of his own, in London, Stockholm and Geneva, all places which represented former centres of exile for the enemies of tsarism. Trotsky welcomed his post as an opportunity to escape more arduous departmental work. When a colleague asked him what would be done by the Bolsheviks in the way of diplomacy, he replied: 'I will issue a few revolutionary proclamations to the peoples of the world, and then shut up shop.'[23] He had little respect for the conventions of diplomacy as a means of conducting international relations. They served the interests of the old order and had failed to prevent the outbreak of war. The ending of secret diplomacy was regarded as an essential prerequisite for a revolutionary foreign policy. In November 1917 Trotsky declared that such secrecy 'is a necessary tool for a powerful minority ... Imperialism, with its plans of conquest and its robber alliances and deals developed the system of secret diplomacy to the highest level ... The abolition of secret diplomacy is the primary condition for an honest, popular, truly democratic foreign policy.'[24] The commitment was honoured so far as the Tsar's secret agreements were concerned and they were duly published. After that it was soon forgotten as the Bolsheviks began to surround the planning and execution of their own policy with ever more elaborate layers of secrecy.

Trotsky expected that Litvinov would use whatever privileges he could extract from the British as a diplomat to further the revolution. He was well positioned to do so, since both his work in publishing and his marriage had brought him into contact with prominent literary and political figures. His continued presence in London together with other Russians and their links with British revolutionaries provided the rudiments of a network of agents and a nucleus of agitators who could all be involved in clandestine political work. Against the background of growing industrial unrest the Bolsheviks were optimistic that an upheaval was imminent. For a while their enthusiasm pushed aside the view that English socialism was a feeble species, beset by religious influences and an innate conservatism.

Litvinov established himself in a People's Embassy at 82 Victoria Street, London, on the site of what is now a steak house, and awaited a response from the British government. His appointment presented the British with a dilemma. Their attitude to events in Russia had been far from firm or consistent. The War Cabinet, in keeping with the other allied governments, had ignored the Decree on Peace. Their overriding concern was that any separate peace being negotiated by Soviet Russia should not weaken the allied war effort. Some ministers, however, were opposed to any dealings with the new regime and certainly none which entailed recognition. Against those of his colleagues who regarded the Bolsheviks as 'avowed enemies', Balfour had earlier declared that 'it is to our advantage to avoid, as long as possible, an open breach with this crazy system'.[25] The Prime Minister, Lloyd George, supported this view. His main worries were military and strategic. He had no interest in the internal politics of Russia. And while he recognised that there was a 'genuine fear that recognition would involve admitting into Allied countries a swarm of Bolshevik intriguers to foment revolution',[26] he told the War Cabinet that he had 'no fear that Bolshevism was a formidable menace to the internal peace of this country'.[27]

The British government embarked on what Balfour admitted was an irregular arrangement. Although he believed that the Bolsheviks 'would not in the least mind quarrelling with us; they think that they have nothing to gain by keeping on good terms with England' he wanted to avoid a rupture as long as possible.[28] So Litvinov found himself dealing with the British on a strictly unofficial basis through the intermediary of Rex Leeper, a member of the Foreign Office Political Intelligence Department. Theodore Rothstein, who was employed by the British War Office as a translator, also attended some of their meetings. And one lunchtime in January 1918 Litvinov, Rothstein and Leeper were joined in the Lyons' Corner House on the Strand by Robert Bruce Lockhart, who left London three days later for Russia as the head of a British mission to Petrograd.[29] Litvinov's postion was further eased by the British government's decision to allow him to send cipher messages, a privilege normally accorded only to fully accredited diplomats. In fact the British could not do without the facility for their own representatives in Russia and were obliged to concede reciprocal arrangements.

It was, however, Litvinov's political work which proved the most demanding. In Janauary 1918 he addressed the Labour Party conference and wrote for the *Daily Herald*. He appointed John Maclean as Soviet Consul in Glasgow, met Tom Bell and Arthur McManus, of the Socialist Labour Party – future leaders of the British Communist Party – and fraternised with the Fabians Sidney and Beatrice Webb. The Home Secretary reported regularly to his Cabinet colleagues on some of Litvinov's less public activities. In the middle of February, after 'endeavouring to tamper with the discipline of British troops', and writing an article for the *Woolwich Pioneer* which incited munitions workers to revolution, Litvinov was warned about his behaviour.[30] Within two weeks he attempted to undermine the discipline of Russian Jews serving in the British and Canadian armed forces, set up a propaganda bureau in the East End and began to form a detachment of Red Guards in London.[31]

Litvinov also maintained his contacts among the remaining Russian Bolsheviks in London and prepared to expand his activities as additional agents and resources arrived from the Soviet Union. But his plans were rudely disrupted. In February the police raided the Communist Club in Soho and found thirty-eight Russians assembled there. In the register of members they discovered Litvinov's name under his alias of Harrison. All but one of those present were arrested. The exception was a Russian who had arrived in the country only twenty four hours earlier.[32]

The released man had been in the company of Lev Kamenev who was supposedly on his way to Paris, via Norway and Aberdeen. An English cheque for £5,000 was confiscated and he was allowed to proceed to London where Litvinov introduced him to his circle of political acquaintances, including the Webbs. Kamenev was an early example, as well as being one of the more senior figures, of the Bolsheviks' use over the next few years of couriers to deliver funds or instructions to revolutionary groups in Britain. Many were apprehended on or shortly after entering the country but some were to play a critical role in the early days of Soviet intrigue.

Throughout 1918 relations between the Soviet Union and Britain deteriorated. At the beginning of March the German–Soviet Peace Treaty was concluded at Brest-Litovsk. Any lingering hope of a continuing Soviet contribution to the war vanished. Less than a week later the first British troops, 130 Royal Marines, landed at Murmansk and nearly two years of allied intervention in Russia began. In the summer a joint British, American and French force landed at Archangel, the Japanese moved into East Siberia and a joint Japanese, American and British contingent disembarked at Vladivostok. Their combined impact on the civil war in Russia was negligible. Despite committing several thousand troops and providing the counter-revolutionary armies with over £100 miilion worth of military equipment, the British government began to lose heart in the enterprise by the end of the following year.

Inevitably Russian attitudes to the Western powers hardened. In August 1918 some 200 British and French residents in Moscow were detained by the Cheka, the political police force charged with the task of stamping out counter-revolutionary opposition. At the end of the month an attempt was made in Moscow to assassinate Lenin and Uritsky, the director of the Cheka in Petrograd, was murdered. The following day the British Embassy in Petrograd was stormed and the Naval Attaché, Captain Crombie, was killed. Lockhart was arrested. And on the instructions of Lenin, the Cheka unleashed its first campaign of terror. Over the next six weeks the Soviet authorities admitted that the Petrograd Cheka executed over 800 people.[33]

In London Litvinov was detained by the British government. Through Leeper the Foreign Office asked him to telegraph Chicerin to secure the release of all British subjects held in Russia. When satisfactory arrangements were made Litvinov and fifty other Russians, including wives and families, were allowed to depart. The party which left Aberdeen for Norway on 26 September included one probable Englishman, Ian Gilbert, and his wife[34] and Nikolai Klishko, who was to become a Cheka and Comintern agent.[35] Klishko, a 38-year-old Petrograd University-educated engineer, had lived in Britain since 1907 and had worked for Vickers. He had also been active in émigré circles and his house had been used as a centre for Russian revolutionaries.[36] Despite this record he was allowed to return to England less than two years later as a member of the Trade Delegation. Litvinov himself was at the same time denied entry to head the delegation. He was, however, destined to follow Chicerin: his period of detention by the British authorities was succeeded by his later appointment as People's Commissar for Foreign Affairs.

With Litvinov and his entourage removed, the Bolsheviks had to improvise in order to advance their cause in Britain. During the next two years a succession of agents and couriers tried to slip into the country. Their nationalities were various. In February 1919 the police arrested a Russian named Myer Hyman who betrayed two other Bolshevik agents, Max Segal, who had brought £4,000 with him from

Moscow and Jules Soermus, a violinist.[37] All three were tried and deported. In June of that year, two more couriers were detained. A Russian–American, Jacob Nosivitsky was held on arrival at Liverpool and taken to London. There he was interviewed by the redoutable Sir Basil Thompson, the head of the Home Office Directorate of Intelligence, and 'turned' to become a double agent. Nosivitsky identified Rothstein as a Russian agent and he was persuaded to act as a courier between Rothstein and the Soviet representative in the USA as well as providing information on the Communist International, the Comintern.[38]

During that same month a Norwegian, Axel Zachiaressen, was also detained when he landed in Britain. He carried a locked box which he said he had been asked to convey from Stockholm. It was found to contain £6,000 intended for Sylvia Pankhurst, who admitted having received £280 for her journal. Zachiaressen also carried with him a list of extremists in Britain. On 18 July 1919 he met the fate of most failed Bolshevik agents and was deported.[39]

In October 1920 a 21-year-old Finn, Erkki Veltheim was arrested leaving the home in Chalk Farm, London of Colonel L'Estrange Malone, a Liberal MP of pronounced Communist sympathies.[40] Veltheim had been in England for six months, having entered as a stowaway and used at least three aliases.[41] Among documents in his posession were some relating to a Red Officers' course being organised by Colonel Malone, and correspondence for delivery to Lenin and Zinoviev from Sylvia Pankhurst. Veltheim was sentenced to six months' hard labour and deportation. In November Malone was also sentenced to six months' imprisonment following an inflammatory speech he made at a meeting held in the Albert Hall on the third anniversary of the Bolshevik revolution.[42]

Other couriers included a Norwegian, Anker Pettersen, who was arrested at South Shields in December 1920 with two British subjects, John Bell and Basil Taylor. A donkeyman on the SS *Derby*, Pettersen was regarded by the police as 'an important link in the Bolshevik courier system' and he was sentenced to three months hard labour.[43] A number of Soviet emissaries who came to England to assist in the unification of the revolutionary groups evaded arrest. One, a 32-year-old Estonian woman named Salme Murrik, who arrived in 1920, remained to marry Rajani Palme Dutt, the half-Indian, half-Swedish graduate of Balliol who became one of the leading intellectuals of the British Communist Party.[44]

The most important Soviet agent in Britain at this time was Theodore Rothstein. Born in 1871, he came to England with his father when he was 20. Four years later he joined Hyndman's SDF.[45] Rothstein had the doubtful distinction of probably being the first man to work covertly for the Soviet Union while, by virtue of his War Office job, being employed in the British civil service. Many of his activities were closely monitored and were reported to the Cabinet in 1919 and 1920 by Sir Basil Thomson in his weekly reports on the activities of revolutionary organisations. Rothstein distributed funds to at least seven organisations of the extreme left, including the British Socialist Party, the Workers' Socialist Federation, to whose leader Sylvia Pankhurst he gave £10 per week to finance *Dreadnought*, and the Hands Off Russsia Campaign when the hire of a hall for one its meetings cost £500. He gave some £20 per week to the Glasgow Socialist Research Bureau, provided funds for Walton Newbold and his wife to enable them to lecture to the Independent Labour Party, and gave various sums to the Communist Unity Campaign, the People's Russia Information Bureau, which was set up in July 1918 with Sylvia Pankhurst as treasurer, and the Socialist Labour Party, two of whose parliamentary candidates he allegedly financed in the 1918 general election. His close associates included Albert Inkpin, a future general secretary of the British Communist Party and Zelda Cahan. Rothstein also sent money to organisations in France and to Sinn Fein in Ireland. Some of the money came from diamonds sent from Russia. His operation was a family affair conducted in some style: when in London he resided at his mother's house in Highgate and he spent the summer lodged in a converted Pullman railway carriage at Windermere in the Lake District. He was assisted by his son Andrew, then a Brackenbury scholar at Balliol College, Oxford.[46]

After joining the Soviet Trade Delegation in 1920 Theodore Rothstein left London in August of that year. Understandably, the British government resolved never to allow him into the country again. In November, however, he was appointed Soviet representative in Teheran and arrived there the following April two months after the signing of a Soviet–Persian Treaty. For the next eighteen months he continued to be a thorn in the side of British interests until he was withdrawn to Russia in November 1922.[47]

Rothstein and the other Bolshevik agents in Britain from 1917–20 had one immediate target: to bring about the formation of a united revolutionary party which would be loyal to Soviet Russia. The pace of discussions, involving several small groups led by the BSP, accelerated in the middle of 1919 after a Russian envoy visited Britain to press for early unification. To encourage them towards a pro-Soviet conclusion most of the main participants, but particularly the BSP and the

Socialist Labour Party, received financial subsidies and under his 'John Bryan' pseudonym Rothstein produced the desired propaganda. Typically, Sylvia Pankhurst acted on her own initiative. In July 1919 she wrote to Lenin for guidance. His reply did not entirely please her: Lenin said that British revolutionaries should not renounce participation in parliamentary elections but if they did it should not delay the formation of a Communist Party.[48] Pankhurst also visited the Comintern Bureau in Amsterdam and in 1920 formed her own Communist Party. Any advantage was lost when, in October 1920, she was sentenced to six months' imprisonment for publishing seditious articles. By the time of her release circumstances had changed. A Communist unity convention held in London at the end of July 1920 was followed in January 1921 by a second convention at Leeds and the Communist Party of Great Britain was born.

The Soviet Union had acted as midwife to the new party and was to dominate its outlook in the formative years of its infancy. The provision of Bolshevik funds, political guidance and propaganda ensured that the new party would comply with Soviet wishes. Nor were the 5,000 or so members of the CPGB reluctant to be tied to the Soviet line; they wanted to emulate the Bolshevik example of a successful revolution and take their place in the ranks of the Comintern.

What the Bolsheviks, British and Russian, hoped to exploit was the social and industrial ferment in the country after the war. Political unrest had spread across Europe as the old order crumbled in the wake of the conflict: at the beginning of 1919 the Spartacist uprising in Berlin was put down with the deaths of Rosa Luxembourg and Karl Liebknecht; in the spring a short-lived Soviet regime emerged in Munich and another survived for six months under Bela Kun in Hungary. Not everyone shared Lloyd George's optimism that Britain faced no serious danger from the contagion of Bolshevist revolution. From King George V, through the Conservative ranks to the press there was a profound and instinctive dislike for the Bolsheviks and all their works. And there was evidence enough of grounds for concern. Discontent among demobilised servicemen led to mutinies in units at Folkestone and Rhyl. The Minister of Labour declared in May 1919 that discharged soldiers were 'in a dangerous mood and tainted with Bolshevism'.[49] He reported that a society of discharged soldiers in Glasgow was said to have converted itself to something like a 'Soviet' and to be in touch with the Bolsheviks. The threat of serious dislocation had appeared to increase with the formation of the Triple Alliance of miners, railwaymen and transport workers in February 1919. Troops were sent into Glasgow in the face of strikes and disorder, the police went on strike in Liverpool and in September a railway dispute ended in victory for the strikers.

In 1920 the prospect of a general strike grew sharply during the Soviet–Polish War. Early in the year Polish forces invaded the Ukraine. Their action brought to the surface widespread fears that Britain might again be drawn into a European land war, and focused latent sympathy for the Bolsheviks among the working class. In May dockers refused to load munitions destined for Polish forces. Around the country 350 Councils of Action were formed to oppose any move to intervene on the Poles' behalf in face of a Soviet counterattack – a course which Winston Churchill and Lloyd George favoured. But the issue was never put to the test: in August the Poles defeated the Soviets, who retreated. This crisis over, the miners struck in October, a short dispute which was again settled on terms favourable to the strikers, but not before the government had secured the passing of the Emergency Powers Act.

The war and the accompanying unrest coincided with the arrival in London of a Soviet delegation to negotiate a trade agreement with the British government. With the White generals Kolchak and Denikin defeated at the beginning of 1920 and allied forces withdrawn, the civil war in the Soviet Union was virtually at an end. Both the Soviet Union and Britain wished to redefine their relationship. The Soviet delegation to the talks arrived in London in May 1920 and set up office in High Holborn. It was to have been led by Litvinov but the British had not forgiven him for his behaviour two years ealier and he remained in Copenhagen. The first to arrive were Solomon Rozovsky, Viktor Nogin, a member of the Central Committee and Nikolai Klishko of the Cheka. They were followed by Leonid Krasin, the Commissar for Trade and Transport, who became the effective head of the delegation. He had worked closely with Lenin in exile before the revolution and among other responsibilities, which had included setting up an underground printing press in Baku and a laboratory to produce terrorist bombs, had supervised the collection of funds for the Bolsheviks by legal and illegal means.[50] In return for a verbal promise by Krasin not to 'interfere in any way in the politics or internal affairs of the country', the members of the delegation were allowed free movement and full use of diplomatic communications facilities, including cyphers, couriers and diplomatic bag. The first phase of the negotiations lasted until July when Krasin departed for fresh instructions from Moscow.

But the British soon realised that the Soviets had not honoured their undertaking of non-interference. Krasin had been in contact with the main parties involved in the formation of the British Communist Party, while Klishko had been dealing with Theodore Rothstein who was still in the country, and funds were provided for the Hands Off Russia Campaign which was heavily involved in the Polish question. The British were aware of their activities largely through the interception of Soviet communications, and when Krasin met Lloyd George at the end of June he received a stern lecture on his wrongdoings from the British Prime Minister.

These strictures did not, however, elicit from the Soviet delegation any gestures of contrition. When Krasin returned to London in August he was accompanied by Kamenev, a member of the Politburo and head of the Soviet and Communist hierarchies in Moscow. They carried with them a quantity of diamonds and other precious stones. The enduring political cliché about 'Moscow gold' as a source of funding for miniscule fringe organisations trying to wage the class war in Britain, has its origins in this period when its existence was an inescapable fact of political life.

Some of the responsibility rested with Francis Meynell, a director of the recently founded socialist newspaper, the *Daily Herald*. In the spring of 1920 Krasin, Klishko and Nogin had met its editor, the future Labour Party leader, George Lansbury, to discuss the provision of Soviet funds for the paper. When no agreement was reached Meynell visited Litvinov in Copenhagen to enlist his support. The 30-year-old director 'knew and admired' the Russian, whose English wife Ivy contributed poetry to the *Herald* and was a close friend of Meynell's sister Viola.[51] On his first visit to Copenhagen Meynell handed over a 'present from Ivy' in London, a tie with a message from Rothstein inside. In return Litvinov gave him a tobacco pouch containing a string of pearls. Meynell put the jewels into a jar of butter and presented it to Rothstein on his return to England. Meynell placed other jewels inside some chocolates and posted the box to the philosopher Cyril Joad, from whom he later retrieved them.

On his next visit to Copenhagen Meynell secured from Litvinov £75,000 worth of jewels to finance the *Daily Herald*. Unfortunately for the would-be secret courier, the *Herald*'s directors unanimously rejected the offer and Meynell resigned his post. The jewels, meanwhile, had been sold through Hatton Garden dealers who immediately recognised their distinctive Russian cut. As Meynell records, word of their sale soon got back to Thomson at Scotland Yard.[52] According to one of the latter's reports, Hatton Garden dealers had said diamonds and other precious stones worth nearly £2,000,000 had appeared on the English market.[53] Meynell subsequently handed over the proceeds from his own transaction to Klishko at the Trade Delegation. Happily for the Cheka agent and his colleagues, however, there was no shortage of other potential recipients, including the Communist Party and various leftist groups and magazines, such as Pankhurst's *Dreadnought*.

During 1920 Kamenev and Krasin also met leaders of the Councils of Action and attended a Fabian summer school. In her diaries Beatrice Webb described the tall Krasin, with 'his finely chiselled features', as a 'veritable aristocrat of intellect and bearing'.[54] Thompson however took a less idealised view: 'it is now quite clear,' he reported in September, 'that Messrs Kamenev and Krasin are almost solely concerned with propaganda.'[55] He estimated that at least £100,000 of Russian money had been spent on revolutionary propaganda in the first nine months of the year. Without these subsidies, Thomson said he believed that neither the Communist Party nor the *Daily Herald* would have existed. Altogether, he thought that the Trade Delegation had become 'a greater menace to the stability of this country than anything that has happened since the armistice'.[56]

These two sharply contrasting views of the Bolshevik presence in London – written within a short time of each other – illustrate at an early stage two of the main themes that were to dominate for a generation. One, from the sophisticated intelligentsia, portrayed a nobility of purpose in the Soviet Union and its representatives while the other, from a down-to-earth official, saw that same individual as a schemer and a trafficker in an alien ideology.

The collection of intercepted communications gathered by the British amply confirmed Soviet duplicity on a range of issues, including their subversive activities in India, Afghanistan and Persia, and their intentions on Poland. In August Lenin had instructed Kamenev to make a detailed statement of policy on Poland for publication over the signature of a British Communist and the following week Chicerin told Kamenev that British workers should form detachments to fight in Poland. This activity had to be undertaken 'absolutely unofficially and confidentially'.[57] The inevitable conclusion to these events was the expulsion of Kamenev on 20 September 1920. Krasin and the rest of the delegation were allowed to remain but the talks were frozen until November.

The dual role of the Trade Delegation in London during the second half of 1920 illustrated some of the contradictions that underlay Soviet policy at the time. Its attitude to Britain was at best ambivalent. The Bolsheviks perceived Britain as a leading enemy of their revolution. Yet it was the first major power with whom the Bolsheviks sought diplomatic relations after November 1917. Moreover, the presence of a Bolshevik community in Britain provided the basis of both formal representation and a network of communications and agents which could be put to the future service of the revolution. And when they extracted from the British an arrangement which conferred some diplomatic privileges on their semi-official representatives, the Bolsheviks used them for purposes of political subversion. They soon discovered how easy it was in an open society to practise deception. The paradox may not have surprised them, for in their view of history the formal freedoms of bourgeois democracy contain the seeds of their own destruction and the birth of socialism. What may have come as more of a shock was the accompanying irony that as soon as subversion began to have any visible effect and impinged upon the consciousness of those in the mainstream of political life it was rapidly detected and exposed. The inner resilience of democracy, and its own self-defence mechanisms, had to be reckoned with and a means of undermining those fortifications had to be found. As a technique of bringing about revolutionary advance, crude political agitation therefore had its limitations in a country such as Britain, where the masses were at best apathetic and certainly untutored in socialism, and the authorities were, in their own way, ever vigilant.

A considerable gulf existed between the extent of Bolshevik ambitions and their capacity to realise them. One of their more urgent tasks was to forge the institutions which would both defend the revolution at home and carry it across the world.

ORGANS OF THE REVOLUTION

The Bolsheviks lost no time in providing the means to finance and promote revolution in the West. In December 1917 two million rubles were placed 'at the disposal of the representatives abroad of the Commissariat of Foreign Affairs for the needs of the revolutionary movement'.[58] The commissariat, known by an acronym from its Russian title as the Narkomindel, established a section for international propaganda. This produced a daily newspaper in German and included a British section under Boris Reinstein, a Russian who held American citizenship. After the signing of the Treaty of Brest-Litovsk Trotsky resigned as Commissar for Foreign Affairs and handed over to Chicerin. Although he began the less spectacular task of building up the Commissariat as a more formally structured organisation, responsibility for major foreign policy decisions passed increasingly into the hands of the Politburo. One of the weapons the Narkomindel lacked was any effective intelligence apparatus.

The origins of the Soviet intelligence agencies lay in the regime's internal security forces and in the military. The existence of an all-powerful force to maintain despotism had long been a feature of Russian history and submission to authority, spiritual and temporal, had been the lot of the Russian masses through the centuries. One of the earliest instruments of repression was the Oprichnina, formed by Ivan the Terrible in the second half of the sixteenth century. It waged a campaign of terror against the boyars, whose landholdings and status Ivan wished to curb. Its counterpart on the eve of the revolution was the Ochrana, which Tsar Alexander II had created in 1881. With some ingenuity and resourcefulness the Ochrana sought out the many enemies of tsarism both in Russia and abroad. Its agents infiltrated the Bolshevik movement at the highest levels: one of them, Roman Malinovsky, a member of the tsarist parliament, the Duma, served on the Bolshevik Central Committee in 1911. Lenin defended him when he was first accused of working for the Ochrana, but at the end of 1918 when the tsarist files had been opened Malinovsky was tried by a revolutionary tribunal and shot. When they established their own internal security agency the Bolsheviks drew freely on the lessons they had learnt from the Ochrana's methods of operation and their own experiences underground.

On 20 December 1917 a resolution from the Council of People's Commissars established the All-Russian Extraordinary Commission for Combating Counter-Revolution and Sabotage. The tasks of this body, known as the Cheka, were:

1. To suppress and liquidate all attempts and acts of counter-revolution and sabotage throughout Russia, from whatever quarter.
2. To hand over for trial by revolutionary tribunal all saboteurs and counter-revolutionaries, and to work out means of combating them;
3. The Commission solely carries out preliminary investigation, insofar as is necessary for suppression.[59]

The first head of the Cheka was Felix Dzerzhinsky, a 41-year-old product of the Polish gentry. An ascetic figure, he had spent nearly a quarter of his life in tsarist gaols. At the end of 1917 he had a staff of only 120 under his control and exercised no judicial power. By the end of March of the next year, when he installed his headquarters in a former insurance office in Moscow's Bolshaia Lubianka near the Kremlin, Dzerzhinky's power base was poised to expand. The assassination of Uritsky and the attempt on Lenin's life at the end of August precipitated the first Cheka-led 'Red Terror'. Over the next twelve months, as the civil war intensified, Dzerzhinsky acquired new powers and added greatly to his resources: the Cheka dispensed summary justice; organised its own troops and border guards; operated special units within the Red Army; was responsible for transport and railway security; ran a network of provincial Chekas and had laid the foundations of the future 'Gulag', the Soviet Union's prison and forced labour camps. Although there are no definitive figures for the numbers of persons killed by the Cheka in the early years of the revolution, recent estimates suggest that up to February 1922 it was responsible for the deaths of about 280,000 people, half of whom were executed while the other half died in the suppression of insurrection.[60] By 1921 it employed some 30,000 civilian staff and over 100,000 troops. By comparison the Ochrana, a much smaller organisation, was responsible for somewhere in the region of 14,000 deaths during the fifty years before the overthrow of tsarism in February 1917.

Within two years the Cheka had raised to new heights the baleful Russian tradition of repression. The roots of autocracy lie deep in the character of Russia's rulers and institutions. The creation of the Cheka, however, was an ideological requirement and an immediate political necessity for the new breed of Bolshevik leaders. If the nature of man was to be remoulded, the social and economic order of the world to be overturned and the political map of the globe to be redrawn on Communist terms, the Soviet regime had need of a body to execute without mercy or favour the moulding, turning and drawing. The rise of the Cheka and its apparatus of suppression was not therefore an accident nor an aberration but an integral element of the revolutionary process. The Cheka was also essential to the survival of the regime. At the beginning of the civil war the Bolsheviks' hold over much of the massive land empire they had inherited was tenuous in the extreme. Besides the allied forces and the White armies there were peasant revolts and troublesome opposition groups, Mensheviks, anarchists and social revolutionaries, to deal with. This combination of tradition, doctrinal imperative and expediency engendered the creation of a massive machinery of institutionalised terror at the heart of the Soviet system. Through many phases, purges and changes the functions of the Cheka have passed through various agencies, known collectively as the 'organs' – the GPU, OGPU, NKVD, MVD, and MGB – to descend to the KGB of today.

The Cheka's first ventures into foreign territory took shape with the establishment of a foreign department, the INO, in December 1920.

INO agents worked among *émigré* organisations outside the Soviet Union, gathered intelligence on foreign countries and supervised Soviet staff posted abroad. A parallel counter-espionage section, the KRO, maintained a watch on foreigners in Russia. During 1918 a separate military intelligence organisation emerged as part of the Red Army. It was created by Trotsky during 1918 while he was Commissar for War, assisted by an English officer, Captain George Hill, of the British Mission in Moscow. Their immediate task was to set up an intelligence section, the Third Department of the Soviet General Staff, to track German army movements. That department grew into what is now the GRU, the Chief Intelligence Directorate of the Soviet Army. Its history has been a chequered one and more than once its independence has been shattered by the intervention of the superior 'organs'. It was, however, responsible for some of the Soviet Union's more imaginative espionage operations in the inter-war years when it was closely linked with the Comintern.

Central though they were to the future of the revolution these instruments of repression and control were themselves insufficient to lead the workers of the world to socialism. In 1914 Lenin had expressed his desire to see the establishment of a new International to unite proletarian revolutionaries across the world. When he returned to Russia in the spring of 1917 the call featured in his famous April Theses. By the beginning of 1919 Trotsky was ready with a letter of invitation to thirty-nine groups, including the British Socialist Party, the Socialist Labour Party and revolutionary shop stewards among others, to create a 'general fighting organ for permanent coordination and systematic leadership of the movement'.[61]

The founding Congress of the Third Commmunist International – known as the Comintern – opened in Moscow in March 1919. Only five of the fifty delegates had travelled from Western European countries to attend. No British group sent a delegate. Joe Fineberg, recently returned from England, acted as the non-voting delegate of the BSP without any basis of authority whatsoever. The congress issued ringing declarations of intent and called on the 'Workers of All Countries' to rise in revolt. To prepare for this event, Rutgers the Dutch delegate was instructed to set up a Western European Bureau in Amsterdam, which he did by the end of the year. But the bureau had a short life. It was dissolved in the middle of 1920, when its place was taken by the Western European Secretariat which had been established in Berlin in the autumn of 1919.

Over the next year the Bolsheviks despatched Comintern agents to many Western countries to guide sympathetic elements along the

Soviet path. Through these couriers, the efforts of resident agents like Rothstein and links forged initially through the Comintern's bureau in Amsterdam, the Comintern built up its connections in Britain. The result was that a twelve-strong British delegation was among the 217 delegates from forty-one countries who attended the Second Congress in July 1920. It included Sylvia Pankhurst, and several who were to become prominent in the CPGB, such as J. T. Murphy, Willie Gallacher and F. Quelch who also became a member of the Comintern Executive Committee.

The main achievement of the congress was to adopt the 'Twenty-one Conditions', the rules for membership of the Comintern, most of which were drawn up by Lenin. Among the duties imposed on member parties were: ending all associations with reformist movements; securing all important posts in trade unions; carrying out propaganda and forming Communist cells in trade unions and other workers' organisations; organising their parties under the Communist name with a Communist programme according to the principles of democratic centralism and with a secret apparatus; combining legal with illegal activities, ready for activation in time of civil war. Parties were obliged to carry out propaganda in support of revolution, including the army as one of their audiences and to frame their programmes according to Comintern policy.[62]

The Twenty-one Conditions established beyond all doubt Soviet leadership of the Comintern. As that grip tightened in the years ahead the Comintern became discredited. Assertions by the Soviet Union of the Comintern's independence were greeted with derision by Western governments. For a time, however, it enjoyed a reputation as one of the main vehicles of Communist inspired subversion around the globe. Its apparent success at the Second Comintern Congress in bringing together so many revolutionaries from different backgrounds immediately spawned a range of specialised activities. In July 1920 a Comintern-run Congress of Eastern Peoples at Baku urged the subjects of the British Empire to 'rise as one man for the holy war against the English conquerors'.[63] At the end of 1920 a Red International of Labour Unions, known as the Profintern, was formed with J. T. Murphy on its executive committee and as head of its British bureau. And when he came home from Russia in December he was provided with the customary Russian subsidy to help launch the new organisation.

To control the despatch of funds and envoys from Comintern headquarters in Moscow, an International Liaison Department, the OMS, was set up under Ossip Piatnitsky who had learned his craft distributing illegal propaganda in Russia under the Tsars. According to Samuel Ginsberg, a senior Soviet intelligence officer who defected to the West in 1937 under the name of Walter Krivitsky, Piatnisky built up a 'world-wide network of permanently stationed agents responsible to him'.[64] Formally, Piatnitsky was the financial secretary of the Comintern Executive Committee and his work as head of the OMS was little publicised. However, he provided the groundwork for other branches of Soviet intelligence to exploit when the Comintern's importance was reduced from the end of the 1920s.

In its early years the Comintern represented the embodiment of the Bolsheviks' aspirations for global revolution. Its message was proclaimed from political platforms across Europe and Asia. There was no attempt to conceal its purpose. That would have been self-defeating and while Soviet foreign policy was couched in the same primitive expressions of revolutionary zeal there was no reason for reticence. Yet there was every reason to conceal the methods to be adopted, since these inevitably meant the subversion of the political systems of countries which might not wish to be subverted. The Soviet Union was already learning that its experiment in reconstructing the art of diplomacy as a form of higher agitation was flawed, both in conception and execution. The Comintern was another way around the problem. Its purpose amounted to an attempt to export revolution, not through the formal foreign policy of the Soviet state but through an alternative institution created for the political mobilisation of the masses under disguised Soviet leadership. But the disguise was ineffective and the approach came to much the same: the use of clandestine means to put into practice openly declared objectives. Despite the contradiction those objectives could not be realised except by heavy reliance on the secret and the underhand.

In the first flush of revolution the Soviet Union therefore embarked upon devising the instruments which would most readily adapt to covert ways of operating. Soviet leaders were not looking then for the means to conduct espionage, in the sense of the acquisition of governmental and military secrets or the planting of 'moles' to influence decision-making. Their purpose was political. But the political techniques they drew upon were not those associated with open debate and the electoral processes of a democracy. They were the skills of the underground agitator pitting his wits against all-pervasive despotism. And there were no more experienced operators in the arts of clandestine politics than the Bolshevik leaders themselves. The result was that many of the early Soviet attempts to subvert Western democracies were not noted for their subtlety; some of their methods seemed naively inappropriate in a Western context. But a more important effect in the longer run was that the task of exploiting the weaknesses of democratic societies fell increasingly into the hands of those in the Soviet Union who knew most about the darker aspects of political manipulation – the agencies who were responsible for intelligence and internal security.

At the same time, the Comintern's role as the party of the world revolution was increasingly destined to conflict with the demands of a redefined Soviet foreign policy which depended on the development of trade and the winning of international recognition. For the first three years after the revolution there seemed no discrepancy between the twin aims of defending and consolidating the revolution at home and disseminating it abroad. But the Bolsheviks' dreams that the whole of Europe was about to be engulfed in a revolutionary conflagration were vanishing fast. In Germany and Hungary socialist triumphs in 1920 were short lived. The prophecies Chicerin made as he shook off the dust of an English prison were evaporating in a cloud of rhetoric, despite the gold and the intriguing.

By 1920 the intitial assumptions of Soviet policy were being challenged, by force of cirumstance and from within the regime. If the Soviet Union was to survive it had to to move out of its international isolation and build up its economy, shattered by war and revolution and disturbance within. The fledgling state needed Western trade, technology and finance. The path of pure revolution was hardly a secure basis on which to achieve international cooperation towards economic recovery. A clash was looming between the interests of the Soviet state and revolutionary ideology; conflict arose between differing strategies of how to defend the revolution at home and how to relate that effort to the spread of Soviet influence abroad, and between the role of diplomacy and the uses of covert methods such as political manipulation and espionage to achieve policy objectives. These strains were to develop sharply in the decade ahead, most dramatically in the wider context of the struggle between Stalin and Trotsky, and were to have an important bearing on Soviet attitudes and behaviour towards Britain throughout the 1920s.

2 Trade, Raids and Propaganda

AGREEMENT AND PROTEST

In 1921 the Soviet Union succeeded in making the first breach in the walls of hostility and distrust which surrounded it. But it was a far from complete demolition. Although the Soviet regime had taken the first steps towards effective trading and diplomatic relationships with the capitalist world, Western suspicions of its intentions remained as strong as ever. When the Soviet and British governments signed a trade agreement in London on 16 March 1921, its fourteen clauses were subject to the condition that:

> ... each party refrains from hostile action or undertakings against the other and from conducting outside of its own borders any official propaganda, direct or indirect, against the institutions of the British Empire or of the Soviet Republic respectively, and more particularly that the Russian Soviet Government refrains from any attempt by military or diplomatic or any other form of action or propaganda to encourage any of the peoples of Asia in any form of hostile action against British interests or the British Empire, especially in India or in the independent state of Afghanistan.[1]

The signing of the agreement came at a critical moment for the Soviet leadership. The year had begun badly, with widespread uprisings among a population which was enduring the severest hardships. In addition to the ravages of war, famine and disease had claimed millions of lives in the previous two years, the currency had collapsed and industrial production had shrunk to less than 20 per cent of its pre-war levels. As the misery of the workers and peasants increased, they suffered the added blows of massive repression, perpetrated by the regime that stood in their name. At the beginning of March 1921, on the eve of the party's Tenth Congress in Moscow, sailors and soldiers at the Baltic base of Kronstadt mutinied. Following repeated artillery bombardment, the Red Army stormed the rebels' stronghold on an island fortress and reclaimed it, leaving several thousand mutineers dead.

At the congress Lenin announced that War Communism had been abandoned in favour of a New Economic Policy. The peasantry was to be allowed to trade its surplus products in a limited reintroduction of local private enterprise and requisitioning was to be replaced by a tax in kind on agricultural products. The trade agreement with Britain, the first of half a dozen to be concluded with Western European countries in the coming year, was the international counterpart to the introduction of NEP at home. The policy was hailed as a new beginning. And the Soviet Union's desperate need for foreign trade and a measure of internal stability was accompanied by an immediate softening of the call for world revolution.

In June 1921 the Third Congress of the Comintern opened in Moscow, with over 500 delegates from forty-eight countries. It sounded what has widely been described as a retreat from revolution. Lenin declared that the Comintern had passed from tactics of assault to tactics of siege, with infiltration taking the place of armed struggle.[2] The 'Theses on Tactics' adopted by the Congress conceded that the Comintern had 'not everywhere advanced far enough' and that in England 'despite the concentration of its forces into a single communist party [nor] has the English communist movement succeeded in becoming a mass party'.[3] It had also failed to gain affiliation to the Labour Party, which Lenin had recommended. The English delegation reportedly received a cold reception at the congresses. Tom Quelch who had been provided with an office in Moscow for a year, returned home because the Russians considered the English movement was 'negligible', according to the Home Office's informant who had heard it from Ralph Fox, another British Communist who was to work in Comintern headquarters.[4]

Despite these setbacks, funding by Moscow of British Communists, with all its associated machinations, continued. Unconfirmed reports from Riga reached the British authorities in May 1921 that £2,000 a month was being spent on agitation in Britain.[5] A separate sum of £4,000 had gone to the Profintern's British Bureau at the end of March. In addition, evidence was mounting of the involvement of the Soviet Trade Delegation in subversive activity. A letter from the secretary of the Profintern in Moscow to the secretary of the British Bureau bore the delegation's stamp on the envelope, dated 1 June 1921, of its offices at 128 New Bond Street in the West End.[6] Further material fell into the hands of the British which pointed to extensive Soviet subversion in Asia.

The patience of the British government soon ran out. On 7 September 1921 Lord Curzon, the Foreign Secretary, delivered a memorandum of protest to the Soviet government, complaining that 'hostile action' was continuing unabated. The catalogue of misdeeds included the importation of large sums of money into Persia where Rothstein had a staff of 100, and into Afghanistan. Unfortunately, it also included intelligence from sources on the continent which purported to prove Soviet support for Sinn Fein 'germ cells'. Not for the last time the British acted on the basis of material of doubtful authenticity and Litvinov had no difficulty in dismissing the charges as 'based on false information and forgeries'.[7]

Little deterred by the British blunder, the Soviet Union persisted in its efforts to build up the disappointingly weak British Communist Party. Moves were in hand to develop the CPGB and others like it to make it conform more closely to Bolshevik norms of organisation and policy. A three-man commisssion was set up to prepare a report on the Bolshevisation of the CPGB. Under the name of George Brown, the Comintern's representative in Britain Michael Borodin watched over the process and the parallel restructuring of the Profintern. In August 1922, however, he was arrested in Glasgow and deported for contraventions of the Aliens Act. Borodin had also attended a Profintern meeting in London in July where he met among others, Harry Pollitt who was to become the CPGB's general secretary in 1929, Tom Quelch and Tom Mann, the veteran president of the British Bureau.[8] J. T. Murphy recalled Borodin as a 'tall, well-built, swarthy complexioned man', an excellent linguist who had spent time in Holland, Mexico and the US, and one of more expert and persuasive of all the so-called 'emissaries' of Lenin he had met.[9]

Like other British Communist leaders, Murphy was a frequent visitor to Moscow. He went there in 1921, 1922 and 1923 and stayed for a longer period in 1926. Delegations also attended congresses and committee meetings of the Comintern and Profintern. On occasion, party leaders were summoned to Moscow to give account of themselves. In 1921 the entire executive committee travelled there; ten of its members were also in Moscow two years later to present their report on reorganisation. The same year the leaders of the British section of the Profintern also made the journey east. A number of British Communists worked in Comintern headquarters, including one Rathbone, a research worker, George Hardy who was the representative of the Natonal Minority Movement at Profintern headquarters, Rose Cohen who was on the Comintern staff in 1923–4 and Ralph Fox, a member of Comintern's Colonial Department in 1925. Bob Stewart, a member of the party's executive who stood as a candidate in the general election of October 1924 before going to work in Ireland for the

Workers' International Relief Organisation, spent time in Moscow as a British representative employed on Comintern Executive Committee business. He was followed in 1924 by E. H. Brown who had been the CPGB organiser in North East England and then in Yorkshire.[10]

Foreign Communists visiting Moscow stayed at the Lux Hotel in Tverskaia Street, just off Red Square. At the beginning of 1923 when he was working for the GRU, Walter Krivitsky lived in the hotel as part of his duties. The Soviet government, he recorded, kept

> 'a close watch upon the Hotel Lux, in order to discover exactly what the comrades in every country are saying and doing, to know their attitude towards the Soviet government and towards the warring factions in the Bolshevik party. For this purpose the Hotel Lux is honeycombed with OGPU agents registered as guests and residents.[11]

Its cosmopolitan atmosphere opened up numerous contacts between revolutionaries from all parts of the world and in all probability led some of them to their first encounters with Soviet intelligence agencies. When J. T. Murphy resided there in 1926 his room was four doors away from that of M. N. Roy, the Indian Communist, and Germans, Americans, Finns and a Japanese were elsewhere in the hotel.[12]

None of these Moscow visits or appointments meant any reduction in the number of Comintern agents sent to Britain. Many were closely observed by the authorities. A Norwegian called Friis who arrived in Britain in 1921 with £1000, attended meetings with Indian revolutionaries in London and with the CPGB.[13] The successor to Borodin, according to the British Special Branch was one Jack or Johnnie Walker. He carried with him a letter referring to money that was to be passed through Peter Miller, a cypher clerk in the Trade Mission or Berzin, second in command at the mission. However, since the letter stated that Walker was from the 'department of the World-Wide Socialist International of Communist Germ-Cells',[14] the British may have been advised to regard him with caution in view of their earlier experience. Another courier was despatched to organise the Young Communist League: Sigi Bamatter, who arrived in Britain in July 1923, also used the name George Brown and a second alias of Williams.[15]

After a lull at the end of 1921, fresh reports reached the Special Branch of renewed payments for British Communists. A sum of £2,500 for the CPGB's propaganda work in the first quarter of 1922 was followed by a sum of £6,000 for twelve months at the beginning of 1923,

£250 for Walton Newbold's propaganda expenses at the beginning of that year and the allocation of smaller sums for the Young Communist League and the Profintern transmitted through the bureau in Berlin.[16]

During the early 1920s the Soviet Union also began to employ the tactic of the 'united front', to appeal beyond the immediate ranks of committed Communists. Its adoption then was the forerunner of a more widespread offensive a decade later. In 1921 a National Unemployed Workers' Movement was set up under a Communist engineering worker, Wal Hannington. The following year it became known as the National Minority Movement, with Harry Pollitt installed as its general secretary by 1924 and fortified with large-scale subsidies from the Soviet Union. It effectively took over the role of the British Bureau of the Profintern and until its decline at the end of the decade and final dissolution in 1933 was the leading Communist-run front organisation in Britain. After 1925 the Minority Movement was joined by the National Left-Wing Movement, which campaigned for the acceptance of Communists in Labour constituency parties. It, too, received Comintern funds – some £4000 in 1925 – but was disbanded in 1929 with its aims unattainable and the postures of the 'united front' temporarily abandoned.[17]

During the first wave of united front activity Communist inspired organisations appeared also on an international level. In September 1921 a German Communist, Willi Munzenberg, founded the International Workers' Aid Society ostensibly to raise money for the starving Soviet population.[18] Its British section – Workers' International Relief – was the one Stewart went to work for in Ireland. Munzenberg's career as the global impressario of communism, as publisher, organiser and propagandist, ended with his expulsion from the German Communist Party in 1939 and his murder – probably on Stalin's orders – the following year in France. His 'Innocents' Clubs' to attract left-wing intellectuals and idealists outside the Communist parties of Europe developed a formula which the Soviet Union used repeatedly before the Second World War and after. Among his other early creations were the League Against Imperialism, with headquarters in Berlin and branches in most major Western countries, and the Communist Youth International, which had emerged from an existing socialist youth organisation. In Britain the CYI found its most enthusiatic supporters not among working-class youth but the privileged undergraduates of the ancient universities.

The first Communist cell at Cambridge was in existence in 1921, ten years earlier than has often been assumed. The growth of Marxism among young intellectuals was a widely-recognised symptom of the

1930s, part of a response to the rise of Nazism and the growing threat of war. But the seeds of communism in the universities were sown a decade earlier. In the 1920s the Communists included: at Balliol College, Oxford, Andrew Rothstein, the son of Theodore, Tom Wintringham who shortly after leaving university went to Moscow on behalf of the Foreign Office, and Rajani Palme Dutt who served on the CPGB's three-man 'Bolshevisation' commission in 1922. Elsewhere to be found were John Strachey, the Communist apologist of the 1930s (who never actually joined the party), as well as party stalwarts such as Emile Burns, Maurice Dobb and Comintern worker Ralph Fox. As Andrew Boyle has noted: 'nearly two-thirds of prominent British Communists during the twenties had studied at Oxford or Cambridge.'[19]

These early Oxbridge Communists were not, however, merely isolated individuals. Their first organised cell at Cambridge was noted by the British authorities at the beginning of 1921. In one of his reports Thomson declared that 'parlour bolshevism' was making some headway among undergraduates and that one C. W. Brook was secretary of the twelve-member Cambridge branch of the CPGB and the Cambridge University Socialist Society.[20] Towards the end of the year the leaders of Communist activity in the universities were identified as 19-year-old Arthur Reade who edited a small magazine called *Free* (formerly *New*) *Oxford*, Charles Gray, another Balliol student, and Maurice Dobb at Cambridge.[21] Dobb, who visited the Soviet Union in 1922, was to become one of the leading economic theorists of the CPGB as well as a talentɪspotter for Soviet intelligence in the 1930s. In a letter to one Arthur Nott of the CYI Reade had written that: 'our object is to stir up a communist nucleus among the 'varsity men who will be going out as schoolmasters, scientific workers, literary men and professional and intellectual workers in general that they may take their place in the Revolutionary working-class movement.'[22] He also noted that he had disagreed with Dobb, who seemed to have a different idea of how the university Communist movement should function. Reade stated that Dobb had written to him: 'I think it is essential for the university groups to be secret.'[23] Reade said he couldn't understand what was to be gained from the policy of secrecy as the Socialist societies already amounted to Communist societies. Within a month he found out one possible reason when he was sent down and his associate Gray suffered the same fate for a two-term period.[24] Reade went to work for the magazine *Labour Monthly*, which had been founded in 1921 and was edited by Rajani Palme Dutt. He was also in contact with the Labour Research Department, formed in the same year and run by a mixture of Fabians and Marxists, which the Special Branch believed was in receipt of money from Moscow.[25] The *Free Oxford* magazine also tried to obtain Soviet funds through the Berlin Bureau of the CYI.[26]

Because that early Communist activity has hitherto been overlooked, together with the links that bound it to Soviet supported organisations, some investigators into the origins of Cambridge communism have looked elsewhere for evidence. Their attention has focused on Peter Kapitza, a Russian physicist who arrived in Cambridge in 1921 as part of a scientific purchasing team. He accepted an invitation to stay on in Cambridge, and for the next thirteen years he worked at the Cavendish Laboratory on atomic research alongside Rutherford. Such was his contribution that in 1929 Kapitza became the first foreigner for nearly 200 years to become a Fellow of the Royal Society. He spent most summers in Russia on holiday but in 1934 the Soviet government refused to allow him to return to England. Kapitza's services were required in Russia and every facility was provided to enable him to develop the research he had begun in England. The next year the Soviet government was able to buy the contents of his laboratory in Cambridge and ship them to Moscow where Kapitza was the Head of the Institute of Physical Problems at the Soviet Academy of Sciences. There he became one of the leading figures in Soviet atomic research over the next two decades.

In his book *Spycatcher*, the former MI5 scientific adviser, Peter Wright, tells that he suspected Kapitza of having been a recruiter for Soviet intelligence. Kapitza remained close to the Soviet government and 'on several occasions was observed receiving Soviet intelligence officers in his rooms'.[27] On his final return to the Soviet Union Kapitza received visiting British scientists at his dacha. Ultimately however the case of Kapitza was, says Wright, 'just another loose end'.[28] The writer Richard Deacon, however, has no doubts. He maintains Kapitza was recruited by Michael Trilisser, the head of the Cheka's foreign department INO, and throughout his time in England was an agent of Soviet intelligence whose presence 'marked the modest beginning of what was to become a steady infiltration of Cambridge University by Soviet government agents over the next fifteen years'.[29] If that were so, it is surprising it has not been commented upon by many other writers on Soviet espionage in Britain.

One who does deal in some detail with Kapitza is Andrew Sinclair. In his study of intelligence and treason in the universities he points out that when Kapitza's equipment was removed from Cambridge for the Soviet Union responsibility for its transfer was placed in the hands of the London head of Soviet Intelligence, Samuel Cahan,[30] nominally a

First Secretary at the Soviet Embassy in London. But Sinclair stops short of suggesting that Kapitza was in effect a spy. Instead, he draws attention to the historic significance of the Russian scientist's atomic research, and to the Kapitza Club at Cambridge, an informal group of scientists who met weekly to discuss their findings. Among the scientific community at the time were several Communist sympathisers such as J. D. Bernal and Roy Pascal, and others whose work was of immense interest to the Soviet Union for military as well as peaceful purposes.

Some of them, as well as Kapitza himself, met Nikolai Bukharin, Zinoviev's successor as head of the Comintern when he came to London in the summer of 1931 with seven Soviet scientists for an international congress. There were protests in the press about the admission of Bukharin and the whole event was observed by the police who intercepted telegrams sent from the congress to Moscow.[31]

Whether Kapitza was in any formal sense an agent of Soviet intelligence is open to question. He was not, in any case, the progenitor of Cambridge's Communist connection. But undeniably he had access to areas of research and to scientists in whom the Soviet authorities were greatly interested. And there is little doubt that his first loyalty lay with his homeland. To say that he was 'kidnapped' by the Soviet government in 1934 on the personal orders of Stalin – as has been suggested[32] – is to overlook that fact. The Kapitza case is significant in the study of Soviet espionage in Britain as one of the earliest alleged examples. Its treatment highlights the difficulty of defining what is and what is not a covert intelligence operation, what constitutes evidence of such activity. The differing opinions of present-day writers confirm that on many of these basic questions there is no real agreement and often no verifiable proof on which to base a definite conclusion.

Kapitza apart, it remains that between 1920 and 1922 all the elements of later controversies were taking shape in the universities: the network of dedicated Marxist intellectuals who nurtured the ambition to take communism out into the world through the professions, combined with an expression of the need for secrecy and the existence of covert encouragement from the Soviet Union, which was engaged in gearing up its intelligence gathering resources for the future.

The size and the power of the Cheka were rapidly expanding. By the middle of 1921 it had some 261,000 members made up of 30,000 civilian staff, 137,000 troops and 94,288 frontier guards.[33] In February

1922, however, the Politburo formally dissolved the Cheka and transferred its functions to a new State Political Administration (GPU) which was to be subordinated to the People's Commissariat of Internal Affairs, the NKVD. Dzerzhinsky was to become the Chairman of the GPU and Vice-Chairman of the NKVD. In practice, the changes imposed no inhibitions on the powers of the security forces. They were still able to arrest at will, banish without trial and carry out unlimited searches and investigations and execute suspects on their own initiative.

Further changes in the Soviet regime enhanced the status of the security police. In November 1923, just over eighteen months after Stalin had been appointed party General Secretary, a new constitution for the Soviet Union was introduced. And what had begun six years previously as an 'Extraordinary Commission' became formalised as the Unified State Political Administration, the OGPU. This permanent body was attached to the Council of Ministers, outside the NKVD's control. Dzerzhinsky retained his position as Chairman and in 1924 enhanced his own personal power when he became Chairman of the Supreme Council for National Economy.[34]

His position illustrates how, during this period, there were many overlapping functions between the various institutions of the Soviet state. The Cheka and the OGPU were beginning to play an important part in foreign affairs – not so much in policy matters but in administration, such as the nomination of the overseas representatives who were being appointed in various countries following the signing of trade agreements. The Cheka/OGPU also began to place its own agents within those establishments. Those who adopted the cover of a diplomatic secretary or attaché but in reality were part of a Cheka section which became known as 'Legals' and their sections as Residencies.[35] The section head was the Resident. This arrangement set a pattern that has existed to the present day. The terminology also prompted the adoption of the corresponding label of 'Illegals' which was applied to Soviet intelligence agents who penetrated foreign countries without diplomatic status and often under false identities.

To carry out their work abroad the Cheka/OGPU also utilised the Comintern's extensive contacts and the resources of military intelligence, the GRU. Dzerzhinsky himself represented the Communist Party at early Comintern congresses. Later, Trilisser, the head of INO, was a member of the International Relations Section of the Comintern, and Joseph Unshlikht, who had attended the 1907 Party Congress in London and became one of Dzerzhinsky's deputies, sat on the Comintern executive committee.[36] In foreign stations duties often overlapped: Georges Agabekov, who worked under Trilisser in the 1920s before defecting to the West, recalled that Apressoff, a lawyer who was Soviet Consul at Meshed in Persia was at the same time the Intelligence Resident and the Comintern representative.[37]

In Britain the trading bodies which sprang up in the wake of the 1921 agreement also became involved in propaganda activities. In September 1922 a 50 lb. bundle of literature including the *Theses of the Comintern* were found in the Surrey Docks lying near the SS *Vladimir Russanoff*, a ship belonging to the All-Russian Co-operative Society, the principal Soviet trading company in Britain, generally known as Arcos. One of the crew who spoke English had copies of Communist magazines in his locker, which he said had been given to him by a stranger who came on board.[38] The contents of the *Comintern Theses* were regraded by the authorities as dangerously seditious: in June the previous year Albert Inkpin, general secretary of the CPGB, received six months' hard labour for publishing a translation of the Theses.[39]

Anxious to avoid the fiasco of the 1921 protest, the British government assembled a more thorough dossier of charges against the Soviet Union. In May 1923 Lord Curzon authorised the delivery of a 26-point memorandum of protest to the Soviet government. The 'Curzon Memorandum' complained that the undertaking to refrain from hostile action under the 1921 Trade Agreement had 'from the start been consistently and flagrantly violated by the Soviet government'.[40] It cited examples of Soviet and Comintern agitation in India, Afghanistan and Persia, and referred to similar instances in Egypt, Turkey, the British Dominions and within Great Britain itself. It also protested about the death in the Soviet Union in 1920 of a British agent, C. F. Davison, and the imprisonment in the same year of Stan Harding, another agent, as well as the detention by the Soviet Union of two British trawlers. In reply Litvinov denied responsibility for the fate of the two Britsh agents and for the work of the Comintern but accepted the rest and embarked on a policy of cautious reconciliation with Britain. His measured response placed the Soviet Union in an advantageous position after the British general election held at the end of the year.

RECOGNITION AND RECRIMINATION

In January 1924 Ramsay MacDonald became Britain's first Labour Prime Minister. Nine days after taking office his minority government recognised the Soviet regime. Christian Rakovsky, who had arrived in

London the previous September to replace Krasin at the head of the Trade Delegation, became Chargé d'Affaires.

During the next three years the Soviet Union pursued a twofold policy towards Britain: first to use full diplomatic relations to develop trade between the two countries; and secondly, mainly through the Comintern, to provide support for the British Communist Party in increasing its influence in the trade unions and Labour Party. The two aims were destined to intertwine and finally to conflict. The latter necessarily entailed the continuation of covert methods as used in the preceding six years. But now more convenient channels existed in the Soviet diplomatic and trading organisations in London. A series of incidents from 1924–7 exposed the relationships between the various agencies at the Soviet Union's disposal and the essentially subversive nature of its political goals. The story of these events – from the arrest of a Communist editor in 1924, through the Communist trial of 1925 to the Arcos Raid in 1927 – has been told many times and need only be recounted here for the light they throw on Soviet aims and methods.

The Soviet Union's newfound relationship with Britain did not immediately appear to disturb the Comintern. A new representative was despatched to Britain in 1924: D. Petrovsky, who went under the name of A. J. Bennett.[41] He was to remain in Britain undetected for some five years and in 1928 accompanied the British contingent at the Comintern's Sixth Congress.[42] At the Fifth Congress held in Moscow in June and July 1924 a resolution on the task of the British Communist Party called on it to 'mobilise the broadest masses of the English proletariat' to exert pressure on the 'petty-bourgeois and treacherous' Labour leadership.[43] Zinoviev, however, complained that the movement had not developed as quickly as he expected and once again urged the British Communists to seek affiliation to the Labour Party. The Soviet Union additionally wanted the Communist Party to play a more central role in the mainstream of the trade unions, at a time of great industrial unrest.

But a broad spectrum of Labour Party opinion was no less suspicious of the Russians than were the Conservatives. In April the Labour government set up an Industrial Unrest Committee under J. R. Clynes to consider the extent of hidden Communist influence in recent docks and transport strikes. During its deliberations the Home Secretary told his colleagues that £60,000 had been provided by the Soviet Union for the British Communist Party up to March 1922, with a similar sum allocated that year, and £2,500 for expenses during the last general election.[44] The committee reported that although there was little evidence that the Communist Party had initiated any dispute, it had actively intervened in strikes and had received substantial financial assistance from the Comintern. Despite that, the committee concluded that the CPGB remained in great financial difficulty and its influence could be exaggerated. It therefore saw no useful purpose in initiating legal proceedings although they could not be ruled out in the future.[45]

Less than four months later, however, in August 1924 the government acted when the Attorney General instigated the arrest of J. R. Campbell, the editor of the *Workers' Weekly*, the CPGB's official journal. Campbell had been carrying out an anti-war campaign in accordance with Comintern policy, during which he had published an article calling on soldiers to join the workers in smashing capitalism and urging them 'don't shoot'.[46] The British government regarded this as an offence under the Incitement to Mutiny Act of 1797. But eight days later on 13 August the charges were withdrawn. An outcry ensued from the Conservative opposition and the press. They linked the government's change of mind to the Anglo-Soviet Treaties then being finalised, which provided for a loan to the Soviet Union by Britain. A Commons debate after the summer recess resulted in a defeat for the Labour government and the calling of a new general election. It was to turn on the very question of Soviet interference in British affairs.

On 25 October 1924, four days before the general election the *Daily Mail* published the contents of a letter which purported to come from Gregory Zinoviev, the President of the Comintern, to the CPGB. In lurid language the letter called for the formation of Communist cells in the army. It was accepted as genuine by the Foreign Office and the press. The contents certainly conformed to the main thrust of Comintern policy at the time. At least two other letters from Zinoviev to the British Communist Party had come into the possession of the British authorities in the early summer of 1924.[47] On both those occasions the Labour government had not doubted their authenticity but had decided to take no action. Yet the circulation of such a letter at a politically sensitive moment seemed calculated to play into the hands of the most fervent of anti-Communists. It did precisely that, for the election resulted in a crushing defeat for MacDonald and the return to office of the Conservatives under Baldwin. On balance, it now seems probable that the letter was a forgery, the work of a group of White Russians in Berlin. In the absence of any original, the internal evidence of the published version – quirks of terminology such as references to the 'Third Communist International' instead of the Third International – point to its being a fake.

The incoming Conservative government shelved the Anglo-Soviet Treaty but continued to maintain diplomatic relations with the Soviet Union. The Locarno Treaty completed at the end of 1925 as a non-aggression pact between Britain, France and Germany seemed to bring the guarantee of peace in Europe. At home, industrial militancy remained a potential threat to recovery. Trade union affairs became a major focus of interest for the Soviet Union. Its policy was again conducted on two levels: first was an official policy of open cultivation and the promotion of friendly relations between British unions and their Soviet equivalents. Tomsky, the Soviet trade union leader, addressed the TUC and in November 1924 a TUC delegation visited Moscow. This paved the way for a conference between British and Russian trade unions the following April which inaugurated an Anglo-Russian Joint Trade Union Council.

Parallel to this initiative was the familiar process of secret funding and political control. Once again the Comintern handled this aspect of Soviet policy, directed towards the CPGB and the National Minority Movement. Events on the industrial front encouraged them greatly. On 25 July 1925, Red Friday, the government retreated before the threat of a miners' strike. A. J. Cook, the miners' Marxist leader, was jubilant.

Alarmed, the government began to prepare measures to win any future confrontation. Above all, however, it feared that disaffection would extend to the armed forces. In October 1925 the police raided the CPGB offices in King Street, Covent Garden together with those of the National Minority Movement and the Young Communist League in Great Ormond Street and *Workers' Weekly* in Fleet Street. Altogether twelve party members were arrested, including general secretary Albert Inkpin, J. R. Campbell, J. T. Murphy, Tom Wintringham, Willie Gallacher, Wal Hannington, Arthur McManus, Harry Politt, Tom Bell and Robin Page Arnot of the Labour Research Department. They were all found guilty of sedition under the Incitement to Mutiny Act; five received sentences of twelve months' imprisonment and the other seven six months.[48]

In the following year the government published a collection of 'Communist Papers', consisting of fifty-two items discovered in the raids. Included was correspondence for 1925 between the Comintern and the CPGB, the Young Communist League and the National Minority Movement. There was clear evidence of extensive Soviet involvement in the affairs of the CPGB at all levels. There were, for example, letters from the Organisation Bureau of the Comintern to the CPGB about recruitment and the reorganisation of the party on a factory nucleus basis, plans for campaigning and training and observations on the 'inadequacy' of the CPGB's organisation. The party was told in December 1925 that six places would be reserved for its members among the forty party workers from different countries who would attend an eighteen-month to two-year course at the Lenin School in Moscow. Those nominated to attend would be expected to have some political experience, show a knowledge of the three volumes of *Das Kapital* and speak either French or German.[49]

The opening of the Lenin School was in fact postponed, but the papers revealed that several British Communists had attended a conference in Amsterdam in July 1925 with Indian and continental revolutionaries. Among those present at that meeting were Percy Glading, who went to India on Comintern business earlier in the year and who, in 1938, was convicted of espionage for the Soviet Union, M. N. Roy, Clemens Palme Dutt, Rajani's brother who was to play an important part in recruitment at the universities in the 1930s and Henricus Sneevliet, the Comintern's Dutch representative, who before he broke with Stalin worked with Soviet agents to set up 'illegal' espionage networks in Britain at the end of the 1920s. Glading was followed to India by other British Communists including George Allison and a Cambridge graduate, Phillip Spratt. Like Glading Allison was later convicted in Britain of spying for the Soviet Union.[50]

Comintern leaders retained high hopes that their British followers were on the brink of a major breakthrough. After the failure of a Comintern-backed revolution in Germany in October 1923, they turned their attention to Britain. Zinoviev believed the masses were becoming more revolutionary and he held up Britain as a shining example of how to apply 'united front' tactics.[51] Communist Party membership was rising and at a conference in March 1926 the Minority Movement claimed to speak for over 950,000 workers.[52] And although the Labour Party had rejected affiliation by the CPGB, banned its members from standing as Labour parliamentary candidates and prevented them from joining constituency parties, the National Left-Wing Movement was attempting to do in the political sphere what the Minority Movement appeared to have achieved in the trade unions.

The OGPU had also scored a victory against Britain and Russian counter-revolutionaries in the West through its manipulation of an organisation known as 'The Trust', which anti-Communists believed was a cover for efforts to subvert the Bolshevik regime. Instead it was totally controlled by the Soviet secret service, whose agents were able to monitor the movements of their enemies and lure them back into

Russia where they were seized. One of the most famous of all British secret agents, Sidney Reilly, fell victim to the trick at the end of 1925, when he was arrested inside the Soviet Union and subsequently executed.[53]

One of the less well-known Soviet initiatives of the time centred on Boris Ogareff, the son of a Russian princess named Marie Mestchersky. A report in Home Office files for December 1926 records that according to the French Ministry of Foreign Affairs he was a Bolshevik agent 'who had been commissioned to recruit ex-British officers in France'.[54] Married to an Australian, Ruth Grierson, the 42-year-old Ogareff lived in Boulogne but for the previous two years had run an office in Paris ostensibly as a representative for a firm of fire-extinguisher manufacturers. His bizzare assignment on behalf of the Red Army appears to have made little headway, but it is one of the earliest examples of the use by the Soviet Union of a commercial operation in the West as a cover for illicit activities. In the years ahead it was to become a much-repeated formula.

When the explosion in Britain came, in the shape of the general strike in 1926, the CPGB and its Soviet masters seemed quite unprepared for it – unlike the British government. The Soviet Union's misjudgement of British attitudes was illustrated when its cheque for £200,000 to the TUC was ignominiously returned. The uncompromising anti-Communist Home Secretary, Joynson-Hicks, sought to prove that the Communists had made other, more successful interventions in the strike. He alleged that A. J. Cook had been party to Soviet plans to precipitate an upheaval when he had met Losovsky, the Profintern general secretary in Berlin the previous summer, and asserted that among other preparations £25,000 had been sent to the Minority Movement in March 1926. Joynson-Hicks was, however, obliged to withdraw his main charge that the Co-operative Wholesale Society had received £300,000 for strike funds from the Arcos trading organisation.[55] Beyond dispute was that in their strike which continued for another six months the miners received over £1,250,000 from Soviet sources. But the contributions from Moscow were to no avail. Within nine days the general strike was over, hopes of a British revolution vanished and Communist fortunes went into decline.

The accusations levelled by Joynson-Hicks against Arcos during the general strike served however as the prelude to events over the next year, when the trading organisation stood at the centre of a major crisis in Anglo-Soviet relations. Since the agreement of 1921 the Soviet Union's trade with Britain had steadily grown. By 1926 a quarter of the

Soviet Union's imports came from Britain. The Soviet commercial presence in the country had also expanded to comprise some 35 concerns by
1927. Besides Arcos, which had been set up in 1921, other organisations
covered the range of business life, from banks, shipping companies,
and oil, textiles and timber businesses to several general export-import
agencies. Individual companies included the All Union Textile
Syndicate, the Bank for Russian Trade, Central Association of Flax
Growers Ltd, Transcaucasian State Import and Export Trading Office,
Ukrainian Co-operative Ltd, Drug Manufacturing State Trust and the
Moscow Municipality Handicraft Department.[56] Between them they
employed in the region of 575 people, of whom about 350 were Soviet
citizens. A further thirty-one Soviet citizens worked in the Soviet
Legation at Chesham House in Chesham Place and another fifty-three
in the trade mission offices, which it shared with Arcos at Soviet House
in the City of London at 49 Moorgate. The remainder of the staff were
mostly British. Altogether 224 British subjects worked for Arcos and
associate organisations, eighteen were employed in the Legation and
twenty-seven in the trade mission.[57]

Among the British employees were several Communist Party
members. These included Alexander Squair, who was secretary of the
Arcos employees' trade union known as Mestkom, F. Quelch,
F. Priestley and W. Duncan, who were to figure in investigations by the
British government in 1928 of transactions involving the Moscow
Narodny Bank in London. Earlier, in 1923 the Trade Delegation had
employed six former police officers who had been involved in the police
strikes of 1919. One of them, ex-sergeant Arthur Lakey was, according
to the Special Branch, based at New Bond Street as chief private
enquiry agent for Nikolai Klishko, the OGPU agent who was attached
to the mission.[58] Klishko was not alone among the Soviet representatives in London in being more concerned with politics than trade.
Krasin, who had replaced Rakovsky as Chargé d'Affaires died at the
end of 1926 and was succeeded by Rosengolz, a Red Army propaganda
specialist.

In February 1927 the British government sent a note of 'protest and
warning' to Moscow about Soviet interference in British affairs during
the miners' strike and its subversive activities in China.[59] Tory
politicians were becoming agitated once more and were looking for an
excuse to break off diplomatic relations with the Soviet Union. Events
accelerated in the spring. In April the Soviet mission in Peking was
raided. And resentment was growing at the prospect of a £10 million
loan which the Soviet Union was negotiating from the Midland Bank.

Justification came with evidence that the Soviet Union was engaged in espionage to obtain military secrets. Early in the year an RAF man was convicted for stealing two documents. George Monkland, a former army officer who was now a Lloyds' underwriter reported to the authorities that he had been approached by another ex-officer called Wilfred McCartney and asked to provide information on arms shipments. The Scottish-born McCartney had enlisted in the Royal Army Medical Corps in 1915 at the age of sixteen. He was later commissioned in the infantry and left the army at the end of the war. In 1921 he had inherited £20,000 from his father which he proceeded to squander, acquiring convictions for shopbreaking, assault on the police and for being drunk and disorderly. In April 1927 he had joined the Communist Party, a month after beginning his espionage career. But the net quickly tightened around him. The government supplied Monkland with an obsolete RAF training manual for McCartney to pass on to his contact, Georg Hansen, a German student who had come to Britain in July 1927 ostensibly to attend the Regent School of Languages in London. In November McCartney and Hansen were both arrested and the following January were each sentenced to ten years' imprisonment.[60] But by then circumstances had changed radically.

Eager to raise the stakes, Joynson-Hicks told the Cabinet on 11 May 1927 that a British army signals manual had been seen at the Arcos office by an English employee. The document which was classified confidential was entitled: 'Descriptions of and Instructions for Wireless Telegraphy'.[61] The following day the British police raided the Moorgate premises and began a search that was to last three days. *The Times* commented that it was 'doubtful whether there are more massive strong rooms outside the Bank of England' than those in the specially constructed £300,000 Arcos building, with their thick concrete walls and steel doors with elaborate locks and bolts.[62] But the signals manual was not found. The only classified British government papers to be discovered were two relatively unimportant RAF documents.

Undaunted, Prime Minister Baldwin informed the House of Commons on 24 May that:

Both military espionage and subversive activities throughout the British Empire and North and South America were directed and carried out from Soviet House.

No effective differentiation of rooms or duties was observed as between the members of the Trade Delegation and the employees of Arcos and both these organisations have been involved in anti-British espionage and propaganda.[63]

Baldwin's assertions were based on additional material provided by the interception of wireless communications between the Soviet establishments in London and Moscow. In one celebrated telegram from Rosengolz to the Narkomindel in Moscow on 13 April 1927, the Soviet Chargé d'Affaires declared that: 'I doubt very much the possibility of a raid on our embassy. I would however consider it a very useful measure of precaution to suspend for a time the forwarding by post of documents of friends, 'neighbours', and so forth from London to Moscow and vice versa.'[64]

Baldwin said that in the raid the police had found a quantity of documents in the photostat room in the possession of one Robert Koling or Kaulin, and more material in the cipher room with Anton Miller the clerk there. Elsewhere, in the secret staff records a memorandum dated 23 December 1926 was discovered, addressed to Comrade Burakova of the Secret Section, from Jilinsky who combined duties in charge of the staff allotments department in the Trade Delegation with those of, in Baldwin's words, the 'principal espionage and secret propaganda agent for Europe'.[65] This note revealed that Koling's job had been to act as a courier between Soviet House in the City and the Legation at Chesham House in the West End. Koling emerged as a man with a long history of political activity. After emigrating from Riga in 1905 he had worked as a shoemaker and a sailor before joining the tsarist army in the war. After a period in German captivity he joined the Red Trade Union of Sailors and eventually came to Britain where he joined the Blyth branch of the Communist Party in 1925.[66] His agitational work had evidently continued since he joined the trade mission. On him was found correspondence from the Profintern to Communists in Britain and America and membership forms for the Minority Movement filled in by seamen whose support had been canvassed in Russian ports. In the possession of the cipher clerk, Miller, the police found a list of secret cover addresses for communication with Communist parties in the USA, several South American countries, South Africa, Australia and Canada.

Among Baldwin's additional complaints were accusations of anti-British activity in China, in which Borodin, the former Comintern representative in England, was instrumental. The Soviet Union insisted, however, through Litvinov in Moscow and Rosengolz in London that Borodin was 'a private individual who is not and never had been in the service of the Soviet government.'[67]

A selection of documents removed from Soviet house was hurriedly published by the government as a White Paper. They highlighted the

Soviet Union's attempts to recruit British sailors and train them on Arcos ships in political agitation. In November 1926 Karl Bahn had written to Jilinsky that he wished to make 'these ships of ours a base for training politically-conscious seamen, who, after preliminary training, could be sent to other British ships'.[68] Bahn complained, however, that so far the results had been far from satisfactory: the CPGB 'recommends none but the refuse of the Labour Party, people who are not seamen'. One man, Adams, was described as 'a good orator but a bad stoker',[69] and another stoker, named Harris, who had been recommended by one of the Rothsteins, drank and was mistrustful. By contrast, a man called Morris on the SS *Korvik*, who had been recruited during a seamen's strike, had written for *Workers' Weekly* and as soon as he had learnt to work better as a seaman would be ready to join an English ship.

The importance of seamen to the Soviet Union was confirmed by a later defector, Richard Krebs, who took on the name Jan Valtin. A sailor and former member of the German Communist Party, he worked in the Political Bureau of the Comintern's International of Seamen and Maritime Workers in the early 1930s. The Bureau's tasks were to engage in revolutionary activity, maintain world-wide communications links among revolutionaries and carry out marine espionage.[70]

Rosengolz's protestations of innocence of the accusations made against the Soviet representatives in London and his countercharge that the police had beaten up at least one of his staff, were brushed aside. At the end of May 1927 the British government severed diplomatic relations with the Soviet Union and expelled members of the Legation, the Trade Delegation and the Soviet employees of Arcos and its associate companies. By 23 June Joynson-Hicks was able to tell parliament that thirty out of thirty-one officials from the main Soviet mission had left Britain, of the fifty-three members of the Trade Delegation forty-three had departed with forty-eight of the 350 Soviet citizens employed in the trading organisations.[71] In Moscow Litvinov said that the British action was no casual or unexpected event but the logical outcome of an anti-Soviet policy pursued by the government.

The repercussions of the Arcos raid were widespread. The related McCartney–Hansen case was the first instance of Soviet military espionage to reach the British courts. The Anglo-Soviet trade union council was dissolved. Support for the Communist Party fell sharply. Governments in several countries took action against Soviet organisations.[72] In Beirut, French police raided the Arcos office there, which according to the documents found, was a subsidiary of the London operation.[73] Investigations rumbled on for several years in some cases. It was not until August 1931 that the Argentinian authorities closed the Soviet trading organisation in Buenos Aires. According to the local chief of police, in his report to the Argentinian Minister of the Interior, a copy of which found its way to the British Foreign Office, interest in the activities of the Russians had first been aroused as a result of the raid in London.[74]

It has sometimes been depicted that the Arcos raid was a botched job which served only to provide an excuse for Tory politicians to rid the country of the Bolsheviks. It is true that Joynson-Hicks and others like him, and much of the press, wanted the excuse. It is equally true that the police failed to find the particular document they were looking for. But what they did find was ample evidence that the trade mission and Arcos had been heavily involved in subversive political activity in Britain and the Empire. The successful prosecution of McCartney and Hansen confirmed that the Soviet Union was beginning to carry out espionage. If there was any miscalculation it was by the Soviet Union not by the British Home Secretary or the police. It had tried to mix revolutionary agitation with trade and diplomacy and it had failed. The Soviet Union's primary aim was to build a centralised industrial economy, for which it badly needed Western trade and expertise. Trying at the same time to undermine the political structures of Western countries could only defeat that principal objective. Britain's major error came in the aftermath of the raid itself when Baldwin unwisely revealed the contents of secret messages from the Soviet Embassy to Moscow. The disclosure alerted the Soviet government of the total lack of security surrounding its transmissions and it promptly switched to a system of codes that the British failed to decipher.

Soviet ambivalence in its international relations, between the drive for economic progress and the residual lingering for world-wide upheaval, reflected the struggles that were taking place inside Russia. Lenin had died in January 1924 and Dzerzhinsky in 1926. A new era was dawning in the history of the Soviet Union and in its relationships with the world. Stalin was tightening his grip on the instruments of government and pushing aside potential rivals. Those who were associated with the failure to spread Bolshevism outside Russia were among the first to be isolated as left-wing adventurers. In 1926 Trotsky, the apostle of universal revolution and Zinoviev, President of the Comintern, were removed from the Politburo. In November 1927 both were expelled from the Soviet Communist Party. Eventually, fresh means of weakening the capitalist powers would emerge. They would be more suited to the doctrine of 'Socialism in One Country' which dictated that the interests of the Soviet state would prevail over revolutionary excesses.

3   The Age of the 'Illegals'

OLD HABITS, NEW DIRECTIONS

In the aftermath of the diplomatic breach of 1927 the Soviet Union was forced onto the defensive. Its advantageous trade with Britain had been jeopardised and prospects of improved relations with many other countries had been severely damaged. A host of Soviet diplomatic and political weaknesses had been exposed. It could neither keep its embassies' wireless communications secret nor drive Britain or any other Western country to the edge of revolution. A reassessment of how it conducted its foreign relations was called for. Domestic considerations also pointed to a change of emphasis. Stalin was launching the first Five-Year Plan, aimed at the intensive industrialisation of the Soviet economy, to be followed by the enforced collectivisation of agriculture. Alleged deviationists – not only Trotsky and his followers on the left but Bukharin and the head of the Soviet trade unions, Tomsky, on the right – were being mercilessly purged. Socialism in one country was under way.

Yet this strategy implied no softening of attitudes to the West. Indeed they showed all the immediate signs of hardening. In July 1927 Stalin warned that a 'frenzied struggle' for markets was taking place between the capitalist nations which would result in a 'new imperialist war'.[1] In response the workers must launch a fresh revolutionary offensive and demonstrate their hostility to capitalists and social democrats alike.

The role of the Comintern, the world party of the revolution, posed particular problems for Stalin. It was proving an effective instrument in the subordination of foreign Communist parties to the will of the Soviet Union and, to an extent, in mobilising popular support for Communist causes. But by the same token it was becoming discredited as a puppet of Moscow. The Comintern's failure to translate subversive manipulation into genuine socialist revolution, whether in Germany, China, Britain or India – and to be repeatedly exposed in the act of failing – earned it the contempt of Stalin. In 1927 he reputedly declared: 'Who are these Comintern people? They are nothing but hirelings on our Soviet pay-roll. In ninety years they will never make a revolution anywhere.'[2] Henceforth its activities would be determined by Stalin's conception of Soviet national interest, not according to the whims of free-booting propagandists. Wherever possible the Comintern's member parties were reorganised under leaders whom Stalin and his henchmen could trust. In Britain, its client, the CPGB faced a bleak future on the political fringes. The British Communists' revolutionary opportunity in the General Strike of 1926 had passed. And although both militancy and the 'united fronts' were past their peak, a reconstituted party embarked on a phase of aggressive sectarianism and attacked moderate socialists in the Labour Party as 'social fascists'.

If Britain imagined that her action in May 1927 would lead to any moderation of Soviet behaviour she was, therefore, much mistaken. Many of the habits of the previous ten years persisted. Joynson-Hicks, for one, did not expect it otherwise. Indeed, he would probably have been intensely disappointed if the Soviet Union had mended her ways overnight. He did not have long to wait before he sensed fresh intrigues. In March 1928 two £10 Bank of England notes found on Michael Burke, an Irishman arrested for illegal possession of firearms, had been traced back to the Bank for Russian Trade in London. Joynson-Hicks ordered an investigation which after four weeks uncovered two sets of transactions carried out by British Communist employees of the London branch of the Moscow Narodny Bank and Soviet trading organisations in London.[3]

The first involved Quelch and Priestley, two English employees of Centrosoyus, one of the Soviet trading bodies which remained in London after 1927. Both individuals were members of the CPGB. Quelch worked in the Centrosoyus tea department and Priestley, who had earlier been employed by the Arcos Steamship Company, now worked in the accounts department. During the second half of 1927 they had changed £10,300 worth of £5 notes for £1 notes through the Moscow Norodny Bank. Most of the money found its way to the Communist Party. The original £5 notes were traced to an amount of £20,000 handed personally to Shannin, then the Commercial Attaché at the Soviet Embassy, on 25 May 1927 – the day after Mr Baldwin's statement on the outcome of the Arcos raid – by the Narodny Bank's assistant cashier. The money came from the account of a company in Berlin on which Shannin had authority to draw. The German capital was the centre of the Comintern's operations for the whole of Western Europe and after the break of 1927 became for a time one of the places from which activities against Britain were directed.[4]

Among other deals involving Quelch and Priestley £1,500 was paid into a joint account opened for them by Alexander Squair, the former secretary of Mestkom, the trade union for Soviet employees in Britain, ostensibly for the purpose of clearing up the union's affairs. Quelch, who had been to the Soviet Union in October 1927 for the celebrations of the tenth anniversary of the Bolshevik revolution also held an account at the Moscow Narodny Bank, in the name of an English periodical on behalf of the Soviet newspaper, *Pravda*. In total, Quelch and Priestley were involved in transactions involving £13,796 drawn from Soviet sources between July and November 1927.

The second case concerned William Duncan, a 26-year-old Aberdonian. He had joined the CPGB in 1923 and had been on the executive of the Young Communist League and the secretary of a section of the National Minority Movement. Unemployed, he came to London in 1924 and on the recommendation of Andrew Rothstein found work with the Moscow Narodny Bank as a messenger. He was promoted to a clerk's job in the foreign exchange department where he was able to sell large quantities of dollars either to foreign exchange brokers or to the bank's own cashier, which he then exchanged for notes to pass on to the Communist Party. Over a six-month period up to April 1928 he was able to provide the CPGB with £14,202 in this way. Altogether, the transactions of the three men amounted to £27,998, all of which went into Communist funds. The directors of the Narodny Bank in London were interviewed in the inquiry and their denial of any knowledge of the deals was accepted by the British government. No action was taken against the bank, which dismissed Duncan from his post.

The affair was once again less than a complete success for Joynson-Hicks. He had failed to make the key connection, to prove that the Soviet government and its banks in London were fully involved in the cases of the three British Communists and the Irish gunman. However, the revelation that English Communists employed by Soviet institutions had been used as a channel for funding the CPGB and its satellites served to make his political point. Joynson-Hicks reinforced this by announcing that separate inquiries by the Metropolitan Police over the previous six to eight months, before the Burke case, had revealed that money for various Communist organisations in Britain had been channelled through the bank. His view of Soviet intentions was shared unequivocally by the Foreign Office. A secret Foreign Office memorandum in March 1929, for example, commented that Soviet foreign policy had 'not altered one jot or tittle. World Revolution remains the avowed objective, and their agents continue to foment agitation and unrest in every country, especially in Asia. Communist cells and centres are maintained everywhere abroad, and money seems always forthcoming to promote sedition.'[5] The Soviet Union drew its own conclusions from the experience, which contributed towards a protracted rethink of the wisdom of involving local Communist organisations in clandestine operations.

But within two months the Anglo-Soviet breach came to an end. The trigger was a shift in British domestic politics rather than any new initiative by the Soviet Union. In May 1929, exactly two years after the Arcos raid Labour emerged from a general election as the largest party and, with Liberal support, Ramsay MacDonald formed his second minority government. He proceeded with great caution to heal the rift with the Soviet Union. Only when he had secured parliamentary approval did he re-establish diplomatic relations. This had to wait until after the summer recess in November, when the Commons voted by 374 votes to 199 for an exchange of ambassadors. For the Soviet Union, Gregory Sokolnikov took up appointment in London despite King George V's refusal to receive him, and established a temporary residence on a six-month lease at 40 Grosvenor Square in Mayfair.[6] Trade promptly revived and over the next six months the two governments negotiated temporary commercial and fisheries agreements. As a conciliatory gesture the Soviet Union gave renewed pledges to refrain from disruptive activity in any part of the British Empire. Never again, even during the Soviet–Nazi pact nor at the height of the cold war, would the two countries sever their diplomatic links.

The relationship was, however, icy and formal. And it was soon Labour's turn to detect the hand of Soviet interference. By May 1930, the Foreign Secretary, Arthur Henderson was confronted with a barrage of parliamentary questions about Soviet propaganda and the behaviour of the Comintern. He summoned Sokolnikov to the Foreign Office and told him that he regarded the situation as 'grave' and the cause of much anxiety. The Soviet Ambassador denied that his government was providing funds for the British Communist Party or that any trade or embassy officials were acting improperly.[7] The government was not convinced and a Cabinet committee on the 'Alleged Propaganda Activities of the Third International and the Soviet Government' was set up. In October 1930 the committee reported that 'those whose duty it is to watch over activities hostile to this country' had accumulated a mass of documentary evidence that the pledges of good conduct given by the Soviet Union the previous year had been broken. The report concluded, however, that as propaganda of this sort was a vital part of the Soviet Union's proclaimed doctrines and intentions it was 'perhaps ... nothing surprising'. It recommended that a break in relations should be avoided but that remonstrations should be made to the Soviet government.[8]

More drastic action might have seemed futile in the midst of a mounting economic crisis. Wall Street had collapsed in October 1929 sending shock waves across the Western world. Stalin forecast the collapse of capitalism, while he struggled at home with two years of famine and the misery and economic dislocation brought about by his ruthless uprooting of the Soviet peasantry. In the summer of 1931 the Labour government fell and Ramsay MacDonald earned the undying hatred of socialists everywhere by leading a Tory-dominated National Government. In one week in September 1931, as the new administration took Britain off the gold standard, the Japanese invaded Manchuria, while China protested helpless at the League of Nations, and the Royal Navy fleet mutinied at Invergordon. The foundations of the post-war world trembled. Conservative statesmen feared that the forces of international communism would give the crumbling edifice a final push.

In Britain Communist agents were despatched to foment unrest in the navy. The government viewed their activity with the utmost alarm. In the ensuing months several hundred sailors were discharged from the service. Two men received gaol sentences for attempting to persuade a naval rating to draft a seditious pamphlet. One, a former Fife miner, George Allison, member of the CPGB Central Commmittee and acting general secretary of the National Minority Movement, who had led the British delegation to the fifth Profintern Congress in Moscow in August 1930[9] and was one of the Comintern's agents in India in 1925, was sentenced to three years' imprisonment, and the other, a *Daily Worker* journalist, William Shepherd, to twenty months.[10] The case was one example of extensive Communist efforts to spread propaganda among the armed forces during the 1930s. The main vehicles were pamphlets, and journals such as *Red Signal*, aimed at naval personnel, and *Soldiers' Voice*. But Communist involvement in the more serious business of sabotage was less easy to confirm. In March 1936 the First Lord of the Admiralty reported that there had been eight cases of sabotage in defence establishments in the previous three years: in Devonport, Chatham, Portsmouth and Sheerness. Although in two cases there were strong reasons for suspecting a known Communist it was impossible to obtain proof.[11]

The party faced the storms of the 1930s under its new

Moscow-approved leadership. Like the earlier phase of 'Leninisation' the process of 'Stalinisation' was intended to make British communism a more effective revolutionary instrument and one more responsive to Soviet dictates. At a special party congress held at Leeds in November 1929 a 'Stalinised' Politburo formally took control. Old party leaders, including Inkpin, Gallacher, Campbell and Murphy were ousted from their positions and within two years Murphy had left the party altogether.[12] At the helm were the remote academic, Rajani Palme Dutt and his social opposite, the north-country boilermaker, Harry Pollitt. A prominent Young Communist League member, William Rust was deputed to edit a new *Daily Worker* newspaper which began publication in January 1930.

A new generation of Communists was being trained at the Lenin School in Moscow which had opened in 1926. According to Walter Krivitsky, the school was subsidised by the Comintern's International Liaison Department, the OMS.[13] Among its earliest students was Percy Glading who attended a six-month course there from October 1929.[14] At about the same time two Welsh Communists, Charles Stead and Leonard Jeffries were at the school; on their return they took a major responsibility for the Communist Party in South Wales.[15]

Many of these developments were watched closely by the Special Branch of the Metropolitan Police. At the beginning of 1930 it received a report from an unnamed individual who had attended a course at the Lenin School at the same time as Glading and the two Welshmen:

> We were having eleven or twelve hours a day in the cleaning commissions ... we had to write our biography, parentage, schooling, etc. and then when one joined the party, what work he has done for the party, what positions he has held and what disagreements he has had with the party and finally any mistakes he had made. Some of us had a job trying to think out how and which mistakes we had made, anyhow we managed to get this out and handed it to the commission. Then in due course we were called up and there we had to relate our biography ... questions were asked such as ... what is the essence of the Right danger? What is the essence of Trotskyism? And a thousand and one questions. If you have been in the army then another fusillade of questions are forthcoming. Some comrades were examined for about five hours.[16]

At the end of January 1930 with the *Daily Worker* just a month old, the Special Branch was able to report to the Home Office on the newspaper's possible sources of funding: 'There was no absolute evidence that the Third International has financed or is financing the

Daily Worker ... but there is proof that it has approved of measures for financing it.'[17] It was pointed out that Page Arnot, who was highly regarded in Moscow had raised the question of 'providing the means' for a Communist daily paper in Britain at a Comintern executive meeting as early as 1928. Various resolutions had been passed to make money available and in December 1929 the Special Branch had learnt from 'a reliable and well-informed source' that £30,000 was to be despatched for the purpose.

The new leaders soon faced a crisis in the party itself. During the slump the CPGB had grown rapidly from a low point of just over 2,500 members at the end of 1930 to a peak of 9,000 at the beginning of 1932. But membership then began to fall as quickly as it had risen. The general election of November 1931 highlighted its weakness when the Party's twenty-six candidates collected only 75,000 votes between them and none was elected. During 1932 the party, and the Comintern, held discussions with the Independent Labour Party which had broken from Labour in July of that year. But the ILP's leaders, including Fenner Brockway and James Maxton were critical of Communist rigidity and the talks collapsed. At the same time the first British Trotskyists emerged, in a small group led by Reg Groves in Balham. Finally in 1933 the Minority Movement, which had become a shadow of an organisation, was dissolved.

The policy of extreme sectarianism was reducing Western communism to impotence. In Germany, where the largest of all the Western parties threw away what chances it had of stopping the rise of Hitler, this course proved catastrophic. Alienated from the mainstream of the Labour movement and with membership dropping the much smaller British party again incurred the wrath of Moscow. The Comintern accused it of a mechanical approach to the class struggle, of neglecting work in the trade unions and the immediate demands of the working class.[18]

At the end of 1931 the Comintern sent one of its agents, Richard Krebs to England to confront the party hierarchy. After his later defection to the West, as Jan Valtin, he recorded that the CPGB was 'led by a corrupt clique of bureaucrats looting not only the Comintern treasury but the pockets of their own rank and file'.[19] It 'had almost no income of its own. Perhaps 5 per cent of its recorded members paid dues. Every phase of party activity was dependent on subsidies from Moscow.'[20] Valtin met Harry Pollitt and set about overhauling the party's operations. He had four assistants: Joe Keenan, a 'hard-boiled Australian', a New Zealander called Red McGrath, Patrick Murphy, 'one of the few hard-drinking, hard-fighting Irishmen' left in the service of Soviet intelligence, and Cilly, a young continental woman who had worked in Arcos before 1927. Valtin described her as 'tall and dark, coolly-independent and chic'.[21] He claims to have brought about the removal of several officials, including George Hardy 'a soft-footed foxy schemer' who had worked for the Comintern in Moscow, India, China, South Africa and the USA. Despite elaborate security precautions, including the possession of three passports – one Dutch, one Norwegian and one American – Valtin was eventually arrested and deported. He attempted to regain entry to Britain through both Newcastle and Glasgow but without success. The failure of his mission illustrated the difficulties of operating in Britain and confirmed the shortcomings of the CPGB. It showed little promise as a political party or as a force for revolution, and there were too many hazards attached to its use as a vehicle for covert activity. Some of its members were, however, deployed for subversive purposes under a legitimate cover.

Previously neglected files in British government archives reveal how the Soviet Union used the reopening of diplomatic relations to begin a fresh round of espionage and subversion through its trading organisations. Contrary to widespread belief, Arcos and many of the other trading bodies were not disbanded in 1927 but were allowed to continue in existence on a reduced level. Arcos itself moved from Moorgate to Bush House, now home of the BBC World Service. After the resumption of relations in 1929 its fortunes rose and it expanded once again, alongside a reconstituted and enlarged Trade Delegation.

In June 1931 Captain Guy Liddell, then in the Special Branch of Scotland Yard, and after the Second World War the Deputy Director General of MI5, wrote to the Foreign Office about the intelligence connections of various members of the Soviet Trade Delegation.[22] Its top official, Saul Bron, the former chairman of the Amtorg trading organisation in the USA was 'entirely controlled by officials of the GPU'. Victor Karpov who had arrived in Britain in 1930 as the chief clerk of Arcos, previously worked in the NKVD and was 'regarded on good authority as the principal GPU agent within the Soviet institutions here'. Shortly after this report Karpov returned to Moscow to join the powerful organ of internal control, the Workers' and Peasants' Inspectorate.

Among other staff in the Trade Delegation with intelligence or Soviet Communist Party connections were: Eugene Goikhbarg, a CPSU member and officially legal adviser to the delegation, whose wife Rebecca was a manager at the head office of Russian Oil Products; Vladislav Kuratov-Leder, an engineer and economist who had worked in the Political Department of the Commissariat for War and retained close ties with Soviet military circles and was said to be 'greatly feared in all the Soviet institutions here'; Krishian Saulit, another member of the Soviet Communist Party who once worked in the special department of the Seventh Army; Yosif Schneerson, ostensibly an Arcos engineer who was a former CPSU and Comintern worker and said to be Karpov's chief assistant, and was allegedly involved in subsidising strikes in Britain and arranging contacts between Soviet organisations and British Communists; Peter Tsurupa, an official of the CPSU Central Committee, who originally came to Britain as secretary to the Managing Director of Arcos; Vera Volik, the wife of the manager of the butter department of the Selosoyous trading body, was 'reliably reported' to be an agent of OGPU's foreign section; and Fanny Robbins, the Russian-born wife of a Communist called W. A. Robbins who had been employed for several years by Arcos as a sales clerk. Robbins' task was organising British employees of the Soviet institutions. Liddell wrote that it might interest the Foreign Office to see 'the extent to which the Trade Delegation offices at Bush House, who are of course immune, have become filled up with GPU agents and other undesirables.' But the diplomatic and political mood had changed sufficiently since 1927 for there to be no repeat of the mass expulsion of Soviet officials and no break in relations.

One of the leading Soviet trading companies in Britain, Russian Oil Products Ltd, also came under close scrutiny from the British government. The company existed to import cheap Russian oil into Britain and Ireland but the Foreign Office believed that its policy of undercutting competitors disorganised the oil trade in Britain and that it was so incompetently run that it had 'never been able to show a profit in any but a cooked balance sheet'.[23]

A report by the British Foreign Office prepared in February 1932 stated that since 1929 there were 'unmistakable signs that Moscow proposed to use Russian Oil Products as a channel for extensive Communist activities in this country, its main possibilities lying in the fact that it had a transport system of its own covering depots all over the country.'[24] At the end of 1929 when it had been in operation for five years, it was believed that one-third of the company's staff were Communists. According to the Foreign Office the OGPU had written to the Soviet Consul in London in February 1930 instructing him to purge the company of outside elements and install an exclusively Communist staff. At the beginning of the next year it had 1,337 employees, including forty-five Russians in London and seven in the provinces. The directors and senior staff were believed to be trusted members of the Soviet Communist Party and the manager at Avonmouth, Kulikoff was said to have worked for the OGPU. By July 1931 nearly 600 members of the CPGB and the Communist League of Youth were employed by the organisation. This Communist workforce, including clerks, drivers, salesmen and accountants, was deployed in a nationwide chain of more than a score of depots and offices in major cities and ports including Glasgow, Aberdeen, Hull, Sheffield, Castleford, Birmingham, Nottingham, Gloucester, Bristol, Cardiff, Dublin, Brighton, Plymouth, and Barking and Battersea in London. Branch offices served as meeting places and the depots were used as distribution centres for Communist literature. Because of the location of its establishments and the nature of its staff, the Foreign Office noted that the main concern of MI5 and the Home Office was the danger that the company and its staff might become involved in sabotage, and a copy of the memorandum was sent to Sir Vernon Kell the Director-General of MI5. But Russian Oil Products continued to function for the rest of the decade. In 1940 the Foreign Office informed Sir Alfred Faulkner that the company had 'a thoroughly bad reputation', and was 'probably concentrating on espionage and subversive activities'.[25]

Despite the unwillingness to embark on another round of expulsions, with all the associated disturbance to diplomatic relations, it remains clear from the material in the files of the Foreign Office and the reports submitted by the Special Branch that subversive Soviet activity, conducted through the trade organisations and involving members of the Communist Party, continued throughout the 1930s. But the use of either of these channels had its limitations, as the experiences of 1927 in China as well as Britain and the affair of the banknotes the following year had demonstrated. The Soviet intelligence agencies were well aware that their activities were being watched and the risks of detection remained high; indeed, they had a healthy respect at the time for the efficiency of the British police and secret services, as several former agents were to testify.[26] Some of the British members of staff of the various Soviet organisations were almost certainly working for MI5 or the Special Branch and were the source of Liddell's and others' information.

The Soviet response to these difficulties was to establish a network of agents under the direction of intelligence officers who would operate independently of local Communist parties or the legal Soviet missions. These were the 'illegals', the spy controllers and couriers who roamed the world, and Western Europe in particular, in the years up to the

Second World War. They posed, not as diplomats or as official Soviet trading representatives, but as independent businessmen or journalists. But where were such people to be found? There were few suitable Russians who could maintain a convincing façade in any Western country while carrying out the work of a secret agent. Those early Bolsheviks who had lived in the West as exiles before 1917 were too well known, or now occupied high office in the Soviet regime – if they had not incurred the displeasure of Stalin.

The Soviet leader and his intelligence chiefs had to face up to the fact that the main source of expertise in undercover work in the West remained the Comintern. Its agents, like Theodore Rothstein and Michael Borodin, were active before the OGPU's INO (foreign) department was established and while the GRU was still preoccupied with the civil war at home. Their business, and that of their successors, was organising local Communists for revolution. But as the revolutions had failed to happen or had been beaten off, the importance of the Comintern diminished and it was ceasing to be an independent force with a primary role in clandestine activity. Instead of the Comintern's increasingly hollow slogans, Stalin wanted his agents in the West to bring him scientific and technical information, and military and diplomatic intelligence. This was work for the OGPU and the GRU, but they lacked the skills. They first had to acquire them, and the manpower for prospective 'illegal' operatives, from the Comintern.

These changing requirements signalled a period of great fluidity between the three main Soviet organisations directly concerned: the OMS, the international liaison section of the Comintern; the INO, the foreign department of the OGPU; and military intelligence, the GRU, sometimes referred to as the Fourth Bureau of the Soviet General Staff. The background is of central importance in the evolution of Soviet intelligence and its activities in Britain. Elizabeth Poretsky was the widow of a one-time Comintern, GRU and finally NKVD agent, the Polish Communist Ignace Poretsky, also known as Ignace Reiss. In her account of the period she says that: 'it was common practice for people to switch back and forth between the Red Army and the Comintern. The INO on the other hand had scarcely any contacts with the European parties and made strenuous efforts to recruit from the Fourth Department and the Comintern.'[27] It was not uncommon for officers, her own husband included, to work in turn for the Comintern, the GRU and for the NKVD, the successor to the OGPU, according to which organisation was in the ascendant. The dominant agency was able to obtain the staff it needed at the expense of the other two, and individuals with personal knowledge of the West were much in demand.

While Trilisser headed the OGPU's foreign section, the INO, and Piatnitsky was in charge of the Comintern's OMS section, relations between the two organisations were amicable enough. The Comintern provided the OGPU with information and useful items such as genuine foreign passports.[28] After Trilisser's departure in 1930, his successors, notably Abram Slutsky from 1935, and following him, Alexandr Shpigelglass in 1938, poached Comintern and GRU officers for their own networks.

The constant changes in organisation and personnel meant that there was little operational uniformity. Poretsky convincingly maintains that:

> The picture of Soviet espionage operations given by writers without firsthand experience is of a fairly rigid pattern laid down by order from Moscow, operating through networks organised along much the same lines in each country and closely supervised from the centre. This is more or less accurate – though considerably over-simplified for the period which followed the great purges of the 1930s, but it is completely untrue of the earlier years.'[29]

One operational rule that was not strictly observed concerned the use of local Communist parties for intelligence purposes. Georges Agabekov claimed that as early as 1927 the OGPU gave instructions for its representatives to abstain from relations with native Communists abroad or with the Comintern.[30] As we have seen, there were some sound reasons for doing this, and they grew in importance in the years before the Second World War.

Some of the most important long-term Soviet spies, such as the Cambridge 'moles' were directed away from any form of contact with the CPGB, and in some cases instructed to cultivate a right-wing image, forswearing all expressions of sympathy with socialism. They functioned as secret Communists whose true loyalties had to be concealed at all costs. They occupied even more sensitive positions in the heart of British government than any individuals on the party's own secret list, who retained but did not disclose their membership. By contrast, there were numerous examples over the next decade and a half of British Communists, and members of foreign Communist parties in exile in Britain, being drawn into the Soviet secret services, as agents, couriers or talent-spotters. The party organisation itself, however, was not usually involved in any of these operations.

A distinction should be drawn between the agents, those individuals recruited to spy, and the intelligence officers who controlled them.

Whereas there was a partial, but far from complete, move away from using known Communists as actual spies, many of the controllers had a background of Communist activity. After proving their worth in their own national parties, most of the individual members of foreign Communist parties who became Soviet intelligence officers were first brought on to the staff of the Comintern or one of its associated organisations such as the Profintern and the Communist Youth International. Some were simply recruited in the corridors of the Hotel Lux during visits to Moscow. From the Comintern they graduated to intelligence work as Soviet priorities changed. But because of the INO's reluctance to use declared party members as agents or officers, it was the military wing, the GRU, which first reaped the benefits of the Comintern's resources and experience, and capitalised on its decline by poaching the available talent. From the mid-1920s onwards, the GRU was prepared to turn Comintern revolutionaries away from fruitless political propaganda to intelligence gathering, or running their own agents as 'illegal' spy controllers or couriers.

This sequence of events, and the contrasting approaches of the OGPU and the GRU, explains why such a high proportion of the 'illegal' Soviet intelligence officers who operated in western Europe and in Asia from the mid-1920s onwards were foreign, that is, non-Russian nationals, and worked specifically for Soviet military intelligence. They were drawn from the pool of dedicated Comintern activists in the West, whose ways they understood and where they had gained experience of 'underground' activity. In dispatching them abroad the GRU took one major precaution: the 'illegals' were sent, whenever possible, to countries other than their own.

The German Communist Party, the KPD, was a major source of recruits for posts around the world. Among those of its members who subsequently took part in intelligence activity in Britain were Jan Valtin, Richard Sorge, the master spy in China and Japan, and, later, at least three members of the Kuczynski family, and the atom spy, Klaus Fuchs. All of them were originally members of the KPD. Sorge joined the party in 1919, Valtin in 1923, Ursula Kuczynski in 1926, her brother Jürgen in 1930 and Fuchs in 1933. The failure of the Communist revolution of 1923, followed by the rise of Hitler, forced many KPD members to flee Germany, and seek employment in the Comintern and ultimately in the Soviet intelligence services. Sorge followed a classic career path, through all the phases, from the KPD, to the Comintern, to the GRU and finally to the NKVD.

Soviet 'illegal' activity in Britain began in earnest after the diplomatic break of 1927. With the removal of all official Soviet representatives it became impossible for a time to mount any operations under a 'legal' resident. The Comintern continued to maintain an undercover representative there, the remarkable Petrovsky, who remained undetected for five years. In 1929 it sent Richard Sorge to Britain to 'study the labour movement, the status of the British Communist Party and the political and economic conditions.'[31] Shortly after that he was transferred to the control of the GRU and in January 1930 began his Far Eastern career in Shanghai.

In 'illegal' operations it became common practice to direct agents from outside the borders of the target country. Hence, the OGPU reputedly directed its work against Britain from Berlin, under a Dr Goldstein, who had previously worked in the Balkans and Constantinople.[32] The GRU's effort against Britain after 1927 was run from Amsterdam by Ignace Porestsky and his wife Elizabeth. The Dutch Communist, Henryk Sneevliet, who had met numerous British Communists through his work in the Comintern, provided Poretsky with a list of addresses in England, as well as arranging contacts for him in Holland.[33] Another associate of Sneevliet's, Jef Swart, was put in charge of a small stationery and office equipment business to provide cover and enough income to support Poretsky's visits abroad. But all did not go well. The business was neglected, and Sneevliet's wife, Sima, left him to live with Swart. Eventually Swart took Sima and her baby daughter to the Soviet Union, where he became engaged in intelligence work. Back in Amsterdam there were added operational disasters for the Poretskys, and growing disillusion, which combined to force them to wind up their attempt to spy on Britain from Holland and return to Moscow.

One of their problems arose from contacts with the Irish, who, according to Elizabeth Poretsky, 'turned out to be of little use and in fact were the unwitting cause of trouble'.[34] A meeting her husband held with one of these Irish contacts was watched by the police and sketches of them both were made, which were reproduced in the British press.

Her version conflicts, however, in certain respects with accounts that appeared in May 1930. Sava Popovitch, an artist and former captain in the Serbian artillery, recounted how he had been approached by 'Bolshevik agents posing as art experts'.[35] They had demanded, in return for payment, plans of the latest British tank, naval training instructions, some secret Royal Air Force documents and confidential industrial information. Popovitch admitted that he had had some earlier contacts with British Communists. He came to England in 1917, having been wounded in the war, and went to Cambridge to look after

Serbian students there and run a relief fund. After the war he settled in London as an artist and later worked on *Burlington Magazine*. In 1922 he was approached by Clemens Palme Dutt, who asked him to join the committee of a Council of Action and to translate some documents. Popovitch said he was warned off by Scotland Yard and heard nothing further from Communist sources until July 1929 when he was introduced to a Russian art expert while on holiday in Paris.

As a result of that meeting he went to Berlin to see a Herr Staal, who had an Amsterdam address, and a Herr Dungarht, who lived in the German capital. They offered him £30 a month to attend art sales in London. On his return to London Popovitch received a letter telling him to meet a man called Maguire at a club in Albermarle Street in the West End. He carried out his instructions and handed Maguire a letter from Berlin. The Serbian described his latest contact as a Canadian of Russian extraction, aged about 36, and a writer and artist by profession. Maguire paid him £90 in US dollars. Later Popovitch met Staal, who also went under the name of Peters, in Amsterdam. Sketches of both Maguire, thin faced and with receding light hair, and Staal, who had a long nose and wavy hair, were reproduced in the *Daily Mail* on 15 May 1930. This account seems too much of a coincidence not to be the incident referred to by Elizabeth Poretsky, despite her omission of any reference to Popovitch and other discrepancies such as the substitution of an art business for office equipment. The latter may be explained by the fact that Poretsky's predecessor in Holland, Max Friedman, ran an art gallery,[36] and it may have still been in use at the time of Popovitch's meetings.

The link between Soviet espionage in Holland and the art world was to reoccur at several points during the next ten years: a wealthy Dutch agent for the Soviet Union, named Henri Pieck, was a professional painter; in the mid-1930s, the NKVD's Resident in Holland, Walter Krivitsky, masqueraded as an Austrian art dealer, Dr Martin Lessner, with a gallery at 32 Celebestraat in the Hague;[37] earlier another GRU agent, Hans Galleni, ran a business in the Hague as an artists' supplier. The art world offered an international arena in which frequent visits abroad and the laundering of funds could comfortably be explained. Later it also may have provided a convenient cover for Soviet intelligence officers to meet their English agent, the art historian, Anthony Blunt.

There were many overlapping connections between these Dutch based 'illegals' and their various agents. Galleni, who has been credited with recruiting the first Soviet spy inside the Foreign Office, was a multilingual former member of the Swiss Communist Party. He joined the GRU as early as 1921 and operated from France, Belgium and the Hague. In Holland he was said to have been in touch with another GRU 'illegal' there, who was a genuine artist.[38] This was probably Henri Pieck, who may have been persuaded to act as a Soviet agent by Ignace Poretsky.

Galleni's British agent was E. C. Oldham, a former army captain who worked as a clerk in the Foreign Office. Disgruntled with his low pay and position, Oldham approached the Soviet Embassy in Paris during 1928. When he returned to London he was contacted by Galleni who persuaded him to hand over details of Foreign Office communications procedures and codes. His betrayal continued until 1932 when he resigned. A year later he was found dead in his house in Kensington, suffocated by gas.[39]

According to two former American intelligence officers, Corson and Crowley, in about 1930 Galleni met and culitvated Captain John King, a Foreign Office cypher clerk.[40] King, too, became a Soviet spy inside Whitehall and was gaoled for ten years in 1939, although his offence was not disclosed until 1956. Peter Wright, however, suggests that Pieck recruited Captain King,[41] while E. H. Cookridge claims recruitment was the work of a British Communist, Douglas Springhall.[42] The full extent of Galleni's activities and his relationships with other Soviet 'illegals' based in Holland – Poretsky, Friedman and Pieck – are ultimately uncertain. Like so many of his contemporaries he is said to have vanished in Stalin's purges.

The Dutch 'illegals' threw up other clues regarding the early penetration of Britain's intelligence agencies. In his investigations in the 1960s into pre-war Soviet spy rings, Wright interviewed the widows of Poretsky and Pieck. They both identified photographs of Dickie Ellis, a member of the Secret Intelligence Service (MI6), who was suspected of spying for the Soviet Union. Nigel West records that Ellis admitted to passing information to Nazi Germany but not to the Soviet Union, while Chapman Pincher is convinced that Ellis was working for both and Richard Deacon says it was neither.[43]

Clearly not all these interpretations can be correct. The evidence is inconclusive. It seems probable that in the 1930s GRU 'illegal' officers based in Holland were running at least two, and perhaps three, spies in the Foreign Office and MI6, before the entry of Maclean and others of the Cambridge ring later in the decade. It is sometimes more, not less, revealing of the nature of Soviet intelligence operations at that time to recognise that in fact the picture was not always clear-cut. There was a high turnover among the Soviet operatives who tried to recruit and run spies in Britain, partly due to the existence of different networks operated by different agencies, partly to the successes of the British authorities, and later to the toll of the purges. The intensity of activity gathered pace the closer war in Europe loomed and the picture became even murkier. It may not always matter which of a gallery of shadowy continentals subverted which individual. However, disentangling the facts has an intrinsic historical value and it is also of special importance in evaluating the results achieved by the 'illegals' in their attempts to recruit long-term 'moles' within the heart of the British ruling classes, the effects of which were to leave a mark on society for a generation.

Soviet interest in young, upper middle-class intellectuals was a direct consequence of the failure of the British Communist Party to produce a working-class revolution. Alexander Orlov, a senior Soviet intelligence officer, who defected to the West in 1938, later noted that '… in the early 1930s, the NKVD's residentura concentrated their energies on recruitment of young men of influential families. The political climate was very favourable for such an undertaking … when the young men reached the stage when their thinking made them ripe for joining the Communist Party, they were told that they could be much more useful if they stayed away from the party, concealed their political views, and entered the "revolutionary underground".'[44] As potential future rulers of the British Empire, these chosen individuals would, in the fullness of time, be able to provide the Soviet Union with intelligence of the highest order, influence in the most select circles, and ultimately help destroy imperialism from within. With revolution removed from the agenda, here was a longer-term strategy that called for determination, subtlety and patience.

The opening of the 1930s was a crucial time, when world politics entered a period of extreme uncertainty and Western intellectuals were showing signs of deep discontent with the response of democracy to economic slump and the rise of fascism. In Britain the focus of Soviet interest was Cambridge, where the Communist cell was re-established in 1931. The story of the Cambridge spies is a peculiarly English tale of snobbery, homosexuality, and tribalism, of an elite of Marxist aesthetes within an elite of the privileged intelligentsia, of secret social codes and coteries, and of public faces which concealed private truths. The explanations for their actions are psychological as much as political. Their motives, and the circumstances of their devotion to the Soviet Union, have been examined many times, in all their aspects.[45] What is of concern here is the light that the affair throws on Soviet objectives.

In June 1931 Clemens Palme Dutt was said to have been

instrumental in bringing together Marxist dons and undergraduates to form a new Communist group at Cambridge University.[46] This gathering was followed at Easter 1932 by a meeting at James Klugmann's Hampstead home of Communists from Oxford, Cambridge, the London School of Economics and London University, together with members of the CPGB. One of those present was Douglas Springhall, who had been discharged from the navy in 1924 for seditious conduct. A leading figure in the Young Communist League, he was to play a central role as a talent-spotter and intermediary between the Communist Party and Soviet intelligence. He rose to become the wartime national organiser of the CPGB, until, as we shall see, he was arrested for espionage in 1943. The years between 1931 and 1933 also saw the greatest concentration at Cambridge of those who in their various ways served the Soviet interest in later life; Philby went up in 1929, Burgess and Klugmann in 1930 and Maclean in 1931. Blunt, Dobb, Pascall and J. D. Bernal were dons and Maurice Cornforth was studying for a doctorate.

In all the known cases, the transition from Marxist intellectual to Soviet spy was accomplished in stages. The conversion to Marxism was followed by a period in which the individual, probably unknown to himself, was being selected and his suitability assessed. At this point, the initial moves were often made by committed dons and overt British Communists, not by Russians or foreign 'illegals'. They had nurtured their subjects in their conversion to Marxism until they were ready for initiation into a higher realm of duty. Maurice Dobb and James Klugmann, together with Douglas Springhall, performed the roles of guide and mentor. It is very probable that each had his own contacts with members of the Soviet intelligence services and was in a position to make introductions and offer recommendations.

Springhall has been credited with the actual recruitment of Kim Philby into espionage.[47] This is unlikely. His role would have stopped short of anything that could be described as the formal enrolment of any targeted individual into Soviet intelligence; he would have been limited to spotting likely recruits and arranging meetings with an agent controller, who in turn would form his own view of the candidate in a probationary period before entrusting the potential agent to any major task. Klugmann, who was one of the acknowledged leaders of Cambridge communism in the early 1930s, was also involved in talent spotting for the Soviet Union. His targets included an Oxford undergraduate named Bernard Floud, who later became a Labour MP and was a Granada Television executive for twelve years. When Harold Wilson wished to offer him a junior ministerial post in 1967,

Floud was interviewed by the Security Service. Shortly after the interview he committed suicide.[48]

Another key figure at this stage was Anthony Blunt. He was several years older than many of those with whom he is often linked. He went to Cambridge as an undergraduate in 1926, three years ahead of Philby, for example, joined the secret society of the Apostles in 1928 and was elected a Fellow of Trinity in 1932. He claimed to have been converted to Marxism only in about 1935, but was probably already working on two people who were to spy for the Soviet Union during the war, John Cairncross, who had been at Cambridge for two years, and Leo Long, who went up in that year. By 1937 Blunt had left Cambridge to join the Warburg Institute in London. He also had a hand in initial approaches to Guy Burgess and the attempted enlistment of a wealthy American undergraduate, Michael Straight. Straight went up to Trinity College in 1934 after a year at the London School of Economics. There he had been persuaded to join the Socialist Society by Peter Floud, the brother of Bernard. Early in 1935 Straight joined a Communist cell at Cambridge. Altogether he estimates that about a quarter of the 200 members of the Socialist Society in Cambridge when he arrived were Communists, and a similar proportion of the 600 or so who were Socialist Society members three years later when he left.[49]

The links formed at university were cemented elsewhere. Philby went to Paris and Vienna in the summer of 1933, where he met Soviet intelligence officers and the woman who was to be his first wife, the Comintern agent, Lizi Friedman. Burgess made the pilgrimage to Moscow in 1934 followed by Blunt, already a Marxist, a year later. All pursued active intelligence careers thereafter, having passed through the processes of selection and assessment in Cambridge and overseas.

Some commentators have maintained the Cambridge spies made contact with Soviet intelligence through officials of the Soviet Embassy or the Trade Delegation in London. Philby is said to have had his first such encounter in 1932 at a safe house at 3 Rosary Gardens, in Kensington, where Springhall introduced him to two Soviet Embassy officials, Tolonsky and Askalov.[50] Philby and Donald Maclean are also alleged to have met Samuel Cahan of the Embassy.[51] The house in Rosary Gardens was, however, the address of the Soviet Consulate. As such it was probably watched by the British police and MI5, and was a highly unsafe place in which to arrange a meeting with a potential secret agent. Although, as noted above, official Soviet institutions in London continued to provide a base for espionage on a scale that has not hitherto been appreciated, it would have made more sense from the Soviet point of view to direct the Cambridge spies after 1933 through the 'illegals' who were moving from the continent to infiltrate Britain in growing numbers.

APPROACH TO WAR

The Soviet response to the rise of Hitler was far from decisive. Moscow's instructions to the German Communist Party in the middle of 1932, to mount an anti-Nazi 'united front', came too late to prevent Hitler from becoming Chancellor the following January. A subsequent shift in Soviet policy came only gradually. In September 1934 the Soviet Union joined the League of Nations, with the positive encouragement of Britain and France. Anglo-Soviet relations warmed, following the difficulties of 1933 when six British engineers working in Russia for the Metropolitan-Vickers company were arrested on charges of espionage and sabotage. In March 1935 Anthony Eden, then a junior minister in the Foreign Office travelled to Moscow, from Prague and Warsaw, while his superior, Sir John Simon was in Berlin. It was the first visit by any member of the British government to the Soviet Union. Four months later the seventh, and last, Comintern Congress reflected the new Soviet thinking, in its proclamation of the policy of the 'Popular Front'.

The new Comintern line was not, however, a sudden departure. It had been evolving over the previous two years, in a faltering, fitful fashion. For the British Communist Party cooperation with others on the left offered a possible means of escaping its political isolation. The approaches to the Independent Labour Party in 1932 were a symptom of the changing mood. Although they were unwilling partners, there were others who were beginning to look to communism as a means of resisting the fascist tide. As early as the end of 1931 the MP, John Strachey, had signalled a trend. After leaving, successively, the Labour Party and Mosley's New Party, he wrote to Rajani Palme Dutt and Andrew Rothstein, and talked to the CPGB general secretary, Harry Pollitt and to the Soviet Ambassador, Sokolnikov, about the possibility of becoming a member of the Communist Party.[52] In the event he did not join but over the next three years he became, in the words of his biographer, 'the most articulate spokesman for Marxism in Britain',[53] with the publication of three books, *The Coming Struggle for Power* in November 1931, *The Menace of Fascism* a year later, and *The Nature of the Capitalist Crisis* in 1935.

Strachey became one of the leading 'fellow travellers' of the decade. He stood in the forefront of that assortment of politicians, lawyers, writers and scientists who supported the Soviet line from outside the Communist Party. They included intellectual luminaries like H.G. Wells, George Bernard Shaw, and the Webbs, who lauded the paradise of socialist planning represented by Soviet civilisation. In March 1936 Strachey joined forces with Professor Harold Laski of the London School of Economics in Victor Gollancz's Left Book Club. That same year Sir Stafford Cripps founded the Socialist League, which for a time provided a forum for Labour Party left-wingers, the ILP and the Communist Party, and he followed it a year later with the launch of the *Tribune* newspaper.

During 1936 the need for anti-fascist unity seemed all the more pressing. In October the Battle of Cable Street led to the Public Order Act, to curb Mosley's British Union of Fascists. In France a Popular Front government was formed. But elsewhere the skies were darkening. In March Hitler had occupied the Rhineland, and in July the Spanish Civil War had begun with the revolt of General Franco's forces. Dramatically the fight against fascism intensified. Around 2,000 volunteers – trade unionists and poets, Communists and Labour Party members – went from Britain to enlist in the International Brigade. Among them were several who feature in this narrative, such as Tom Wintringham, one of the first Oxford Communists and a defendant in the 1925 Communist trial, who commanded the British Battalion, Ralph Fox, the former Comintern worker, who was killed in Spain in 1936, Wilfred McCartney, the gaoled agent of 1927, Fred Copeman, a discharged Invergordon mutineer, Alexander Foote, recruited by the GRU on his return to England in 1938, and the ubiquitous Douglas Springhall. By contrast, Kim Philby stood aloof from the left's enthusiasm for the Spanish Republicans and went out to report the war for *The Times* from the Francoist side.

These various developments suited the CPGB perfectly. It enjoyed the rare satisfaction of carrying out the wishes of its Soviet sponsors and prospering at the same time. Anti-fascists, Socialists, internationalists and academic social engineers could all find something in the Communist cause. Party membership raced ahead – from 5,800 in December 1934 to 11,500 in October 1936 and up to a record 17,756 in July 1939. The party reopened its campaign for affiliation to the Labour Party.

As the menace of Hitler grew, the Soviet Union was able to improve its own international standing. At the League of Nations, Litvinov preached the virtues of 'collective security'. The slight thaw in relations with Britain was followed in May 1935 by a pact between the Soviet Union and France, guaranteeing mutual assistance in the event of aggression against either country. But these diplomatic initiatives could not bring Stalin all that he sought to enable him to press ahead with the socialist transformation of Russia from a position of confidence and strength. To stay ahead of the rapidly changing situation Stalin also demanded technical, military and diplomatic intelligence. The counterpart to the Popular Front and collective diplomacy was, therefore, an increase in Soviet espionage.

In order not to jeopardise the political and diplomatic aspects of Stalin's policy, the actions of the Soviet secret services in the late 1930s continued to be conducted mainly through 'illegal' operations. Soviet Embassies and Trade Missions had a part in the totality of espionage, but together with the national Communist parties they could by and large proceed with other designated tasks without the fear of being compromised to any serious degree. The main contribution of Embassies to the 'illegal' networks was the transmission of documents and messages to Moscow under diplomatic privilege. They also provided supporting services, which carried few risks. There were also some eminently practical reasons for this allocation of duties: in 1939 the Soviet Embassy in London had only nine staff with diplomatic status, compared with twenty each for Germany, Italy and Japan.[54] One way round the problem was to boost the staff levels in the Trade Delegations and concerns like Russian Oil Products. But they were in an exposed position. The alternative was an infusion of 'illegal' controllers and couriers who could make up for the shortfall in manpower without attracting undue suspicion from their British hosts.

For the time being the GRU, the military intelligence service stood in the vanguard of the espionage offensive. Given the nature of much of the information it was trying to obtain it seemed logical that it should take the lead. The GRU had by now also swallowed up most of the old Comintern networks. Between 1935 and 1939 at least seven 'illegal' Soviet controllers or couriers were active in Britain, the majority of them officers of the GRU, and they were responsible for more than thirty known agents.

The GRU's operations in western and central Europe became known as the Red Orchestra, a term first applied by German counter-intelligence.[55] Its activities extended to more than a dozen countries, with the main networks in Germany, France, Belgium, Holland and Switzerland, and connections to espionage rings in Canada and the UK. Peter Wright records that intensive efforts to try to discover the British end of the Red Orchestra have produced few results.[56] A report on its European networks by the USA's Central Intelligence Agency confirms that although Britain was one of the major targets before the outbreak of war, little is known in detail of its activity.[57] Some pieces of the jigsaw do, however, exist.

From about 1935 onwards the GRU established a series of deep cover operations throughout Europe. They functioned through commercial companies – much as Poretsky had done seven or eight years earlier – but on a larger scale. Among the most important were the Foreign Excellent Raincoat Company, based in Belgium, and an import–export agency, Simex, set up in Paris after the German occupation in 1940. In the Red Orchestra, the GRU employed people of many nationalities, very often with professional and linguistic skills that aided their cover. In charge of the network in each country was the Resident, generally a non-Russian GRU officer holding a military rank in the Red Army. To support him he employed couriers, 'cut-outs' who acted as intermediaries between him and his agents, radio operators, and, if circumstances warranted it, someone who maintained the business cover. Some of them also had army ranks conferred upon them. Together they serviced and ran the actual spy, the agent who was the source of the information.

The 'Grand Chef' of the Red Orchestra was Leopold Trepper, who was born in Poland in 1904. After spending nearly a decade and a half in Paris he was arrested by the Gestapo there in 1942. After eighteen months he somehow escaped – some say he became a double agent – and returned to the Soviet Union, where he was promptly incarcerated and only released after the death of Stalin in 1953. He then went to Poland and finally to Israel, where he died in 1977. The leader of the important Swiss network from 1936 until his arrest in 1943 was Alexander Rado, who joined the Communist Party in his native Hungary at the age of 20 in 1919. He, too, survived the war and went to the Soviet Union.

Despite their many diversions, the commercial cover and the false passports, the networks of the Red Orchestra looked wherever practical to Soviet Embassies, Consulates and trade missions to get information safely back to Moscow. The use of the 'legal' apparatus by 'illegal' operatives illustrates the inherent flexibility associated with Soviet intelligence at the time. General observations about their methods can serve only as guidelines. By the end of 1939, however, the 'illegal' officers in the field were forced to use radio to transmit their reports home. This applied throughout the war to those in Britain as well as those in occupied France, Poland and the Low Countries.

According to the CIA, one of the Red Orchestra's first members in Britain was a German called David Ernest Weiss, who was born in

Breslau in 1902 and went to university there. He came to England in 1932 and for most of the next nine years was an active Soviet agent, under the name of Walter Lock, with a flat in Paddington.[58] The CIA refers briefly to one of his contacts as a Wilfred Foulston Vernon, from whom Weiss obtained confidential information during 1936 concerning aeroplane and other war material production.

Vernon was in fact a 35-year-old former army major who had worked in the Air Ministry since 1924. From 1929 he was employed at RAF Farnborough as a technical officer. In October 1937 he was fined £50, on a charge under the Official Secrets Act, for keeping classified documents at his home in Fareham without permission.[59] His cottage was broken into by four men, and the documents removed and taken to Fareham police station where Vernon identified them. They included details of new aeroplanes and the names of others, whose very existence was 'still a matter of the utmost secrecy'. Other documents concerned air exercises and the most secret of all was said to relate to bombing. It was not revealed in court whether Vernon had passed information to Weiss. His lawyer, the Labour MP and Soviet sympathiser, D. N. Pritt, said that the case did not involve espionage.

The four men responsible for the raid on Vernon's cottage were found guilty of burglary in a separate trial and bound over. They were identified as fascist sympathisers, and included a former soldier who said Vernon asked him to help him spread communism in the armed forces, and gave him some Communist literature to distribute.[60] Vernon denied that he had any connections with communism, although he admitted he had once visited Russia. Despite objections from the Civil Service National Whitley Council, which the Home Office ignored,[61] and protests from the *New Statesman*, Vernon was dismissed, and this long-forgotten episode in the history of the Red Orchestra drew to a close.

Weiss had probably not been identified by the British security services at the time, for he had several other subsequent contacts. These included Sam Barron, who went from the London School of Economics to work in the British Embassy in Washington from 1938 to 1941, Frederick Meredith, an Irish Communist, and Andrew King, a member of MI6. King was a Cambridge graduate and a member of the CPGB in the 1930s, and was questioned by MI5 several times after 1951.[62]

Still deeper mystery surrounds the identities of other members of the Red Orchestra in Britain. An operative known only as Harry I met Weiss during 1932. He was followed by Harry II, who directed Weiss's work between 1935 and 1937. Harry I was based in Paris, where, according to the CIA, he used the Soviet Military Attaché to communicate with Moscow.[63] His successor, located in Paris but controlling agents in Britain, was known as Henry Robinson.

Robinson's origins are obscure. He may have been a German Jew called Henry Baumann, who was born in Frankfurt-am-Main in 1897, or he may have come from Belgium. Or his father may have been a Russian whose name really was Robinson. Henry used at least ten other names in a career that spanned twenty years. A member of the German Communist Party in the 1920s, Robinson worked with Munzenberg in the Communist Youth International before moving into intelligence work with the GRU as a courier and liaison officer. During the 1930s he was based for most of the time in Paris, although he was involved in espionage directed against Switzerland, where he had studied in his youth, and Britain.

Robinson's British connections are a source of much speculation. The CIA say that he took over Harry II's networks in England in 1937. According to a British intelligence report in 1966, 'Robinson played an important part in the running of Russian operations in the UK ....'[64] These included the direction of Weiss and his agents. Guy Burgess may have been among them.[65] French intelligence also believed that Philby was another, and other agents included two exiled German Communists working as research engineers for EMI.[66] Leopold Trepper, however, claimed that Robinson had broken with Moscow by 1937, and was never part of the Red Orchestra, although he continued to provide help and information to the Soviet spy networks for another five years.[67]

In 1942 Robinson was arrested by the Gestapo in Paris and executed. Under the floorboards of a hotel room he used, the German forces found a collection of papers, including three Swiss passports in the names of Otto Wehrli, Albert Bucher and Alfred Merian, other identity documents, and codes and messages transmitted by him. Copies of these papers – but not the originals – were taken by the allies at the end of the war and formed the basis of the CIA's account of Robinson's spying activities and of the largely fruitless investigations later carried out by MI5.

The period when Robinson was alleged to have run spies in England, from 1937 to 1940, partly overlapped with the activities of another unidentified Soviet 'illegal', who was known simply as 'Otto'. He disappeared from the scene in 1938 when he was recalled to Moscow, where he perished in the purges. His name has been linked to some of the most important British spies, including most of those recruited at Oxford and Cambridge. 'Otto' was said to have controlled the work of

Philby, Blunt, Maclean, Alister Watson, John Cairncross and Captain
King, as well as others such as the American, Michael Straight and
Jenifer Fischer Williams, an Oxford graduate and associate of Bernard
Floud, who in 1941 married a wartime MI5 officer, later Professor Sir
Hubert Hart.[68] Philby later told British intelligence that the
mysterious 'Otto' was an Austrian named Arnold Deutsch, who came
to Britain in 1934 to do postgraduate work at London University.
Although Deutsch was known to have links with the Comintern, some
– but not all – authorities have discounted the likelihood that he was
'Otto' or that he controlled any of the Cambridge spies.[69] There are
other possibilities: 'Otto' was the first name of one of Robinson's many
aliases, as revealed in one of the passports found in 1942. Intriguingly,
Trepper claims that he was known as 'Otto' in his European operations
before the war.[70] Although Britain figured as one of his major targets,
there is no record that Trepper visited this country, and no evidence to
suggest that he had any responsibility for the Cambridge spies.

The period was undeniably a critical one in their history. By the
middle of the decade the university recruits to Soviet intelligence had
severed all overt links with CPGB and operated as the most secret of
secret Communists. And as they launched their careers, London
became the focal point of their social and professional lives. Maclean
joined the Foreign Office in 1935, ahead of Cairncross, Burgess became
a talks producer at the BBC exactly a year later and in 1937 Blunt left
Cambridge to join the Warburg Institute in London. Philby,
meanwhile, was beginning to establish contacts in journalism before
going to Spain; after his return from Vienna in 1934 he found work on
a small magazine called the *Review of Reviews* and at the end of the
year joined forces with an Austrian postgraduate student at the
London School of Economics, Peter Smolka. Together they ran the
London Continental News Agency, which Smolka sold to Exchange
Telegraph in 1938.[71] After the outbreak of war he joined the Ministry
of Information and, as we shall see, had an important part to play in
the wartime development of Anglo-Soviet relations.

London was also a recruiting ground for the GRU among open
Communists who could be used in espionage networks on the continent.
In September 1938, a 32-year-old Liverpudlian, Alexander Foote
returned from Spain after nearly two years as a volunteer in the
International Brigade. Although not a party member he attended the
CPGB congress in Birmingham that month. He was approached by
Fred Copeman and Douglas Springhall who told him to go to a flat in
St John's Wood. There, in October 1938, an unknown woman gave him
detailed instructions for a meeting outside the general post office in

Geneva. Foote was to wear a white scarf and hold a leather belt in his right hand. As the clock struck 12 noon he would be approached by a woman carrying a string shopping bag with a green parcel in it and holding an orange in her hand. To avoid the danger of mistaken identity, when asked where he had bought the belt, Foote was to reply, in a Paris ironmonger's, and ask where he could get an orange like hers.[72] The script for the rendezvous was typical of the highly contrived exchanges the Soviet spymasters devised to make sure agents did not hand material to or approach the wrong people. When Foote's meeting had taken place as planned he found himself in the service of the GRU.

The woman with the bag and orange was Ursula Kuczynski, an experienced GRU officer a year younger than Foote, who had spent five years on intelligence work in China. Her father, Robert, an economist, her brother, Jürgen, and her sister, Brigitte had lived in England for several years. They were all members of the German Communist Party. Jürgen was highly active in left-wing circles in Britain: he was friendly with the Stracheys, and contributed to *Tribune*, Rajani Palme Dutt's *Labour Monthly* and the Left Book Club. In December 1940, several months after marrying another British member of the GRU's spy network, Bill Beurton, Ursula Kuczynski used her newly-acquired British passport to join the other members of her family in England. She was to remain there for another nine years, during which she, and her brother, were to become deeply involved in a new phase of Soviet espionage against Britain.[73] Foote, meanwhile, trained as a radio operator and worked for the GRU until he was arrested by the Swiss authorities in November 1943.

Increasingly in the second half of the 1930s the GRU's predominance in the operation of networks run by 'illegals' was under threat. The new circumstances arose not because of any revision in working methods, although they were to lead to that. Nor were they prompted by any switch in intelligence priorities, although Nazi Germany was rapidly supplanting the British Empire as the main enemy, nor even as a result of any of its failures in the field. The change came about firstly as a result of events inside the Soviet Union.

In May 1934 the head of the OGPU for the previous eight years, the Polish born Viacheslav Menzhinsky, died, and was succeeded by his deputy, Genrikh Yagoda. The 43-year-old Yagoda was a Jew who had joined the Cheka in 1919. Two months after he took control, the OGPU was formally abolished and its functions transferred to the NKVD, the People's Commissariat of Internal Affairs. The NKVD was also responsible for the preservation of order and state security, border protection, and running labour camps. Yagoda stood at its head. Once more, the bureaucratic changes of name and structure presaged a massive growth in the internal powers of the secret police.

The assassination of Kirov in Leningrad in December 1934 triggered the launching of the great purges that over the next four to five years were to claim the lives of some one million people and lead to the imprisonment of seven to eight million others.[74] The planning and execution of the purges was the responsibility of the NKVD. Many of the surviving Bolsheviks from Lenin's day were eliminated. In January 1935 Zinoviev and Kamenev were tried and imprisoned. But the outcome did not please Stalin and a little over eighteen months later they were retried, with fourteen others, and shot. Yagoda himself was replaced in September 1936 by Nikolai Yezhov, a former member of Stalin's secretariat. Under his direction the terror of the purges reached its peak during the next two years. At the beginning of 1937 Karl Radek, prominent in the early days of the Comintern, and sixteen other defendants, including Sokolnikov, the former Ambassador to Britain, were subjected to a show trial and either executed or banished to labour camps. In March 1938 the largest of the major exhibitions of Soviet justice took place when Bukharin and Yagoda were among twenty-one leading figures accused of espionage, wrecking, and anti-military and anti-state activities. All were found guilty and nineteen were executed.

In the meantime Stalin had turned his attention to the Red Army. In the summer of 1937 Marshal Tukhachevsky and some of his most senior generals were secretly tried and shot. Altogether the purges resulted in the removal of some 90 per cent of the army's generals and 80 per cent of its colonels, including 13 out of 15 army commanders, and 110 of 195 divisional commanders.[75] Military intelligence did not escape. General Berzin, the founding head of the GRU, was shot, and Uritsky, the head from 1935 was arrested in November 1937 and shot soon afterwards. The NKVD was also purged. Yezhov was removed from office and disappeared in July 1938. Its new chairman was Lavrenti Beria, a fellow Georgian of Stalin's, who was in his late thirties. He had served in the secret police for seventeen years and was to remain its supreme figure until after his mentor's death in 1953.

The purges did not stop at the Soviet frontier. The NKVD destroyed leftist opposition elements in Spain in the midst of the civil war. Intelligence agents suspected of Trotskyism or of improper contact with foreigners were recalled to face the camps or the firing squads. Those with a Comintern or GRU background were perilously vulnerable. Some of them had in any case become disillusioned with their task. They considered themselves revolutionary idealists not spies, and as they began to realise that they were caught up in the services of an instrument of tyranny rather than a movement for the liberation of mankind, their enthusiasm understandably waned. And as their dedication to world communism declined, their fears rose.

Several attempted to flee to the safety of the West. Alexander Orlov, the NKVD's head in Spain, made his way safely to the USA in 1938. But not all succeeded. Ignace Poretsky escaped from Paris in July 1937, only to succumb to a hail of bullets on the road to Lausanne a month later. The patience of Stalin's roving gunmen matched their ruthlessness. After nine years in exile, the former OGPU agent in the Middle East, Georges Agabekov, was murdered in Belgium in 1938. A year earlier, Walter Krivitsky, the NKVD's man in Holland, and one time GRU officer and a colleague of Poretsky, had defected. He sought refuge in the USA, but did not have Orlov's good fortune.

Krivitsky dangerously exposed himself by setting himself up as a political commentator and made exaggerated claims about his record.[76] He was also de-briefed by both American and British intelligence services. His information to MI5 identified the cipher clerk, Captain King, and may have pointed to Donald Maclean and Kim Philby. Altogether, Krivitsky listed nearly 100 Soviet agents around the world, of whom sixty-one were working against Britain or British interests.[77] Of these, six were 'legals', under cover of diplomatic or trading organisations, twenty were support workers, specialists in photography, couriers and providers of safe houses, and thirty-five were active agents. Sixteen of the agents were British and the rest were of assorted nationalities. Of the British subjects, Krivitsky stated that eight were active in politics and the trade unions, six were in the civil service and two were in journalism. He refrained, however, from naming names and after several weeks of questioning he returned from London to Washington. There was talk of his being asked for more interviews in London. But it was never to happen. In February 1941 Krivitsky's body was found in his hotel room in Washington. It appeared that he had shot himself but the work of Soviet assassins has been strongly suspected.[78]

Another NKVD officer who perished in the purges, Theodore Maly, was its leading 'illegal' operator in Britain during the second half of the 1930s. In common with many other 'illegals' his life is shrouded in mystery. He was a Hungarian priest who served as an army chaplain in the First World War, or, alternatively, an Austrian who was in the Russian cavalry.[79] Peter Wright states that he was the first controller of Burgess and Philby. Gordon Brook-Shepherd believes Maly ran

Captain King among his British spies. The former American intelligence officers, Corson and Crowley maintain that he was the main Soviet 'illegal' resident in the UK as early as 1930, while Andrew Boyle claims that Maly was sent to Britain to replace the 'legal' Resident, Tolokonsky, in 1935. Like most 'illegals' he used a variety of names, including Paul Hardt, Peters and Stephens. The latter pair were favourite choices among Soviet agents in search of English sounding names. Whatever his background, Maly was almost certainly in England from the middle of the decade until the spring of 1937, when he went to Paris to call on the Poretskys before returning to Moscow and his death.[80]

In England Maly ran the spy ring which became famous in the Woolwich Arsenal case.[81] His task was to obtain secret information on new guns being developed by the navy. To help him he recruited the graduate of the Lenin school, Percy Glading, who had worked at Woolwich as a grinder before the First World War and between 1925 and 1928, when he had been dismissed because of his Communist associations. Since his return from Moscow in 1930, Glading had worked for the Communist Party and the League Against Imperialism, and had helped produce the anti-military newspaper, Soldiers' Voice. He had been unemployed since March 1937. As Maly's agent Glading enlisted three Woolwich employees, Albert Williams, an examiner in the Chief Inspector of Armaments department, George Whomack, an assistant foreman in naval ordnance, and a young chemist, Charles Munday.

Maly's choice of such a well-known Communist as his principal aide was, to say the least, ill-considered. Glading's activities had been shadowed for several years by an MI5 agent named Olga Gray. It was only a matter of time before he and his accomplices were rounded up. Maly himself escaped when he left England in the spring of 1937, only to find a more terrible fate awaiting him in Moscow. His successors, a Mr and Mrs Stephens, who were in reality central Europeans by the name of Brandes, stayed only until November when they departed for Paris. Only in January 1938 were Glading and the three Woolwich employees arrested. At the Old Bailey in March, Glading received a six-year prison sentence, and Williams and Whomack four and three years respectively. Munday was acquitted. The defending lawyers were both Communist sympathisers: the Labour MP, D .N. Pritt, fresh from the Vernon case, and Dudley Collard, who, like Pritt, had been favourably impressed by the displays of Soviet justice he had seen in the show trials on a visit to Moscow.[82]

Maly's approach in the Woolwich case illustrates again the dangers of generalisation about Soviet espionage methods in the pre-war period. During the 1930s Stalin relied first on the GRU and the expertise it had acquired from the Comintern. Most of their operations were carried out by 'illegal' officers who had false identities and were not members of official Soviet organisations or Embassies enjoying diplomatic privilege. But Maly, one of their most experienced officers, was never in the GRU but was an NKVD member throughout his career. Others, such as Sorge, Krivitsky, and Poretsky progressed only later from the GRU to the OGPU and NKVD. Ursula Kuczynski, however, stayed in the GRU for twenty years in the field. The NKVD in particular was discouraged from using local Communists in espionage activity. Yet Maly employed Glading. And other members of the CPGB were at the same time involved with either the NKVD or the GRU – Springhall, for example, and Bob Stewart who acted as a courier.[83] The 'illegals' existed where it was too risky to mount spying from an Embassy or Trade Delegation. But, on the continent at least, they looked to the Embassies for communications and supporting facilities. the control of some agents was switched, from 'illegal' to 'legal' and back again. The removal of some officers and the defection of others during the purge years complicated the picture.

Against this background, the question of exactly how the Cambridge recruits were run in the closing years of the 1930s remains unclear. No fewer than twelve individuals have been identified as the recruiters, and, or, controllers of Kim Philby between 1933 and 1939. These include three members of the CPGB, one Comintern agent, four GRU officers, and four members of the Soviet Embassy and trade mission. Some, at least, were probably not controllers at all, but 'cut-outs' or couriers. By the time war came to Europe, however, the NKVD was asserting itself as the undisputed superior partner in Soviet intelligence and taking charge of the 'moles' inside British government departments. But because of the turmoil resulting from the purges, some of these spies may have been dormant for a while, with no active direction between the departure of their 'illegal' controllers in 1938, or thereabouts, and the installation of a new 'legal' NKVD residency in 1940. On balance regular direction through Henry Robinson's network or the Red Orchestra seems unlikely. Some investigators have suggested continuing contacts with the 'legal' residencies at the Soviet Embassy. In January 1937, Philby was said to have met Samuel Cahan's successor, Vinogradov, nominally a First Secretary at the Soviet Embassy in London, and Mikhail Grinov of the trade mission, shortly before going out to Spain.[84] Earlier Douglas Springhall is alleged to have introduced Philby to Simon Kremer, a GRU officer under the cover of clerk to the Soviet Military Attaché. In 1941, towards the end of his four-year stay in London, Kremer was the controller of Klaus Fuchs and Ursula Kuczynski.[85]

But there is again evidence in official files to indicate that the British police and MI5 kept official Soviet institutions under some degree of surveillance. In January 1939, Karpeltsev, the Chief Engineer at the trade mission, fled the country in order to evade arrest for espionage, while his successor, Doschenko was arrested and expelled at the end of that year.[86] The possibility of another raid on the trade mission offices was discussed in Whitehall at the beginning of 1940. But through Guy Liddell, MI5 advised the Foreign Office against such action as 'there was no specific evidence against any members of the Trade Delegation' since the Doschenko case. MI5 did however say that 'we know on very reliable evidence that it is common for certain sections, particularly the [industrial] inspectorate to engage in espionage activities.'[87] MI5 accepted that Russian inspectors working at Metro-Vickers could, in the ordinary course of their duties, pick up a certain amount of confidential information, but it doubted whether a raid would produce any worthwhile results as the delegation would probably have removed any compromising documents. In any event, the problem was overshadowed by matters of far greater magnitude.

For nearly five years the Soviet Union had supported the creation of a 'united front' against fascism and followed the diplomacy of collective security, the principal exponent of which, Litvinov, became an admired figure at the League of Nations. Stalin however was prepared to take whatever opportunities arose. In April 1939 the Soviet Union proposed to Britain and France the formation of an alliance against aggression. There was a slow response. The two Western powers still retained the hope they might tame Hitler and thus not have to come to an accord with Russian communism. But Stalin had other plans for the security of Russia. In May the diplomatist, Litvinov, was replaced by the harsh, unrelenting figure of Molotov. Within three months the new Commissar for Foreign Affairs had signed a non-aggression pact with his Nazi counterpart, Ribbentrop. Ten days later Germany invaded Poland. The war that began in September 1939 was, so far as the Soviet union was concerned, an 'imperialist war': Communists should not support it. Ever loyal, the CPGB switched its intended line backing the anti-Nazi war, when Springhall conveyed the new wisdom straight from Moscow.[88] In mid-September, Soviet forces occupied eastern Poland with agreement from their new ally. At the end of November Stalin carried his expansionism further by invading Finland. In the spring of 1940 the Soviet Union annexed the Baltic states of Estonia,

Latvia and Lithuania, and in June seized parts of Rumania. In Britain, there was a sharp public reaction against communism. The *Daily Worker* newspaper was banned and in 1940 fellow travellers like Strachey and Laski attacked the Soviet Union. But those who did not weaken in their dedication to the cause of world communism lived to see undreamt-of opportunities for Soviet intelligence operations in Britain during the decade ahead.

4 'On a Better Wicket'

During the war, Soviet penetration of British institutions was at its most extensive. Stalin's agents were at work in the Foreign Office, Secret Intelligence Service (MI6), Security Service (MI5), Special Operations Executive, Security Executive, the Government Code and Cipher School, in military intelligence, the Admiralty, the Ministry of Information, in atomic research establishments and at the BBC. Their success was the sequel to the intense recruitment in the universities during the 1930s. Many of the spies began their entry into some of the most secret areas of government even before war was declared, or during the twenty-two months when the Soviet Union was allied with Nazi Germany. But their rise was greatly facilitated by the sudden transformation in Anglo-Soviet relations in the second half of 1941.

At four o'clock on the morning of 22 June 1941 the first of 160 German divisions swept into Russia. In the preceding months Stalin had disregarded the warnings of an impending invasion given to him by the British government as well as his own intelligence agents, notably Richard Sorge in Japan. The Soviet leader was devastated by the attack. He could not bring himself to tell the population that Hitler had with such awesome force torn up the Nazi–Soviet pact. It was left to Molotov, the author of the ill-fated accord, to broadcast the news later in the day. That evening the British Prime Minister, Winston Churchill also went on the air. 'The Russian danger is therefore our danger,' he declared, 'and the danger of the United States, just as the cause of any Russian fighting for his hearth and home is the cause of free men and free people in every quarter of the globe.'[1]

For Stalin, the war against Hitler was no longer an 'imperialist war' but a great patriotic struggle to save the motherland. Britain's enemy was now his own. But Stalin's suspicions of the West ran deep. They were exceeded only by Churchill's loathing of communism. In his radio speech, the British Prime Minister swallowed his pride in face of the greater peril. He said: 'No one has been a more persistent opponent of communism than I have been for the last twenty five years. I will

77

unsay no word that I have spoken about it, but all this fades away before the spectacle which is now unfolding.' On this basis, with past enmity suspended in an hour of common danger, the wartime alliance was forged.

Contact between the two governments had in fact continued throughout the duration of the Nazi–Soviet pact. The socialist, Sir Stafford Cripps, went to Moscow as British Ambassador in June 1940, in the hope that he spoke a language Soviet leaders might understand. Communication proceeded on several levels: Foreign Secretary Eden tried to feed the Soviet Union with intelligence on Hitler's intended duplicity, and Anglo-Soviet trade talks were resumed. This was despite the anger felt towards Moscow's actions in 1939 and after, and even as service chiefs weighed up the consequences of selective military action against the Soviet Union.

After the German invasion all thought of anti-Soviet action was banished overnight and the existing diplomatic links rapidly built upon. In July, Cripps and Molotov agreed a programme of assistance that was both material and financial. The USA entered the war in December, just as Eden was preparing to visit Moscow. In May 1942 the Anglo-Soviet agreement was enlarged and formalised into a twenty-year treaty between the two powers. After its signing in London, Molotov flew to Washington to meet President Roosevelt, while two months later Churchill had his first encounter with Stalin in Moscow.

The immediate Soviet objective was survival. British military planners did not at first rate the Red Army's chances of throwing back the invader very highly. They gave it a matter of weeks at most before they expected its certain defeat. But they were mistaken and by the spring of 1943, the threat to Moscow had been lifted, the mighty battle for Stalingrad had been won, and the Soviet forces went onto the counter-offensive. They reclaimed two-thirds of their captured territory during the summer. But the Grand Alliance ran far from smoothly. From the beginning Stalin had pressed Churchill and Roosevelt for the opening of a second front to relieve the pressure on Russia. And as the three leaders began to turn their minds to the world after the war, the outlines of future conflicts emerged.

As early as November 1941 Stalin had complained to Churchill that 'there is no definite understanding between our two countries on war aims and on plans for the post-war organisation of peace.'[2] The lack of clarity was entirely to the Soviet leader's advantage. Stalin wanted recognition of his seizures in 1940 and was set on extending his power in eastern Europe, in Poland and East Prussia in particular. How far the detail of his thinking extended, and how early, is open to question.

But, in the early stages of the alliance at least, it was not clear to his new-found allies what his demands would mean beyond border changes. The Soviet Union had given repeated pledges to the effect that it would accept political plurality in post-war Europe. Britain accepted some Soviet aims as it understood them: that Stalin wanted to make Russia secure and prevent Germany from ever again posing a threat to her land and interests. Britain also much desired the continuation of friendly relations with the Soviet Union after the war, however enigmatic and difficult her leaders might be.

Indeed many senior British diplomats believed that the Soviet Union harboured no agressive intentions which would seriously threaten British interests, and that, in any event, exhaustion from the efforts of war would dampen her ambitions. The British Ambassador in Moscow, Sir Archibald Clark Kerr, who had replaced Cripps at the beginning of 1942, believed that after the conflict the Soviet Union 'will probably be prepared to take things quietly for a considerable period of time. There will be a general desire on the part of the population at large for a greater degree of comfort and happiness than was granted them before the war.'[3] Not everyone, it is true, shared this view. Sir Owen O'Malley, Ambassador to the exiled Polish government in London, wrote in the spring of 1943 that he 'would certainly not put it beyond the power of a victorious and dangerous Russia to lay a heavy hand... on Eastern Europe'.[4] But the Permanent Secretary at the Foreign Office, Sir Alexander Cadogan, dismissed his argument as not 'a helpful contribution'. Commenting on O'Malley's paper, another official, William Strang, who was destined to become Permanent Secretary after the war and the first Baron Strang, observed that 'there is a respectable and well-informed opinion that Russia will not, either now, or for some years after the war, aim at the Bolshevisation of Eastern and Central Europe or adopt an aggressive policy elsewehere.'[5] His words encapsulate the predominant view of Soviet strategy held in the Foreign Office during the war.

O'Malley would have found allies elsewhere in Whitehall. As will be examined in detail later, the Security Service (MI5) expressed strong views about the continuing threat of communism; and in 1944 the service chiefs were criticised by the Foreign Office for suggesting that the Soviet Union might emerge from the war as a hostile power.[6]

It was clearly in Stalin's interest to perpetuate the Foreign Office's relaxed view of his intentions. To help his unfolding strategy on its way, the Soviet leader could draw on the hidden resources at his disposal. The main tasks of the Soviet intelligence services in Britain during the war, and of their agents at the centre of the machinery of

British government, can be identified with reasonable certainty. Stalin's first requirement was information on his allies' intentions both in the conduct of the war and regarding their post-war aims. Secondly, he was seeking to influence decision-making from within, most critically in cases where there was a conflict of interest between Britain and the Soviet Union, so that the Soviet case would prevail. Thirdly, Stalin wanted all the technical and military data he could obtain to support his efforts to raise the Soviet Union to great power status in the post-war world, particularly the secrets of the atomic bomb. Finally, his agents could use their positions to complement propaganda activities aimed at influencing public opinion towards a favourable view of the Soviet Union, reinforcing the Soviet line that it intended no threat to the rest of Europe.

To carry out such an ambitious programme of espionage and propaganda required more solid foundations than the Soviet Union had given itself before the war, when so many 'illegal' controllers came in and out of Britain with little continuity. The establishment of the alliance however presented some new possibilities: making full use of the greatly increased official Soviet presence in London after 1941. Henceforth the majority of agents working for the Soviet Union were to be controlled by 'legal' officers under full diplomatic cover. There were, however, some important exceptions to this general rule.

Besides an increase in the numbers of staff at the Soviet Embassy, a separate mission was set up to the allied powers, a Soviet Military Mission came to London (with a corresponding British Military Mission in Moscow), and the NKVD had its own mission to liaise with the Special Operations Executive. In October 1943, the urbane Maisky left London after eleven years as Ambassador and was succeeded by Feodor Gousev, formerly the Soviet envoy in Canada. Among his staff was an NKVD officer named Anatoly Gromov, nominally a Second Secretary and Press Attaché, who was otherwise known as Gorsky, or Henry to his agents. From his arrival in London in 1940, Gromov controlled the work of eight spies, including Burgess, Maclean, Philby and Blunt.[7] When Maclean was posted to the British Embassy in Washington in 1944, Gromov followed, and was replaced by Boris Krotov, who took over the remaining agents in Britain.

The Trade Delegation also continued to dabble in espionage under Dmitry Borisenko. In 1941 it acquired premises in Highgate West Hill in north-west London which had previously been used as a Soviet school and by the Anglo-Soviet Shipping Company. The following year, the future Labour MP, Bernard Floud, who had been recruited by Soviet intelligence at Oxford, moved into a flat in a block adjacent to the Trade Delegation offices, in which members of the delegation's staff also lived. At the time he was working for the Ministry of Information after three years in the army Intelligence Corps.[8]

Other university recruits were making good progress through the British establishment. Donald Maclean was based in the Foreign Office in London from the summer of 1940 when he returned from Paris following the fall of France, until his posting to Washington in 1944. Kim Philby established himself in the Iberian section of MI6 in the autumn of 1941, after a year in Section D, the predecessor of the Special Operations Executive, and a period in SOE's training section. John Cairncross also joined the headquarters staff of MI6 in 1944 from the government Code and Cipher School at Bletchley, where he was able to pass secrets of the 'Ultra' interceptions of German radio traffic to Gromov. In August 1940, with just under a year's experience as an army intelligence officer behind him, Anthony Blunt joined MI5. Soon after, Guy Burgess returned to the BBC after two unsuccessful years in Section D and remained there until 1944 when he went into the Foreign Office News Department. Alister Watson stayed in Admiralty Research throughout the war, while another recruit of Blunt's, a fellow 'Apostle' Leo Long, joined military intelligence.[9]

These spies conveyed to their Soviet masters intelligence of immense value, covering allied military operations and plans, decoded German communications, details of the inner workings of British intelligence and security services, as well as anecdotal information picked up from a range of well-connected sources in London in the course of their sometimes colourful social lives. Once Gromov or Krotov had gathered in the information it was usually transmitted to Moscow by radio. The days when couriers could physically take material to the Soviet Union, or when it could safely go by diplomatic bag, ended with the advance of the German armies across Europe. Churchill, however, had forbidden the interception of Soviet radio traffic from the very inception of the alliance. It was not until after the war that work began on the vast amount of accumulated material, eventually involving the intelligence services of Britain, the USA and Australia. None of it has been made public, but according to Peter Wright, it contained the cryptonyms of some 1,200 individuals, of whom about 800 were believed to refer to Soviet agents around the world. Among those who were identified in the messages were Maclean, Philby, and Blunt, Fuchs and the atom spies in the USA, and others such as the Honourable Ivor Montagu, a *Daily Worker* journalist who was allegedly used by the Soviet Union to provide intelligence on the Labour Party and the CPGB.[10]

British citizens and establishments overseas were also a target for

Soviet intelligence during the war. In New York, several members of British Security Co-ordination, which was responsible for intelligence operations in the Americas, later came under suspicion of having worked for the Soviet Union. One of them, Cedric Belfrage, and his former wife, Mary, were deported from the United States in 1954 after refusing to answer allegations that they were Communists with links to Soviet spy rings. At the hearing over 150 specific questions were put to the 49-year-old Belfrage and he declined to respond to any of them. He had lived in America since before the war, had worked in British Security Co-ordination, from 1941 to 1943, and afterwards became the editor of the radical *National Guardian*. His ex-wife, who worked as a journalist under the name of Molly Castle, refused to testify against him but stated at the time of the deportation hearings that for the previous ten to twelve years (i.e. since the mid-1940s) she had been working against the Communists. The British Consul-General in New York did, however, inform the Foreign Office that 'Mrs Belfrage has all along told us that she admitted membership of the Communist Party in 1937'.[11]

British subjects living and working in the Soviet Union, as well as employees of the British Embassy had long been vulnerable. Soviet attempts to compromise them became ever more desperate after the outbreak of war. Some of the subjects selected by the NKVD had the sense however to report their experiences to British officials and the Ambassador, Cripps, raised several cases with Andrei Vyshinsky, the former chief prosecutor at some of the show trials in the purges, who had become Molotov's deputy in the Foreign Affairs Commissariat.

In August 1940 a Mrs Tamplin, the Latvian-born wife of the manager of a Latvian bank was approached by the NKVD after she applied for an exit visa to accompany her husband to Cairo. She was told to make influential friends in British and foreign society in Egypt and to win over her husband. After being made to sign a piece of paper agreeing to comply with the demands of the secret police, she reported the matter to the British Embassy in Moscow.[12] Another naturalised British subject, Lazar Ram, who was employed by the British Legation first in Korvo and later in Moscow, was accosted in the Hotel National and threatened with dire consequences for his relatives in Latvia if he did not work for the NKVD. In September 1940 Ram was transferred to Turkey. In the same year, John Murray, the clerk to the Air Attaché at the British Embassy, was compromised by the NKVD and subjected to bribery and threats.

Born in Blackpool in 1908 of a Greek father, Murray went to Riga to work in a Greek-owned cigar factory when he was 17 and later ran his own business there. After the business was nationalised, he eventually joined the staff of the British Legation. During 1940 he was visited in Riga by two men from the NKVD who claimed to represent Glavtabec, an official Soviet trading organisation interested in the tobaccco industry. At first British officials felt that Murray was at risk because his parents were living in Latvia, but when they left in the midldle of 1941 the Air Ministry said it had no objections to Murray's continuation in the post. In 1942 the clerk was compromised again when he married the daughter of an NKVD officer and he was finally relieved of his post and sent back to England.[13]

Murray was not the first clerk in the Air Attaché's office to be targeted by Soviet intelligence. The then Foreign Office member, Fitzroy Maclean, noted in October 1940, that a previous clerk, called Hubbard

> made no attempt to disguise tastes which soon caused him to fall an easy victim to the People's Commissariat for Internal Affairs, whom he appears to have supplied with confidential documents from the Air Attaché's safe. His successor, who arrived in response to an appeal for a normal man, was, improbable as it may seem, a Mohammedan, a drunkard and a Communist, whose behaviour ultimately became so strange that he had to be removed from Moscow in a hurry.[14]

These cases, during the war and shortly before it, prefigured the more serious affair in the 1950s, when John Vassall was ensnared by Soviet intelligence while working as a clerk in the Naval Attaché's office in Moscow.

Meanwhile, in London the NKVD was able to set up its own small mission after 1941, under the command of Colonel Chichaev. Its primary purpose was to liaise with the Special Operations Executive (SOE), the sabotage and guerrilla organisation created by Churchill in 1940 to 'set occupied Europe ablaze'. Operational results of the liaison proved patchy. Major-General Colin Gubbins, the head of SOE, told the Foreign Office at the beginning of 1945 that in Poland, Czechoslovakia, Germany and Rumania, cooperation had come to naught and in Turkey relations had been suspended from 1941–4. And when the SOE was able to assist the NKVD, the help was not always appreciated. It enabled a member of the NKVD's London mission, a Major Krassowski, to reach Tito's forces in Yugoslavia, but local SOE officers reported that he 'was completely unappreciative of the efforts made on his behalf'.[15] The SOE was, however, keen to continue working with the NKVD after the war. One of its senior officers wrote in February that the two bodies had a 'treaty' under which the SOE had certain rights and obligations.[16] The SOE's Moscow Mission was in daily touch with the NKVD and SOE chiefs wanted approval for talks in Moscow about peace-time collaboration, including the possibility of a joint study of underground warfare and sabotage in Germany. Even the Foreign Office baulked at the prospect of some of the SOE's ideas and its initiative was curtailed. In the event its plans were never realised as the SOE was wound up after the war.

Continued collaboration with the NKVD would have greatly pleased some of the SOE's less senior officers. In addition to Philby, who was in SOE in its early days, the CPGB member and Soviet intelligence talent-spotter, James Klugmann, was a major in the SOE, stationed in Cairo and concerned with operations in Yugoslavia. Another Communist, John Eyre, was a member of SOE's Albanian intelligence section based in Bari.[17] Ormond Uren, a young captain of the Highland Light Infantry attached to the SOE's Hungarian section in London, passed on details of his work to Douglas Springhall, then National Organiser of the CPGB. In 1943 both men were arrested. Uren was court-martialled and sentenced to seven years' penal servitude and Springhall received a similar term of imprisonment. He had also been receiving information from a clerk in the Air Ministry, Mrs Olive Sheehan, who was gaoled for three months.[18]

On his conviction, Springhall was promptly expelled from the Communist Party and his wife lost her job on the *Daily Worker*. The CPGB leadership was seriously embarrassed by the association with espionage at a time when its membership had soared to a record 56,000 and it was trying to foster a patriotic image in full support of the war effort. Douglas Hyde, a prominent Communist and *Daily Worker* journalist, who broke with the party shortly after the war, noted that Springhall's expulsion had occurred 'not because the party disapproved of his activities' but because of his 'indiscipline and indiscretion',[19] which undermined the foundations of its growing popularity. The fact was, said Hyde, that Communists believed the alliance with Russia was not being put fully into effect:

> The reaction of the average member was 'If they won't supply the information to Russia, we will.' The spying which had gone on during the 'imperialist war' phase was nothing to that which followed. The information came from factories and the Forces, from civil servants and scientists. And the significant thing to recognise is that those who did it were not professional spies; they took big risks in most cases, received no payment whatsoever, and, this is doubly important, did not see themselves as spies and still less as traitors. As party members they would have felt that they were being untrue to themselves and unworthy of the name of communist if they had not done it.[20]

It is impossible now to try to measure the extent of this voluntary, amateur espionage. If Hyde is right, it came as a significant bonus to the systematic efforts of the Soviet Union's own professional agencies and their small army of strategically-placed agents. Yet whatever the value of the information which passed through those informal channels, spying was not part of the Communist Party's allotted wartime role. Indeed it conflicted with it.

Stalin wanted to exploit his alliance with Britain by presenting a less menacing face to 'capitalist' institutions. Soviet propaganda cultivated the image of a nation whose undoubtedly heroic sacrifices had earned it a place among the world powers in a way that would reduce the likelihood that it would in future behave like some international bandit, seizing whatever territory and spoils it could for its own aggrandisement. It was, as noted above, a line largely accepted by the British Foreign Office. Stalin took what steps he could to disarm British suspicions of his intentions and to divert attention from any such unfriendly acts as subversion and espionage.

In May 1943 he formally abolished the much despised Comintern. Some Western observers interpreted the move as a gesture of goodwill. That was no doubt one reason why Stalin disbanded it. In reality the Comintern had long outlived its usefulness as a supposedly separate agency. Revolution in Western Europe was not a foreseeable prospect, and its Communist parties, either *in situ* or whose leaders were safely exiled in Moscow, were under firm Soviet control. Burying the Comintern would affect none of these issues nor limit the Soviet Union in any way. Many of its remaining functions were transferred to a new Foreign Affairs Department of the Soviet Communist Party, the forerunner of the larger and more powerful International Department of the post-Stalin era. Indeed the Comintern's abolition was of symbolic rather than practical importance. Igor Gouzenko, the GRU cipher clerk who defected to the West in Ottawa in 1945, believed that 'the announcement of the dissolution of the Comintern was probably the greatest farce of the Communists in recent years. Only the name was liquidated, with the object of reassuring public opinion in the democratic countries. Actually the Comintern exists and continues to work.'[21]

The pro-Soviet mood of both the British government and the people was there to be exploited. The gains from 'Soviet Weeks' and other celebrations of the alliance were worth any number of Comintern proclamations. Douglas Hyde captured the ironies of one such occasion in Feltham, Middlesex when, 'standing between two flag poles from which flew the Union Jack and the Red Flag, were Mr Maisky, the

Soviet Ambassador, the local city fathers, the Conservative MP, a leading Communist shop steward and others.'[22]

The Communist Party's primary task was to be seen actively supporting the war and the Soviet alliance, and to echo the Soviet Union's call for a second front. Any local scandal caused by its involvement in espionage might therefore have wider repercussions. Spying on one's allies is always likely to cause embarrassment; the risks have to be weighed against the advantages. It was a matter of judgement whether the 'moles' in the British establishment were in danger. In fact they were not because the British weren't looking for them. Spies in the CPGB were more vulnerable, for the reason that this was just the sort of activity that the British had come to expect of the Communist Party over the years. Their discovery might compromise the party's patriotic posture and cast doubts in official British circles about the sincerity of the Soviet Union, destroying its carefully constructed propaganda campaign. The Springhall case therefore re-emphasised the pitfalls for the Soviet Union of employing local parties and their members in sustained espionage operations. His capture was more serious, because of the circumstances and Springhall's own position, than anything that had gone before, including the Glading case. After 1943 the Soviet Union was much less inclined to use party members in such a role.

Foreign Communists exiled in Britain did not face the same inhibitions. They ran the added peril of being interned if their actions attracted the attention of the authorities, but they were unlikely to damage the reputation of the CPGB. To their hosts they were first and foremost alien refugees. The official attitude to them was ambivalent. Those members of the German Communist Party (KPD) who were among the 27,000 Germans interned in Britain in 1940 were detained for their nationality rather than their ideology.[23] By the end of that year the government had changed its mind about the threat they posed and released 20,000, among them Klaus Fuchs, Jürgen Kuczynski, whose friends Pritt, Laski and Strachey had pressed for his freedom, and Hans Kahle, one of the leaders of the KPD in England. The Western allies soon began to utilise some of this talent. In May 1941 Fuchs began work on atomic research in Birmingham, became a naturalised British subject the following year and transferred to America in 1943. Kuczynski, having resumed his political pamphleteering, was recruited in 1944 by the American Office of Strategic Services (OSS), a body analagous to MI6 and SOE, as an economic analyst for the US Strategic Bombing Survey.

For the Soviet Union the presence of such dedicated Communists in

Britain and the USA presented its intelligence services with additional weapons. Jürgen Kuczynski kept in touch with Gromov at the Soviet embassy in London,[24] and arranged an introduction there for Fuchs in 1941 when the latter approached him to offer his services as a spy. Fuch's controller in the second half of that year was Simon Kremer, the GRU man who acted as secretary to the Defence Attaché. Before he left Britain at the end of 1941 Kremer also met Ursula Kuczynski, Jürgen's sister.

After her departure from Geneva in December 1940, Ursula Kuczynski had travelled overland with her two children to Lisbon. After a three-week wait she sailed for Liverpool in January 1941, and after surviving routine questioning on her arrival, went to Oxford to be near her father, Robert. Over the next eighteen months Ursula Kuczynski established herself as a GRU 'illegal', under the innocuous cover of a wife and mother, and the holder of a British passport. She lived in a succession of lodgings until the autumn of 1942 when her husband, Len Beurton, at last joined her from Switzerland; they settled in a house in Oxford which was also occupied by Harold Laski's brother, Neville.[25]

Under the code name, 'Sonja', she took over the control of Fuchs after the departure of Kremer, until Fuchs himself left England in December 1943. She received information from her father and brother, who introduced Hans Kahle to her. Besides being prominent in exile political circles, Kahle was a military correspondent for *Time* and *Fortune* magazines. 'Sonja' also ran an agent called 'James', a working-class RAF officer, who on one occasion supplied her with a newly-invented aircraft part.[26] To pass on this information she travelled regularly to London to meet her own Soviet controller, a succession of individuals who were always referred to as 'Sergei', and transmitted by radio from her home, for which an addditional radio operator called 'Tom' was recruited.[27]

Altogether 'Sonja' lived in England for nearly nine years until her departure for East Germany with Len, in 1950.[28] Of the GRU 'illegals' who began their careers before the war she was one of the last to work in Britain. And unlike Krivitsky, Orlov and the Poretskys, 'Sonja' retained her orthodox Communist faith through the purges and all the twists of Soviet policy. Her own account of her life as a spy first in China and then in Britain should therefore be treated with caution. It glorifies her own role and reveals nothing which might be damaging to the Communist cause. There is no clue in her autobiography which suggests that her main agent in wartime England and after may have been the MI5 officer and future Director-General of the Security Service, Roger Hollis.

HOLLIS, MI5 AND THE SECURITY EXECUTIVE

The war years are crucial to the question of whether Britain's spy-catcher-in-chief was himself a Soviet agent. Hollis entered MI5 a year before the war at the age of 33. He was responsible for monitoring and countering Communist subversion during the war. The successes and failures of that time were therefore directly attributable to his detailed work rather than to his overall, and perhaps remote, direction in later years. Springhall, Uren and other Communists were apprehended while the more dangerous Cambridge spies continued to rise high in Whitehall, and Fuchs obtained clearance to undertake work of the highest secrecy with the added reassurance of British nationality. And during the war 'Sonja', the woman who is said to have recruited Hollis in China, came to England and specifically to Oxford, allegedly for the prime purpose of taking over the direction of Hollis, then serving in MI5's wartime location at nearby Blenheim Palace. Such are the bare bones of the circumstances which, in retrospect, have been held to demonstrate the alleged treachery of Hollis.[29]

Hollis appears an unpromising candidate for the most senior position in British security. The middle of three sons of the Suffragan Bishop of Taunton, Roger Hollis was educated at Clifton College and at Oxford, which he left before taking a degree. Reserved by nature and not enjoying the best of health, his early career was not a success. He spent eight years in China from 1928–36, mainly in Shanghai in the employment of the British American Tobacco Company. 'Sonja', then Mrs Rudolf Hamburger was in China from 1930 to 1935, a member of the same international community in Shanghai. When Hollis returned to England in 1936, already a Soviet agent according to his accusers, he had poor job prospects and was ill with tuberculosis. He did, however, marry the next year and in 1938, through the social connections which were still MI5's main avenue of recruitment, he entered British intelligence.

There is, however, no evidence that Hollis met 'Sonja', either in China or in England, and no evidence of any youthful inclination towards communism, as there was with many of the Cambridge spies. The charge that none of the major Soviet spies active in Britain during the war was detected because Hollis was a spy has yet to be either proved or disproved. The whole affair raises wider questions of the framework in which Hollis was working, how the British authorities perceived the threat of communism at the time, and what they did about it. It also poses the specific question of what were Hollis's duties in the war – whether they were concerned mainly with the CPGB and

its satellites, or with the whole range of Soviet-inspired subversion and
espionage conducted throught all the available 'legal' and 'illegal'
channels. This has been a subject of animated debate between Hollis's
detractors and defenders.[30]

Some hitherto neglected documents relating to the Security Executive, the wartime body which coordinated all aspects of policy on
counter-espionage and counter-subversion, offer new insights into these
questions. They also provide the fullest statement available on MI5's
approach to communism during the war in a paper prepared for the War
Cabinet with the direct involvement of Roger Hollis. As the Security
Executive is so little known its work may require some introduction.

Established by Churchill on 28 May 1940 under the chairmanship of
Viscount Swinton, who as Sir Philip Cunliffe-Lister had been Air
Minister in the Chamberlain government, the Security Executive
brought together the work of a score of government departments and
agencies covering the UK, the dominions and the colonies. It began life
as the Home Defence (Security) Executive but to avoid confusion with
other wartime bodies such as the Ministry of Home Security and the
Home Defence Executive, its name was changed in October 1941.[31]

The Executive's responsibilities embraced the 'defence of national
interests against hostile elements other than the armed forces of the
enemy; in practice against espionage, sabotage and attempts to
procure defeat by subversive activity.'[32] The detailed list of subjects
considered included, under espionage, giving guidance to police on the
techniques of enemy agents, the arrangements with police and
military commands for dealing with them and the facilities for their
interrogation and detention. The Security Executive was also
responsible for preventive measures against sabotage, the control of
chemicals and explosives and arrangements for coordinated investigation and reporting. Under the heading of subversive activities, the
Executive included the British Union of Fascists, the CPGB and its
satellites, Trotskyist organisations and 'pacifist, "religious" and
conscientious objectors' organisations'.[33] It was also responsible for the
policy on the internment of aliens, security relating to detention and
employment of prisoners of war, fifth columnists, identity cards and
passes, and the control of information and communications, ranging
from censorship and the restriction of material from government
departments, to the control of cameras, binoculars, telescopes, radios,
codes, secret inks, pigeons and 'propaganda against careless talk'. The
Executive was further concerned with security measures at military
and government establishments, docks, marshalling yards and
industrial installations, the security of shipping, entry and exit

controls at ports and the protection of British interest in foreign countries.

Few institutions in British history have possessed such wide-ranging powers of control over so many aspects of the nation's life, public and private. Yet there was something typically British in the way the actions of the Security Executive were circumscribed. As the formal description of its functions admitted, the title 'may perhaps be misleading, since the Executive is a coordinating body and does not itself take the operative action to give effect to its recommendations'.[34] It was the Security Executive's job to see that best possible measures were framed and that responsibility for action was accepted by the appropriate department. Some of the agencies most closely concerned with security matters met in a special liaison officers group, which consisted of representatives of the Admiralty, War Office, Home Office, the Home Forces, Ministry of Information, Postal and Telegraph Censorship, MI6, MI5 and the Metropolitan Police, under the chairmanship of Sir Herbert Creedy the Executive's top civil servant. Coordination of security in government departments was further supervised by a panel under the chairmanship of the Secretary to the War Cabinet, with the Secretary of the Security Executive as joint secretary of the panel.

Other senior members and officials included Isaac Foot, the Liberal MP and father of the future leader of the Labour Party as Vice-Chairman, with William Armstrong, later Lord Armstrong, the head of the home civil service and Kenneth, later Lord, Diplock, as joint secretaries.[35] These officials also serviced the Security Executive's sub-committees, three of which were concerned with shipping and ports, and one, under a trade unionist, Alf Wall, dealt with the CPGB. Through the Wall committee, which incorporated information direct from MI5, weekly reports were prepared on Communist activity for the full Executive.

In the autumn of 1941, with the alliance with the Soviet Union just three months old, the Security Executive built on its interest in communism by submitting, via the Home Secretary, a major report on the CPGB to the War Cabinet. It was prepared in September 1941, with the final version being considered at a meeting of the Security Executive on 1 October 1941. The report was drafted not by Wall but by MI5, in 'close consultation' with Lord Swinton, and 'particular care had been taken to check the accuracy of all the statements made'.[36] The comment reflected Swinton's own relations with MI5: as the description of the Executive's functions put it, he had 'certain personal responsibilities with regard to the Security Service and MI6'.[37] In fact,

Churchill had asked Swinton to oversee the activities of the intelligence agencies. One of his first moves was to secure the appointment of Sir David Petrie as Director General of MI5 in November 1940 after an unsatisfactory period following the dismissal five months previously of the long-serving Major-General Sir Vernon Kell.[38]

The report of September/October 1941 was intended as 'a complete appreciation of the Communist Party's aims and methods'.[39] It sought to answer the question of how far the party's professed support of national unity should be accepted at face value. The report's answer was that the Communists' revolutionary aims were in reality unchanged. Since the German invasion of Russia the CPGB had taken the opportunity to escape from its unpopular position and develop a new approach. Although this entailed 'apparent cooperation in the war effort', it included a 'new technique of penetration from within'.[40] The main areas of penetration which concerned the Security Service were in the factories, where Communists were using their calls for increased production as a means of attacking the government and management and gaining recognition. In the trade unions, the CPGB was undermining established bodies by creating its own parallel organisation in the Shop Stewards' National Council. The party had also 'established secret groups of party members amongst journalists and such other professional workers as doctors and lawyers, and they have set up or gained control of a number of bodies which operate without any direct connection with the Communist Party.'[41] Among those specifically mentioned were two which exist today, the Labour Research Department, which had been in receipt of Soviet funds in the 1920s, and the National Council for Civil Liberties.

The more favourable conditions for the spread of communism since June 1941 meant that 'the Communist menace may be considered even more dangerous now than in the past because so many more people are likely to be attracted by its present popular front policy, which the party represents as the only method of obtaining a quick and successful end to the war.'[42] MI5's view that while the CPGB's tactics had changed, its basic aims remained the same was confirmed by the reports of its agents, described as 'information received from the most secret sources, which have proved reliable in the past'.[43]

In a covering note Viscount Swinton endorsed the report's findings and added further emphasis to the 'increased use ... of non-Communist bodies; and new bodies of this kind are being formed, "Aid to Russia" serving as an excellent medium of propaganda and camouflage'.[44] He concluded that: 'It is clear that the Communist game is still the same; but it is being played on a much better wicket.'[45]

Among the members of the Security Service who attended the meeting of the Security Executive of 1 October 1941 which discussed the final version of the report was Roger Hollis. He was listed after his Director-General, Sir David Petrie, and two other colleagues, D. C. H. Abbot and Herbert Hart, the husband of Jenifer Fischer-Williams, who had been in touch with Soviet intelligence before the war. It was customary for Petrie and several senior MI5 officers to go to Security Executive meetings, but Hollis was not, it appears, usually among them. He was, however, present for the whole of that one, which also considered identity cards, controls at ports and entry into Northern Ireland and the position of British and allied subjects in Portugal.[46]

The pattern of Hollis's attendance at meetings of the Security Executive at this time, and in particular the meeting of 1 October, indicates a close personal interest in the memorandum for the war cabinet of the CPGB. Indeed it is very likely that Hollis was one of its authors. This would explain why it was important for him to be on hand for the whole of that meeting, alongside colleagues who were more regular attenders. It also would have been standard practice for the officer, or officers, who had been most closely involved in the drafting of a paper to attend the meeting at which it was to be discussed. The report was of course a combined effort, and the criteria which apply to Hollis might apply equally to Herbert Hart. Whatever the full extent of Hollis's responsibility for the paper's contents, he undoubtedly helped shape what is one of the fullest statements of record of MI5's attitude to the CPGB. It is for these reasons reproduced in full as as appendix (Appendix II).

It is not altogether surprising that MI5 should prepare such a document of the party which was so closely identified with Britain's new wartime ally. What is more revealing are the limits of its scope. The dangers of communism are treated in their political, propaganda and industrial aspects. The sections on the role of the CPGB in industry and the trade unions anticipate many concerns of the post-war era. Missing from the MI5 and Security Executive view of communism is any appreciation of the true significance of the 'secret' Communists who were instructed not to declare their faith by being open members of the CPGB, but to operate as 'moles' within the establishment. Although the concepts of 'penetration from within' and the control through secret party members of non-Communist bodies were recognised, they were not applied to the machinery of government nor to espionage.

Indeed, the report failed to consider the whole question of spying.

There was no mention of the relationship between CPGB members and espionage, nor the role of official Soviet representatives in Britain. There are a number of possible explanations: one is that they were covered in a separate report which remains locked in Whitehall, if it has survived. But there are no clues or cross-references to one. Secondly, there is the possibility that if Hollis was a Soviet agent, as an author of the report he could have suppressed such information. That, however, is unlikely since so many other people were involved in preparing and approving the paper, not least Viscount Swinton himself. Thirdly, it is conceivable that MI5 considered espionage as a matter quite distinct from the political and industrial activities of the CPGB: it simply did not belong in this paper. From that may be drawn another conclusion: that Hollis was not at that stage responsible for both aspects of communism. His primary interest then was in the political elements, national and international perhaps – the Comintern features early on in the report – but it could be concluded that he was not also handling the question of Soviet espionage. If he, or the section of MI5 which was most involved in putting together the paper, had customarily treated those two areas side by side, as related matters under the general heading of Communist threats, they would surely have made some reference to the connection in such a major report. Their failure to establish the link was not due to the treachery or incompetence of any one individual. It was a product of bureaucratic distinctions within MI5, the result of a deeper lack of imagination, and the pressure of more immediate dangers, which affected the whole of the British intelligence and security community. The espionage it was primarily concerned with came from the Nazi enemy not the Soviet ally. These circumstances, and Whitehall's lack of perception, were fully exploited by the Soviet Union during the war.

Just how easily some of its agents were able to function inside British government is illustrated in further material relating to the Security Executive. Towards the end of 1941 the Foreign Office did not send a regular representative to its meetings. As a department it was perhaps not excited by some of the detail, focusing on the mechanics as much as the policy of security, which came before the committee. Two weeks after the report on the CPGB had been submitted, Donald Maclean attended the next meeting of the Security Executive in the company of a slightly more senior colleague, a 32-year-old First Secretary named John Ward who had served in Cairo and Baghdad. The agenda was routine: an item of British and allied subjects in Portugal, the relaxation of restrictions on allied seamen, and the regular report of the Communist Party.[47] The first item is worth noting, for any MI6 input would almost certainly come to Kim Philby's attention as he had recently joined its Iberian section.

For his part Donald Maclean may have had several reasons as a spy for attending. He may have heard about the previous submission of the Communist Party and wanted to find out more. The contacts he could make in such a forum might prove invaluable to a Soviet agent who had returned to London less than eighteen months before. Around the table with Maclean that morning were twenty-four assorted government servants and officers from the armed forces and police. They included Viscount Swinton, Isaac Foot, Sir Herbert Creedy, William Armstrong, four members of MI5, (but not Hollis) and representatives from the War Office, Admiralty, Home Forces GHQ, and the Home Office as well as Major Desmond Morton from the Prime Minister's Office.[48] Maclean would have been more than interested in getting to know the latter, as Morton was one of Churchill's most trusted confidants and sifted all the intelligence reports going into 10 Downing Street.[49]

The General Department of the Foreign Office, in which Maclean was working, had its own links to the intelligence community. Among the matters it dealt with were communications, shipping, censorship and issues of coordination between the allies. In March 1943, for example, Captain Brooke-Booth of MI5 telephoned one of its members to ask for a Foreign Office view of an American request for authority to send some NCOs to Britain to prepare for counter-espionage work in different European countries. One of the department's members, Peter Loxley, discussed it with John Ward, and wrote back to Brooke-Booth that it depended on the nature of the tasks. He also mentioned that he had had an after-dinner conversation about it with Guy Liddell, of MI5, who agreed that it would 'fairly lamentable if, for instance, an allied government in London tumbled to the fact that these US soldiers were being used to obtain information for HMG about allied internal political dissensions.'[50] It is not known what happened to this particular proposal. But it provides a small example of the social and inter-departmental connections of Whitehall at work. For someone like Maclean, it was the simplest thing to tune into the network and add greatly to his value to the Soviet Union.

Hollis, meanwhile, was present at a further meeting of the Security Executive, its 53rd, of the afternoon of 12 November 1941. He stayed, according to the minutes, for the first two items on the agenda: on aliens brought to the UK by force, and, his main area of interest, for a discussion of a Ministry of Information paper concerning its policy towards communism. Petrie, the Director-General of MI5 and

D. C. H. Abbot were present throughout the meeting. The Executive secretariat allowed three-quarters of an hour for consideration of the Ministry of Information paper. It raised various questions of propaganda, diplomatic contacts, and the manipulation of Anglo-Soviet Weeks and exhibitions by British Communists. Neither the paper nor the discussion touched on the problem of Soviet espionage. Once again, that may reveal something about the terms of Hollis's duties at the time.

In retrospect, the main significance of the occasion was that the Ministry of Information's policy on communism was itself prepared by a secret Communist who has since been identified as a Soviet agent: Peter Smollett, otherwise known as Peter Smolka, who had worked with Kim Philby in a small news agency in the mid-1930s. But the true nature of his loyalties did not become apparent for another decade and a half, after his return to his native Austria.[51] During the war he was the head of the Ministry of Information's Russian branch and as such formulated policies to promote Britain's alliance with the Soviet Union. In October 1941 Smollett circulated a paper to a Whitehall conference on propaganda policy towards communism. In the light of that meeting the subject was discussed the following month by the Security Executive. Smollett himself was not present at that meeting and his Ministry was represented by its usual representative, the director of the home division, R. H. Parker.

The Ministry's twofold policy, as set out in Smollett's paper, aimed to:

> Combat such anti-Soviet feeling in Britain as might jeopardise the execution of the policy defined by the Prime Minister, June 22nd. Combat enemy attempts to split national unity over issue of Anglo-Soviet alliance.
>
> Attempt to curb exuberant pro-Soviet propaganda from the Left which might seriously embarrass HMG. Anticipate Communist inspired criticism and prevent initiative from falling into hands of Communist Party.[52]

For a policy formulated by a Communist, the latter objectives might appear self-defeating. But like everything else in the labyrinth of inter-departmental committees, no one individual could expect to have a totally clear run. Smollett, however, as Glees has shown, was a subtle operator.[53] In this instance he had his sights set higher than some controversial manoeuvre which might marginally enhance the status of the CPGB. For the Ministry of Information's solution to prevent the Communist Party exploiting celebrations on the alliance was to join forces with the Soviet Embassy:

> It is intended to develop a close liaison between this Ministry and the Soviet

Embassy which will greatly assist us in dealing rigorously with the English [sic] Communist Party since the attitude of the Soviet government is almost cynically realist about the war position. They appreciate that the assistance which they are to receive is due to the existence of a Capitalist system and they do not propose at this stage to authorise anything which will endanger the capacity of this country to afford them the subventions of which they stand and will stand increasingly in need ...

Negotiations are pending on the subject of the Society for Cultural Relations in the USSR, and it is anticipated that that Society will form a useful instrument of the same character as the British Council already does.

It is the intention of the Ministry ... to refuse all facilities to White Russians and English Reds to speak under the aegis of the Ministry. Negotiations have been taken in hand by Mr Smollett to obtain the services of Soviet speakers from Russia and when this has come to fruition it will be desirable to arrange for them extended tours giving them by arrangement with the appropriate Division here, the maximum amount of radio and Press publicity. These speakers will be strictly under Party discipline and we need not therefore fear any ideological friction.[54]

The views of Petrie, Hollis and other members of the Security Service of this policy are not unfortunately recorded. For the Home Office, Frank Newsam declared that the police should provide information for the Ministry of Communist-inspired activity, particularly when they were operating behind a 'respectable façade'. He also advised against using German or Czech Communists as speakers, since a number of them had been released from internment on condition that they did not take part in any political activity. The chairman, Viscount Swinton said that the Ministry should ask the Cabinet to agree that all requests for recognition of any Anglo-Soviet organisation should be referred to him so he could clear matters with the police or Security Service.

In the end, the strategy devised by Smollett was approved by the Security Executive with only one major amendent. That concerned the proposed use of the Society for Cultural Relations with the USSR. William Armstrong circulated a note to members of the Executive informing them that the Society had been formed in 1927 by a 'small group of left-wing intellectuals, Communists and Russians'. The Metropolitan Police, the note stated, had reported some months earlier that the Society had 1,000 members and that its chairman was the barrister, D. N. Pritt.[55] It is likely that if any Security Service contribution was forthcoming at the meeting it would have endorsed the doubts about this aspect of the plan. For the rest, as Swinton said, it was 'well designed to give effect to government policy'.

Within the limits of its understanding of the threat, MI5 continued to monitor Communist activity throughout the war. The Springhall case

resulted from its surveillance of the CPGB as a subversive political
threat rather than as a specifically counter-espionage operation. Similarly, watch was maintained on foreign Communists for their political
activities. It is not true, as Chapman Pincher has suggested, that MI5
ignored the Kuczynksi family, because someone inside the Security
Service, possibly Hollis, was protecting them.[56] In October 1943 Captain Brooke-Booth of MI5 informed the Foreign Office that the inaugural meeting of the Free German National Committee had taken place,
with Professor Robert Kuczynski in the chair at a meeting attended by
400–500 people.[57] In December Postal and Telegraph Censorship prepared a 72-page dossier of anti-Nazi German exile groups, both Communist and social democratic. This report identified Robert Kuczynski as
the president of the newly formed committee, whose eighteen-member
Provisional Committee included eight members of the KPD and three
sympathisers or camouflaged Communists.[58] Hans Kahle was named as
the leader of the KPD in Britain and a member of the Free German
Committee. On the committee of another KPD 'camouflage organisation', the Free German League of Culture, based in Hampstead, was a
Dr Alfred Kuczynski.

In November 1943, MI5 wanted to grant a licence to a moderate
German trade union magazine, to help prevent the Communists and
the Russians from gaining control of German politics, either outside,
or, ultimately, inside Germany. But the Foreign Office did not find the
MI5 case convincing, thought the German émigrés were unimportant
and that MI5 was 'suffering from so many delusions'.[59] Foreign Office
officials summoned the MI5 officers concerned to discuss it, 'in order to
educate them'. As a result of that meeting the original proposal to
approve the magazine was dropped. It is difficult on the basis of these
examples to accuse the Security Service of ignoring or disguising the
potential dangers of Communism. It may have not have grasped
everything that was at stake, but its awareness during the war was
demonstrably greater that that of the Foreign Office.

Nor did MI5 and the Security Executive neglect other political
groups of the revolutionary left who might have received funds or
encouragement from sources overseas. In January 1940, for example,
Dick White (later Sir Dick, and the only man to head both MI6 and the
Security Service) wrote to the Foreign Office about policies and
funding of the National Revolutionary Marxist Centre, whose
secretary in London was Fenner (later Lord) Brockway.[60] In 1941 the
Security Executive considered the activities of Trotskyists in Britain
and concluded that nothing should be done to lessen the
embarrassment they were causing to the Communist Party.[61] And

three years later, when various Trotskyist groups merged to form the Revolutionary Communist Party, the Home Secretary submitted a memorandum of its strengths and weaknesses to the War Cabinet. He was, however, far from impressed and concluded that there was no evidence of funding from abroad and that the Trotskyists had had little success in penetrating the trade unions. Among the individual leaders named was Ted Grant, the future leader of the Militant Tendency in the Labour Party.[62]

By 1944 Churchill was 'weeding out remorselessly every single known Communist from all our secret organisations.'[63] The initiative achieved only limited results. Whatever criteria were set it would have been impossible to deal with Communists they did not know about. But the two categories of 'secret' Communist, those who did not declare their membership and those who were not card-carrying party members at all, escaped detection. It is now known that at least forty people who held sensitive posts in government service or the armed forces during the war were suspected Soviet agents. None were detected at the time. The British government was simply not attuned to the possibility of their existence because they were part of a wider plan few British officials appeared to comprehend. Without a proper appreciation of the extent of Soviet ambitions, the use and contribution of the 'moles' could never be understood.

Yet, up to 1945 the Foreign Office viewed relations with the Soviet Union through the perspective of the Grand Alliance. Spying did not feature in its conception of the relationship. British politicans and officials hoped that the fraternity born of conflict would somehow survive in peace. But the alliance came into being and existed for one purpose, the defeat of Nazism. Stalin understood that and acted accordingly: his designs for the future, after victory over Nazi Germany, were outside the terms of the alliance. If he could, in his meetings with Churchill and Roosevelt, secure allied compliance for Soviet freedom of action within its designated sphere of influence so much the better. If not, then he would wait, and act alone when the fruits of victory were ripe for the picking. As he pushed back Hitler's armies, he aimed to extend Communist power across central and eastern Europe, to build the security of a land empire of Russia's western borders, and tilt the balance of continental power against the West. The spies in the West were there to provide intelligence and exercise influence in support of these aims. By the time of the major allied conferences at Yalta and Potsdam during 1945, Stalin was strong enough, on the battlefield and in the negotiating chamber, to press home his claims. The West's darkest fears were revived; the alliance was doomed.

5 'The Threat to Western Civilisation'

THE 'TWO CAMPS'

By 1947 there were nearly 250 Soviet officials in Britain. They were
made up of 126 in the Embassy, including 23 people in the Military
Attaché's office, 16 on the staff of the Naval Attaché, 94 in the Trade
Delegation, and 22 in associated companies.[1] To house its expanded
staff, the Soviet government acquired ten-year leases on several
additional Crown properties in Kensington Palace Gardens, including
the offices of the former Polish government in exile. For five houses it
paid a total of £2,650 rent per annum, having secured reductions of
£980 and £400 on two of them by paying the Crown Estate Office a
premium of £2,400.[2] By 1950 the Soviet Union had thirteen service
attachés in London, compared with six British military representatives in Moscow. When the British government decided to reject a
Soviet application for a further increase in its military staff, a Foreign
Office official commented: 'the more of them there are in the country,
the more intelligence they can gather.'[3]

Indeed, increased Soviet representation in Britain after the war had
little to do with the business of improving relations between the two
countries. The 'cold war' was at its chilliest. The Soviet Union
displayed hostility to the capitalist world of an intensity not seen since
the early days of the revolution. Its sentiments were reciprocated with
equal fervour by the West, whose alarm was more acute than it had
been a generation earlier: communism appeared a more menacing
power around the world, its ideological appeal remained strong, and its
leaders were prepared to act with ruthless self-interest, backed by
force, when the occasion demanded. At the end of the war the West had
retained its strategic advantage through possession of the atomic
bomb. But its lead was short lived, as Stalin's hidden cohorts of spies
and scientists set to work.

In the closing years of Stalin's rule, Moscow's world-wide espionage
networks made some of their greatest contributions to the
advancement of Soviet policy. In the USA, Canada and Britain, key
agents – including British subjects such as Klaus Fuchs, Alan Nunn

May and Donald Maclean – provided material which enabled the Soviet Union to close the strategic gap by hastening the development of its own atomic bomb. Diplomats like Maclean and Burgess, who remained in government service after the war, were able to keep Moscow informed about British foreign policy in Europe, the Middle East and Asia and about the state of the Western alliance, while Kim Philby passed across details of the workings of the Secret Intelligence Service, saw to it that anti-Communist initiatives in eastern Europe were destroyed, and helped protect his fellow agents when they were threatened with exposure. In Canada twenty-six people were identified as Soviet agents as a result of documents provided by a defector from the GRU in 1945, and in the USA up to 1951 a score or more spies were unmasked. By contrast, in Britain during the same period only two prosecutions were initiated for espionage offences. And both cases resulted from information received from across the Atlantic. The existence within the British secret services of an unseen guardian, or guardians, became of vital importance for the Soviet Union as it raced against time to catch up with the West's scientific and military know-how. The grand design of which the spies were a part had been signalled by Stalin soon after the war in Europe had finished.

In May 1945, at a victory banquet in the Kremlin, the 66-year-old Soviet leader, who had just under eight more years to live, proposed a toast:

> I drink first of all to the health of the Russian people, because it is the most eminent of all the nations belonging to the Soviet Union. I drink to the health of the Russian people because it has earned in this war the universal recognition as the leading force of the Soviet Union among all the peoples of our country.[4]

Eight months later, in February 1946, Stalin told an audience in the Bolshoi Theatre on the occasion of elections to the Supreme Soviet that: 'Our victory means in the first place that our Soviet system has won ... a form of organisation superior to all others.'[5] Stalin went on to announce a new Five-Year Plan to rebuild an economy whose work-force and productive capacity had been shattered by four years of conflict.

As explanations of how the defeat of Nazi Germany had been made possible, Stalin's two speeches offered some contrasting, even conflicting, themes. The first emphasised the patriotism which Stalin had invoked throughout the war to mobilise and drive his people, a patriotism which was, however, limited to just one of the nationalities of the Soviet Union. But by the beginning of 1946 the patriotism was relegated in favour of a new tribute to Sovietism. Taken together, however, the two speeches heralded the main elements of Stalin's thrust in his final years: a resurgent drive for ideological conformity, which presaged an attack on dissenters and troublesome intellectuals, and an assertive Russian nationalism, at the expense of minorities as diverse as Crimean Tartars, Balkan and Ukrainian nationalists, Jews and Ingush-Chekens. Combined, the two speeches pointed to a new phase of Russian-dominated Soviet imperialism.

Within the Soviet Union, the Communist Party endeavoured to recover the authority it had ceded to the army during the war. A trusted Politburo member, Andrei Zhdanov, who had run Leningrad after the assassination of Kirov in 1934 and had founded a party Propaganda and Agitation Directorate, headed a campaign of cultural repression which outlasted his sudden death in 1948. As part of the modernisation of the Soviet state, the 'People's Commissariats' were remodelled in January 1946 as Ministries. The NKVD, for example, became the MVD, the Ministry of Internal Affairs. This move coincided with changes in the structure of the security and intelligence apparatus which had begun earlier but had been abandoned because of the war. From February 1941 until the German invasion in June, the NKVD had been divided into two distinct branches, the NKVD itself, which was responsible for internal affairs, and the NGB, which looked after security and espionage. In 1946 this division was revived in the new ministries – the MVD and the MGB respectively.

The MVD, Ministry of Internal Affairs, was placed under the direction of Sergei Kruglov, Beria's cunning 45-year-old deputy, who was made an honorary Knight Commander of the British Empire for organising security at the allies' wartime conferences. A party Central Committee member, Vsevolod Merkulov, became the first head of the MGB. He was replaced later in the year by General Viktor Abakumov, the former commander of the notorious 'Smersh' organisation – meaning 'Death to Spies' – which hunted down Soviet army deserters and citizens who had the misfortune to fall into Nazi hands. Beria clung tenaciously to overall control, however, and saw his budget for the two organisations double from 1945 to 1946.[6] Meanwhile, the GRU lost ground and in 1947 its overseas espionage responsibilites, together with some of those run by the MGB, were taken over by Molotov as chairman of a new body, the Committee of Information. This committee survived for only four years, when further power struggles and organisational switches exacted their toll.

After the wartime shows of comradely spirit, Western reaction to

Soviet assertiveness was swift and sharp. Churchill's historic 'iron curtain' speech at Fulton, Missouri in March 1946 reflected the public mood of fear and distrust of Soviet intentions. Foreign Office attitudes also began to harden. In April 1946, Christopher Warner, of the Northern Department which handled Soviet affairs, wrote a memorandum entitled, 'The Soviet Campaign Against This Country and Our Response to it'. He observed that 'Russian aggressiveness threatens British interests all over the world. The Soviet government are carrying out an intensive campaign to weaken, deprecate, and harry this country in every possible way.'[7] A Foreign Office Russia Committee was set up the same month and later came the Information Research Department to disseminate anti-Communist propaganda.

Foreign Secretary Ernest Bevin became one of the government's most forceful opponents of communism. Regular papers circulated to his Cabinet colleagues reveal his concern at the destruction of democracy in eastern Europe by communism and the potential dangers in the West. In February 1948, immediately following the Communist coup in Czechoslovakia, he set out his feelings in a long top secret memorandum to the Cabinet, called 'The Threat to Western Civilisation'. Bevin warned that the Soviet Union was

> actively preparing to extend its hold over the remaining part of continental Europe and subsequently over the Middle East and no doubt the Far East as well. In other words, physical control of the Eurasian land mass and eventual control of the whole world Island is what the Politburo is aiming at – no less a thing than that.[8]

The Foreign Secretary sought the broadest possible unity, in western Europe and the Commonwealth; he feared that it had 'become a matter of the defence of western civilisation or everyone will be swamped'.

Bevin was writing when the Communist march across central Europe seemed inexorable. In an eight-year period, from 1944–52, the Leninist and Stalinist phases of the Communist revolution were compressed into a ruthless programme of subjugation. The methods and pace varied from country to country according to circumstance, but only Tito's Yugoslavia and its wayward neighbour, Albania, escaped control by Moscow. At first an assortment of governments of national unity emerged in the countries of middle Europe from the wreckage of war. Socialists, liberals, and peasant parties combined to try to create working, popular democracies where only fascism and feudalism had trodden before. But the leaders of the exiled Communist parties returning from Moscow to organise their forces had other ideas:

leaders like Gomulka in Poland, Dmitrov in Bulgaria, Rakosi in Hungary and Gottwald in Czechoslovakia squeezed out the moderates and took power for the Communists. But as soon as they had gained control, the Soviet Union instigated a fresh wave of purges in which local party leaders were removed: Gomulka was turned out of office in 1948, leaders of the Bulgarian party were executed the next year, Ana Pauker was ousted in Rumania in 1950 and in 1952 Slansky and thirteen of his colleagues in Czechoslovakia, mostly Jews, were tried and executed.

To maintain the façade of ideological unity, in September 1947 Stalin established a Communist information bureau, known as the Cominform. Not to be confused with the Committee of Information,the Cominform was a more select version of the supposedly buried Comintern. Its membership comprised all the Communist parties of eastern Europe, together with the two largest Western parties, the French and the Italian, who, Stalin believed, might themselves be near to taking power. In fact they were expelled from government in 1947 and their hour of opportunity slid away. No Asian party, not even the Chinese, was admitted to the Cominform, and all smaller Western parties, including the British, were left firmly on the outside. The CPGB had lost 7,000 members in the two years since the end of the war, and 18,000 from its wartime peak of 56,000. It managed, however, to remain a considerable force in some sections of the trade union movement, notably in the docks and mines, and two Communist MPs were returned in the 1945 general election which had resulted in a Labour landslide. Some thought its influence in parliament ran more widely: Douglas Hyde claimed that after the war, the party 'had at least eight or nine "cryptos" in the House of Commons, in addition to our two publicly acknowledged MPs',[9] (who sat on the Labour benches).

The spearhead of Soviet cultural conformity, Zhdanov, was put in charge of the Cominform. At its opening conference, he described the altered alignment of social and political forces which had emerged from the war in uncompromising terms:

> Two camps came into being, the imperialist anti-democratic camp with the basic aim of establishing world domination of American imperialism and routing democracy, and an anti-imperialist democratic camp with the basic aim of disrupting imperialism, stengthening democracy, and eliminating the remnants of Fascism.'[10]

Zhdanov claimed leadership of the anti-imperialist camp for the Soviet Union, which also opposed measures such as the recently launched Marshall Plan for the reconstruction of Europe, and stood for what he described as a 'lasting democratic peace'. The fraternal unity did not last long, however, for within a year of the Cominform's formation Yugoslavia was expelled from membership.

The themes of 'peace' and 'democracy' were to become the catch-phrases of Soviet propaganda for the next forty years. To project them and to enlist support in the West, in the late 1940s the Soviet Union created a host of international organisations, which were not unlike Munzenberg's pre-war 'Innocents' Clubs'. Each catered for a specific section of society and sought to draw in left-wing sympathisers and fellow travellers, and people like Hyde's 'crypto' Communist MPs, with the intention that Communists should not be seen to be too obviously in control.

One of the first bodies to emerge was the World Federation of Trade Unions (WFTU), which originated in a conference held in Paris on British initiative in 1945. But within four years it was apparent, in the words of the British Trades Union Congress, that WFTU had become 'completely dominated by communist organisations which are themselves controlled by the Kremlin and the Cominform'.[11] British, American and Dutch unions withdrew to leave the organisation under undisputed Communist management. By the end of the decade the same fate had befallen a range of umbrella groups, which became recognised as 'front' organisations for Soviet propaganda. Some had been effectively Communist-run from their inception but others, like WFTU, began life on a broader basis.

These various organisations included the World Federation of Democratic Youth, which had been founded at a congress in London in November 1945, the International Union of Students, Women's International Democratic Federation and the International Association of Democratic Lawyers. One body made its headquarters in London. The World Federation of Scientific Workers (WFSW) was established in 1946 with an inaugural conference in London in July. The prime mover behind it was the British body, the Association of Scientific Workers, which had been in existence for nearly thirty years and had a strong left-wing element. In 1939 its membership stood at only 2,000, but with the rapid expansion of scientific work during the war, had risen to 17,211 by the end of 1946.[12] Of these one-third worked in the London area, some 1,582 were employed in the civil service and 1,050 were in the armed forces. After the war the ASW joined the TUC and was also affiliated to the Communist influenced Labour Research Department, the National Council for Civil Liberties and the Society for Cultural Relations with the USSR. One of its leading members was the Cambridge scientist, J. D. Bernal, who was one of three ASW members on the executive of the World Federation. A future president of the WFSW, Dr Eric Burhop, a winner of the Lenin Peace Prize in 1971, was secretary of the Association's Atomic Sciences Committee. In 1946 it set up a special campaign committee to press for a reduction in the gaol sentence for espionage passed on one of its members, Alan Nunn May, who in the 1930s had served on the editorial board of the ASW's journal.[13]

Bernal and Burhop also became prominent members of the largest of the Soviet-dominated propaganda organisations, the World Peace Council (WPC). The WPC's roots lay in a World Congress of Intellectuals for Peace, held at Wroclaw in Poland in August 1948. After further meetings it set up headquarters in Paris as the World Peace Council two years later. But early the next year, the French government expelled both the WPC and the WFTU, because of their Soviet connections. Both organisations spent several years based in Vienna, before again being expelled, after which the WPC finally found a home in Helsinki and the WFTU in Prague. The British supporters of the WPC set up their own British Peace Committee in 1950 with J. G. Crowther as chairman and Bernal as the vice chairman, with support from Labour members, D. N. Pritt, another leading barrister, John Platts Mills, Steve Lawther and S. O. Davies. The journalist, Ivor Montagu, was a member of the WPC's secretariat from its formation until 1967.

Many of them were also active in the various friendship societies which were formed to promote closer links between Britain and the emerging Communist regimes of eastern Europe. Pritt, for example, became president of the Society for Friendship with Bulgaria, to add to his presidency of the Society for Cultural Relations with the USSR.[14] Meetings of these bodies could attract large audiences: in November 1946 a reported 2,000 people attended a British Soviet Friendship Society rally to hear speeches by D. N. Pritt, the Dean of Canterbury, Hewlett Johnson and B. Karavaev, a First Secretary at the Soviet Embassy in London.[15]

The Labour Party leadership moved decisively against all these international 'peace' and 'democratic' organisations and 'friendship' societies. They were included in a list of proscribed bodies which were banned from affiliating to the Labour Party, and individual Labour members were not allowed to join them. The spirit of 'left understands left', which had inspired so many Labour candidates in the 1945 general election as the only sure foundation on which to secure lasting world peace, had all but evaporated, and with it the influence inside the Labour Party of ginger groups like Keep Left, in which Harold

Wilson, Richard Crossman and Ian Mikardo had been involved. In 1948 and 1949 several of the most hardline pro-Soviet MPs were expelled from the party, most of them for sending a telegram of support to Pietro Nenni, the leader of Italy's pro-Communist socialist group, instead of the more moderate socialists under Saragat. The trade unions paralleled the Labour Party's steps to isolate Communist influence and by 1950 the Transport and General Workers Union, the engineers and the clerical workers had all barred Communists from holding office.

Action was not confined to the political level. The Labour government set up special Cabinet sub-committees to examine the Communists' role in industrial disputes and an official report into dock strikes in 1949, when 400,000 working days were lost through industrial action, concluded that the strikes had been 'founded upon the support mainly of members of the Communist Party and their sympathisers'.[16]

Attlee's government also made wide use of the Special Branch and MI5 to monitor Communist activity in the 'front' organisations. One of its concerns was the possible link between domestic communism and clandestine activity directed from Moscow. In October 1950 another Cabinet sub-committee was formed to counter the effects of a Peace Congress planned for the following month in Sheffield. The government believed that the WPC's aims were to enlist support for peace on Soviet terms and to subvert the West's rearmament plans, that it was 'under Comintern direction' and 'had instructed the peace committee and the associated Communist bodies to indulge in acts of sabotage and subversion against the Western powers'.[17]

In the committee the Home Secretary, Chuter Ede, told his colleagues that MI5 had cleared about thirty-five out of 285 people who had applied to attend the congress from abroad. He reported that the Special Branch and MI5 'would be instructed to keep a careful watch over the congress as it was expected that useful information might be derived thereby about the contacts of colonial students and others and Communist agents.'[18] Foreign Secretary Bevin wanted firm steps to prevent the congress from being a success, and said he was supported by the service Chiefs of Staff. The Attorney General, Hartley Shawcross, added that he was disturbed by the prospect of the admission of so many aliens, who included eighty-five from Russia alone. Prime Minister Attlee concluded that although there were no powers to ban the gathering, public opinion would be strongly against the admission of such a large number of aliens to attend it, and it was 'desirable to do everything possible to cripple the congress by severely limiting attendance'.[19] There was, however, to be no ban on whole categories of people such as members of the WFTU, WFSW, the WFDY and other front organisations, and cases were to be looked at individually. Meanwhile, Shawcross and Chuter Ede were to trace the congress's sources of finance. The Labour government's use of the Security Services to monitor and counter the peace movement was just one part of its total response in the rapidly developing intelligence and propaganda struggle between East and West.

WINNERS AND LOSERS

Western knowledge of the extent of Soviet espionage grew immeasurably as a result of information arising from a series of defections by Soviet intelligence officers shortly after the war. The first attempted defection came in August 1945, by an NKVD officer, Konstantin Volkov, who held a consular post in Istanbul. He approached his counterpart in the British Consulate – perhaps imagining he too was an intelligence officer. The Russian offered the names of Soviet spies in Britain in exchange for money and asylum. Among them was an officer who, according to the NKVD man, was currently fulfilling the duties of a head of a section of British counter-intelligence.[20] The British Embassy referred the matter to MI6. Britain's Secret Intelligence Service had awoken early to the dangers of communism and set up an anti-Soviet section in 1944. Its head was a 32-year-old Cambridge graduate who seemed destined to reach the highest levels of the service – Kim Philby. When news of Volkov's approach to the British reached his desk he alerted his Soviet controllers and delayed his own departure for Istanbul for nearly three weeks. When Philby arrived in Turkey, supposedly to facilitate Volkov's escape, the would-be defector was nowhere to be found. The NKVD had been given ample time to spirit him back to Russia; he was never seen or heard of again. But as Philby himself later admitted in his autobiography, the Volkov incident was a 'very narrow squeak indeed'.[21]

Three years later Philby found himself in Turkey again, on his first overseas tour of duty as an MI6 officer, attached to the British Embassy in Istanbul as a First Secretary. During the two years Philby spent in Turkey he was able to set in motion one of the most notorious deeds of his career, when he betrayed Western-backed incursions into Albania at the expense of several hundred lives. He was also able to debrief another defector who had arrived in Istanbul. Ismail

Akhmedov had served for twelve years in the GRU and reached the rank of lieutenant-colonel before fleeing to the West at the age of 38. Akhmedov later said that at the time he found Philby 'so courteous and pleasant, always smiling ... the legitimate British intelligence officer'.[22] What he did not know then was that Philby would pass only a fraction of the information he provided to MI6 headquarters. Akhmedov himself was more fortunate than Volkov, for in 1950 he became a Turkish citizen and later settled in the USA.

But Philby utterly failed to intercept the man destined to become one of the most important defectors of all, a GRU lieutenant named Igor Gouzenko. The revelations he provided about the scale of Soviet espionage in Canada transformed the whole of Western understanding of the problem they faced.[23] Early in September 1945 Gouzenko walked out of the Soviet Embassy in Ottawa, where he had worked for two years as a cipher clerk, with several hundred documents about the GRU's spying operations.

When the material was fully examined, and subjected to enquiry by a Royal Commisssion, it revealed espionage which extended to Canada, the USA, Britain and to the Red Orchestra's Swiss section. The Canadian Prime Minister was utterly dismayed by the disclosures: 'all very terrible and alarming' he wrote in his diary.[24] Sir Alexander Clutterbuck, the British High Commissioner in Canada, told the Dominions Office in London that what had been happening in Canada was 'not an isolated phenomenon but part of an elaborate system extending to many other countries ... Many people see little difference between the Russian method of today and the German methods we have fought two wars to eradicate.'[25] Canada's experience, meticulously described in the 700-page report of the Royal Commission, had a sobering effect on Western governments, and was held up as an illustration of what the Soviet Union was probably doing against each and every one of them.

Gouzenko could in fact give complete information on only one of four parallel intelligence gathering networks run from the Soviet Embassy in Ottawa. In addition to the activities of his own organisation, the GRU, separate operations were run by the NKVD, under Second Secretary, Victor Pavlov, by a naval intelligence unit, and by the Embassy's political section, to which Gouzenko did not have access.[26] The political wing was run by another Second Secretary, Goussarev, who had earlier served as an assistant to Georgi Malenkov, while head of the foreign section of the CPSU Central Committee. Of the Embassy's seventeen diplomatic staff, at least six were primarily concerned with espionage. Their numbers were augmented by clerical staff, chauffeurs and other non-diplomatic personnel who were also part of the espionage residencies. But the Ambassador himself, Gousev, was forbidden to enter the secret room on the second floor of the Embassy where the various intelligence branches were housed and he had no right to see telegrams or correspondence between Moscow and his own nominal subordinates.

Secret Soviet activity in Canada could be traced back to 1924, but it was in 1942 that it seriously began to develop. In that year a Major Sokolov took up an appointment in the country as a factory inspector – a wartime capacity which the British had felt was being used for espionage. In 1943 a full Soviet Mission arrived and in June Colonel Nikolai Zabotin, the Military Attaché, took control of the GRU section, with Gouzenko among his total staff of fourteen; their covers included that of Commercial Attaché and the correspondent of the news agency, TASS.

When Zabotin and his staff set about enlisting Canadian agents, they turned first to local Communists; indeed the Royal Commission found that the 'Communist movement was the principal base within which the espionage network was recruited'.[27] Recruits were described as generally highly educated, and not motivated by financial gain. They included ideologically-committed intellectuals who became drawn into secret membership of the Canadian Communist Party through 'study groups', similar to those which had operated among some of the university Marxists in Britain before the war. They signed no membership forms and were not issued with party cards. But even within the select circles of the study groups only a minority were initiated into illegal espionage activity. Focusing on scientists and academics, one of the GRU's main targets was the Canadian National Research Council, which was engaged in secret work on nuclear physics.

In total, some twenty-six people were identified by the Royal Commission as having had some contact with the Soviet intelligence services in Canada. Of those, eighteen were tried and half were found guilty of espionage offences. Of the original twenty-six, ten had foreign, mainly Russian, origins and six came from Britain. The Europeans included Sam Carr, who was born Scmil Kogan in the Ukraine in 1906. He went to Canada when he was 18, joined the Young Communist League and later the Canadian Communist Party. In 1929 he attended the Lenin Institute in Moscow, at about the same time as Percy Glading from England, and on his return became editor of the Canadian party's journal, the *Clarion*, and the party's organising secretary, a position analagous to that held by Douglas Springhall in the CPGB. One of Carr's main associates was Fred Rose, who was born under the name Rosenberg in Poland in 1907. He had lived in Canada since 1926 and, although he had been gaoled for sedition in 1931 and interned for anti-war activity in 1942, he became an MP the following year. Both Carr and Rose were central figures in the formation of the GRU's Canadian spy rings and they were each sentenced to six years' imprisonment for the part they played.

A three-year prison sentence was passed on one of the British members, Kathleen Willsher, who had the code name 'Elli'. A language graduate of the London School of economics, she went to Canada in 1930 and found work as a stenographer in the British High Commission in Ottawa; later she was promoted to assistant registrar. But from 1936 Miss Willsher had been a member of the Communist Progressive Labour Party, had met Fred Rose and was a member of one of the study groups.

The most important English person to be discovered in the investigations following the Gouzenko defection was the physicist, Alan Nunn May. Born in King's Norton, Warwickshire, Nunn May was a contemporary of Donald Maclean at Cambridge. In 1936, shortly after gaining his doctorate, he visited Leningrad and on his return joined the editorial board of *Scientific Worker*, the journal of the Association of Scientific Workers. In 1942 he joined the Tube Alloys project on atomic research and in June the next year crossed the Atlantic to continue his work in Canada. GRU headquarters in Moscow suggested to Colonel Zabotin that an approach should be made to Nunn May, which was carried out through Fred Rose. By the spring of 1945, under the code name 'Alek', the scientist was passing information to Soviet military intelligence, including a written paper about his work and two samples of enriched uranium. In September 1945, when Nunn May was ready to return home, Moscow gave him detailed instructions for meetings outside the British Museum on three dates the following month. But for reasons which have never become clear, neither he nor his contact kept any of the rendezvous. The British were certainly watching his movements, but it was not until March 1946 that he was arrested and two months later sentenced to ten years' penal servitude. His controller in Canada, Colonel Zabotin, sailed on a Russian ship from New York in December 1945, when it became clear that the Gouzenko affair was turning into a disaster for the GRU. But that was his final journey: Colonel Zabotin vanished, either at sea or in Russia, another victim who paid for failure with his life.[28]

The lessons of the Gouzenko affair were certainly not lost on the

British Chiefs of Staff, who in March 1947, delivered a report to the Cabinet Defence Committee, in which they sought to establish a connection between the Soviet Union's thirst for technical information, the high number of Soviet officials in the country, and the British Communist Party. Baron Tedder, Marshal of the RAF, and Field Marshal Viscount Montgomery for the army, together with R .R. McGregor, the Vice-Chief of Naval Staff, warned Ministers that: 'Present day conditions, including the relaxation of powers and controls under the Defence Regulations are definitely favourable to the development of Russian espionage, and consequently counter-measures are proportionately difficult.'[29]

The military commanders wanted limitations imposed on the numbers of Soviet representatives and members of the Trade Delegation admitted to the country, restrictions on the visits they could make to government establishments and factories, and the exclusion of known members of the British Communist Party from secret work. Soviet officials, they said, were concerned with the collection of information 'as part of their normal function' and their opportunities were increased by the number of Communists employed in research establishments with access to secret information. During the war, maintained the Chiefs of Staff, the course of events:

> tended to make government departments less inclined to exclude Communists from secret work, and, in fact, members of the Communist Party are known to have been placed in positions where they had access to information of considerable secrecy. Many Communists are known to have volunteered to the Communist Party headquarters information about British war production, projects and weapons with the intention that the information should be passed on to the Russians. In addition, certain members of the Communist Party are known to have carried out espionage activities, the products of which were almost certainly destined for the Russians.[30]

The report was far from an unwanted military intervention in political affairs. The Defence Committee, a government Working Party on Subversive Activity, the Joint Intelligence Committee and the Standing Inter-Departmental Committee on Security had all been grappling with various aspects of the problem of Soviet espionage. The Ministry of Defence, for which the Prime Minister was responsible, supported restrictions in the light of the revelations from Canada. Attlee himself said at a Defence Committee meeting in February 1947 that all reasonable steps should be taken to prevent the disclosure of secret information through visits by Soviet officials to government installations. He also supported the removal of Communists from areas of secret work. But he recognised that a ban on known Communists would not be wholly effective since 'some of those who were or might become ... Soviet agents were probably not open members of the Communist Party'.[31] The Home Secretary, Chuter Ede, agreed that while it was possible to exclude Communist Party members from secret work, it would be difficult on a large scale. The greatest risk, he declared, came from scientists who believed that all knowledge should be shared for the common benefit of mankind.

Many factors were therefore working against the Chiefs of Staff and the Ministers, such as Attlee and Bevin, who wished to take the firmest possible line against communism. One of them was the need to promote trade. At the February meeting of the Defence Committee the future Labour Prime Minister, Harold Wilson, then the President of the Board of Trade, expressed enthusiastic support for increased trade with the Soviet Union, which he saw as a 'valuable market for our exports'.[32] He felt that it would be impossible to restrict access by Soviet officials to non-governmental factories, and, on the contrary, they should be encouraged.

Later in the year the Defence Committee had to respond to a succession of orders from the Soviet Union for Rolls Royce jet aircraft engines. These were accompanied by requests to allow Soviet engineers to attend training courses in England. Against opposition from Bevin and MI5, who wanted the Russians excluded altogether, the Derwent and Nene engines were removed from the secret list to enable the sale to be completed and visas were granted for seventeen Russians to come to Britain for six to eight weeks for training.[33]

On the security issues, the eventual outcome was the removal in March 1948 of known Communists and fascists from vital areas of secret work. The introduction of a more systematic scheme of positive vetting did not take place until 1952, by which time perceptions of the espionage threat had changed dramatically and the words uttered by Attlee and Chuter Ede in February 1947 had been proved true.

Despite the loss of the GRU's network in Canada, the alert which saw the beginnings of tighter security measures in Britain and the imprisonment of Nunn May, Soviet atomic espionage on both sides of the Atlantic was able to continue until the end of 1949. Six months after Nunn May's arrest, Klaus Fuchs flew back to England to join the staff of the atomic energy research establishment at Harwell. Before he left Canada he, too, was given instructions for meetings in London, devised by Moscow and relayed through his American contact, Harry

Gold. They had the same comic elaborateness as those given to Foote and other GRU agents: he was to go to Mornington Cresent underground station in London carrying five books tied together with string in one hand and two more books in the other.[34] But again, neither Fuchs nor his controller turned up and it was another year before Fuchs resumed contact with Soviet intelligence. Contact was re-established through Joanna Klopstch, a member of the German Communist Party who had lived in England since 1938. During the next eighteen months Fuchs had a further eight meetings with a new contact, mainly at pubs in the London area, including one possibly with 'Sonja', Ursula Kuczynski.[35] But his career as a Soviet spy was drawing to a close: in 1949 the FBI identified him from decoded intercepts of Soviet radio traffic.[36] He was interrogated by MI5 in December and arrested in February 1950. The next month he was sentenced to fourteen years' imprisonment but was released after nine years and went to join his father in East Germany.[37]

With Fuchs' confession and the subsequent identification of Harry Gold, Fuchs' American contact man, the Soviet atomic spy networks in the USA began to unravel. Over the next twelve months, eight people were arrested in the USA, including Gold himself, a 40-year-old Russian-born laboratory assistant, and David Greenglass, an employee at the Los Alamos research centre, his sister, Ethel and her husband, Julius Rosenberg. The Rosenbergs were executed for conspiracy to commit espionage, while Gold received a thirty-year sentence and Greenglass, fifteen years.

In the spring of 1950, shortly after Fuchs was detained, 'Sonja' finally departed for East Germany, with her British husband, Len Beurton. She was fortunate to have made such a clean escape, to say the least. In 1947 she was interviewed by MI5 officers but allowed to go free: they reportedly told her that they knew she had been a Communist agent, but that they believed she was not one any longer.[38] 'Sonja' blamed Alexander Foote, who had recently returned from East Berlin, for giving her name to the British. Her account, however, reflects Foote's own version of her career, contained in his autobiography, published in 1949. In that, Foote gave her the totally bogus name of 'Maria Shultz' and called her husband, 'Bill Phillips'. He said she had given up espionage work when she left Switzerland for England in a state of disenchantment with the business of spying.[39] But shortly before Foote died in 1956, reputedly deeply disillusioned himself, he is alleged to have prepared a statement in which he castigated the British government for not listening to his earlier warnings about 'Sonja', not putting her under surveillance and generally for showing lamentable ignorance about Soviet intelligence when they questioned him after his return to Britain in 1947.[40] There is, however, a major discrepancy between Foote's published view of 'Sonja' and what is later claimed he told British intelligence about her. None of it throws any real light on the still unanswered questions of why 'Sonja', Fuchs and her other contacts were not identified at an earlier date. The episode does however cast doubt on Foote's reliability as a witness and makes it much less probable that all along he was working for one of the British Secret Services, as has been suggested.[41]

Information from the USA resulting from decoded intercepts of Soviet radio messages also led to the effective demise of the Cambridge spies. The net closed first on Maclean. According to an FBI officer who worked on many of the leading spy cases of the time, it was in 1948 that 'several fragments of deciphered KGB messages indicated that someone in the British Embassy in Washington in 1944–5 had been providing the KGB with high-level cable traffic between the USA and Britain.'[42] That someone, appearing in the messages under the code-name 'Homer', was Donald Maclean, First Secretary at the Embassy from 1944–8. Among his other duties there, he had been secretary of the allies' combined policy committee on atomic development and held a pass which gave him the right of unaccompanied entry to American Atomic Energy Commission buildings. FBI files assert that 'from January 1947 to August 1948 Maclean officially represented the British Embassy on matters dealing with atomic energy. He reportedly had no access to classified scientific information, but he did have full knowledge of the discusssions which took place during that period concerning cooperation between the USA, Canada and England.'[43]

His associate, Burgess, fell under a cloud following a brief but eventful tour of duty in Washington, which lasted from August 1950 to the following April. Burgess had joined the Foreign Office permament staff in 1947 and enjoyed the patronage of the Minister of State, Hector McNeil. After several disastrous experiences in various departments in London, during which his general slovenliness earned him many enemies, he was posted as a Second Secretary to the Washington Embassy, where Philby was already working as MI6's liaison officer with the CIA. Burgess's behaviour grew so erratic that Philby took him under his roof in the vain hope that he might save Burgess from himself. Maclean, meanwhile, had suffered a drunken breakdown in Cairo and went back to London, where after recuperation he was made head of the North American Department of the Foreign Office in the autumn of 1950. For the next five months the three Soviet agents, Burgess, Maclean and Philby, were concerned with Anglo-American relations. Because of their various links with the USA, the subsequent knowledge that all three were traitors arguably had as traumatic an effect on the Americans as it did on the British government service. By the spring of 1951, Burgess engineered his transfer back to London by getting himself booked by the American police for speeding. Events moved quickly when on a Friday at the end of May he collected Maclean from his house at Tatsfield in Surrey and together they fled to France, conveniently avoiding the interrogation of Maclean which had been authorised for the following Monday.[44]

Maclean's timely exit was prompted by the existence of a protector – or protectors – within. Burgess had performed the role but found himself trapped and had to leave too. Philby had kept Maclean informed about the progress of the investigations against him, and on the fringes of the secret world Blunt helped them cover their tracks by removing incriminating letters and personal documents from Burgess's flat. Help came too from their Soviet masters: during the periods when they were in London after the war the Cambridge spies were controlled by Soviet intelligence officers under 'legal' cover at the Embassy; these included Boris Krotov, listed as a Third Secretary from 1943, Yuri Modin, who visited Philby in Beirut in September 1962, four months before his defection, and Filip Kislytsin, who later served in Australia. They also assisted the two diplomats in the arrangements for their onward journey from France to the Soviet Union.

The news of Burgess and Maclean's defection had a shattering effect on British public opinion and launched the national mania for mole hunting. But many leading figures in government were unable to overcome their social and cultural loyalties and to recognise the full implications of treachery within the ranks of the ruling classes. Not until September 1955 did the government publish a White Paper on the Burgess and Maclean affair, which turned out to be a singularly misleading and incomplete document. During the parliamentary debate on it, the Tory Prime Minister, Macmillan, delivered his much-quoted exoneration of Philby as the 'Third Man'. In fact Philby had resigned from MI6 in 1952, and worked for the *Observer* newspaper until he finally defected from Beirut in January 1963. In the meantime, Anthony Blunt, Surveyor of the Queen's Pictures, was interviewed by MI5 a dozen times in as many years after 1951, but this did not stand in the way of his knighthood in 1956. Only in 1964, when Michael Straight, the American he tried to recruit at Cambridge before the war, came forward to denounce his former acquaintances, did Blunt confess and the notorious deal offering him immunity from prosecution was agreed. Of the lesser figures from Cambridge, Cairncross left the Treasury in 1952 and went to live abroad, while the involvement of Watson and Long did not emerge until the testimonies of Straight and Blunt. Up to that point Soviet intelligence officers attached to the London Embassy, including Yuri Modin and Sergei Kondrashev, had made periodic use of both Blunt and Watson, the former for his influential connections in royal circles and the latter because of his continuing research at the Admiralty.[45]

Charges of a sustained attempt to conceal the full extent of Soviet infiltration of the British establishment can be justifiably levelled against Conservative governments after 1951. It remains one of the paradoxes of the story, that the Cambridge group of spies caused their greatest harm during the lifetime of a Socialist administration that was, as Cabinet and Cabinet Committee papers reveal, trying honestly to wrestle with the many facets of Communist-inspired subversion and espionage.

In the Labour government of 1945–51, the Prime Minister, Clement Attlee, and his Foreign Secretary, Ernest Bevin, supported by the service chiefs and MI5, took a strongly anti-Communist line and distrusted Soviet motives and actions on all fronts. From the time of the Gouzenko defection and the Canadian Royal Commission onwards, Attlee's government had searched for effective means of countering the threat, while recognising some of the complexities. Its response was entwined with a bundle of issues, the very genuine fear of an East–West world war, the desire to keep open existing diplomatic links and to encourage non-strategic trade with the Soviet Union, and the limits of the protective measures which could be introduced in a democracy. Espionage was but one consideration on this broader canvas.

In March 1949 the West demonstrated its resolve by breaking the blockade of Berlin, followed a month later by the signing of the North Atlantic Treaty. The unmasking of Klaus Fuchs at the end of the year came too late to prevent the Soviet Union detonating its first atomic bomb in September, at least eighteen months ahead of Western expectations. With that, and with the consolidation of his land empire in Europe, Stalin had made massive strides towards reducing the West's strategic superiority. And the rise of communism in Asia, with the victory of Mao Tse-Tung in China in the same year, and the North Korean invasion of the South in June 1950 dramatically widened the scope of the ideological and military conflict.

In Europe, however, Western resistance appeared to have a

dampening effect on Soviet behaviour. During the winter of 1949–50, the Foreign Office seemed thrown into some confusion by the delicately poised international situation and was far from unanimous in its assessment. The proceedings of its Russia Committee at the time reveal divisions of opinion among its senior officials and also illustrate how far removed from each other the worlds of diplomacy and counter-espionage can be.

On 20 December 1949, for example, the day before Klaus Fuchs was first interviewed by MI5, the department's Deputy Under-Secretary, Sir Gladwyn Jebb, and chairman of the Russia Committee, declared that there was 'a definite lull in the cold war'.[46] A Russian-speaking official, J. H. Watson, disagreed. He thought that it was truer to say that there was

> no acceleration of tempo in the cold war, but there had been no actual decrease in the general intensity with which it was waged ... the main Communist line in Western Europe was to concentrate on the organisation of cadres for the promotion of strikes or sabotage (especially in the transport world) in the event of war.[47]

But few of his colleagues held such a stark view of Soviet aims and, with much sophistication, vacillated between a weary acceptance of Soviet cynicism in international relations and an inclination to clutch at whatever signs they could detect of any tendency to moderation on the part of Stalin and his spokesmen.

Evidence of these attitudes, and of further differences, emerged at the committee's next meeting in January 1950, when Jebb himself said that after Molotov's 'rather stupid and obstinate policy', Vyshinksy seemed to be more subtle and at the same time 'more dishonest, more unscrupulous and more dangerous'.[48] But Graham Harrison, the head of the Northern Department, echoed Jebb's earlier view when he said that Russian attitudes were 'apparently less intransigent', a line the junior Foreign Office minister, Christopher Mayhew took issue with: he believed that Soviet methods had not changed, and they had merely substituted defensive immediate objectives for offensive ones. At the committee's meeting on 9 February 1950, just four days after Fuchs appeared in court, Christopher Warner said there were strong objections to the use of the expressions 'winning' and 'losing' the cold war and he wanted their use forbidden in the Foreign Office.[49] The term, 'the cold war', had itself been eliminated from a paper which had been prepared for a meeting of the top-level Permanent Secretary's Committee.

It appears that what Warner, and others in the Foreign Office objected to, was not that premature claims of success might be made in a struggle that was without any foreseeable end, but the whole notion of a conflict in which there might be victory or defeat for anyone. The prevailing Foreign Office outlook confirms once again that counter-espionage services cannot perform with maximum effectiveness if more influential parts of the policy-making apparatus take a radically different view of the framework into which intelligence and security functions fit.

Foreign Office reservations apart, gains and losses could be counted on both sides. The major losers were the peoples of central and eastern Europe who came under Soviet domination. Stalin behind the barricade of his client states and armed with an atomic bomb, could claim to be a winner. In the West the alarms had rung loud and shrill. For the intelligence and security services the period brought mixed fortunes. In Britain the failure to apprehend Fuchs, Kuczynski and the Cambridge spies early on highlighted the lack of understanding among decision-makers of what they were confronted with, as well as more particular deficiencies in the procedures for vetting government servants and the control of aliens. Some of these failings were partially rectified. But governmental reluctance to admit past errors of judgement only served to fuel popular suspicions of an 'establishment cover-up' and with it the dangers of the hysterical over-reaction which ministers and officials, in their measured way, expressly wished to avoid.

Yet, the West had succeeded, if not in reversing the balance sheet of espionage, at least in minimising the immediate prospect of further damage on such a massive scale. In a little under eighteen months, the Soviet Union had lost its atomic spy ring in the USA, its main source of information on atomic research in England, its two most senior spies in the British Diplomatic Service, and had seen its rising star in the Secret Intelligence Service compromised. The removal of the principal moles effectively curtailed a major strategic initiative in the history of Soviet espionage. Just as the West had frequently had to react to circumstances it had not determined, so it was now the Soviet Union's turn to plan its counter-response to an unfavourable turn of events.

6   The KGB and the 'Long-Range Policy'

AFTER STALIN: THE 'NEW LOOK'

In the months following the death of Stalin in March 1953 Foreign Office officials detected a change of behaviour among Soviet diplomats in London. Members of the Soviet Embassy, or at least some of them, started 'coming out of their shells'.[1] They entertained politicians, civil servants and diplomats of other nationalities at parties and made contact with selected individuals, including Labour and Conservative MPs and Foreign Office staff. One official enjoyed an 'amiable and expensive lunch' at the Dorchester as the guest of a senior member of the Embassy, Georgi Rodionov, and its principal contact man, a Third (later promoted to First) Secretary, Georgi Zhivotovski.[2] They discussed trade and current topics such as the Bermuda Conference, and Zhivotovski asked whether he could meet Foreign Office heads of departments from time to time to exchange views. On another lunch occasion the recently arrived Rodionov enquired about the possibility of visiting Oxford for some sightseeing.

Political contacts were not confined to left-wingers with pro-Soviet leanings. In July 1953 the right-of-centre Tory member, Julian Amery, wrote to the Foreign Office Minister of State, Selwyn Lloyd, to tell him about his dealings with the Russians.[3] Amery, who had attended a film show at the Soviet Embassy with some of his colleagues, invited the newly appointed Ambassador, Yakov Malik, to dinner. To Amery's surprise, he accepted: Malik was accompanied by Rodnikov, while Amery reinforced the British side with two fellow MPs, Christopher Soames, and Robert Boothby, who himself had embarked on a series of unrevealing lunches with Zhivotovski. On the Labour side, former Ministers such as Arthur Bottomley and Kenneth Younger were the objects of Soviet hospitality.

But behind these seemingly innocuous exchanges with such well-known and sociable figures on the political scene there sometimes lurked a more sinister purpose. Towards the end of 1953 the KGB appears to have engineered an approach to a rising Tory politician who later entered parliament and became a Minister in Mr Heath's government in 1970. And when the young man sought guidance on how to handle a rapid succession of ostensibly social contacts initiated by a member of the Soviet Embassy who was in reality an officer of the KGB, an unwary Foreign Office gave ministerial encouragement to the relationship.

Then aged 29, Mr (now Sir) William van Straubenzee, a former major in the Royal Artillery and a newly qualified solicitor, was national Chairman of the Young Conservatives. He was approached in his hotel at Margate during the party conference by Ivan Skripov, an Assistant Press Attaché at the Soviet Embassy. Skripov told Mr van Straubenzee that he had been interested to hear his speech at the conference on the German question. In a contribution during the foreign policy and defence debate, Mr van Straubenzee had said that, as a result of recent visits to Bonn and other European capitals, he had concluded that 'the time is fast approaching when Germany, even Western Germany, is once again going to run Europe'.[4] He believed that present Tory government policy on Germany would mean that 'once again, we shall have in Western Europe the whole of the continent under the domination of one power, the thing we fought against for three hundred years.' In the future, he ended, people 'will wonder how on earth it was that, with our eyes so fixed on the great danger from Russia, we overlooked what is palpably going on under our very noses.'

Skripov subsequently entertained Mr van Straubenzee to lunch at the expensive Á L'Écu de France restaurant in London and invited him to the Soviet Embassy for the celebrations on 7 November of the anniversary of the Bolshevik revolution. Immediately after attending these events, Mr van Straubenzee sensibly reported his contacts with Skripov to a Conservative MP (Sir) Peter Smithers, who in turn referred his comments to the Foreign Office.

In his report Mr van Straubenzee said that he had the impression he had been approached because the Russians were interested in anyone who 'deviated' from the party line. But he also felt that at the Embassy reception, it was 'very obvious indeed that great efforts were made to make my sister and myself at home.'[5] Mr van Straubenzee noted that he had been the sole Tory, alongside Labour members such as Sidney Silverman, Geoffrey Bing and Anthony Wedgwood Benn. He was introduced to a Soviet First Secretary, Serge Kondrashev, and to an unnamed Bulgarian Assistant Military Attaché.

In response, the Foreign Office Minister of State, Sir Anthony

Nutting, thought that van Straubenzee had taken 'an admirable line' with the Russians, and doubted 'if they would consider him susceptible or frameable'.[6] Nutting said he could see no harm, and indeed some advantage, in continuing such contacts. He believed the Russians had a twofold motive: it was part of a Soviet 'new look', which entailed being 'appreciably more forthcoming socially these days'. But, he added, they were also looking for dissensions inside the Conservative Party like those in Labour's ranks.

What the Foreign Office did not appreciate was that both Skripov and Kondrashev were officers of the KGB. Kondrashev was one of the top Soviet spy controllers in London. He was George Blake's case officer, and met Alister Watson, the Admiralty scientist recruited at Cambridge, before later moving to posts at Soviet missions in Austria and West Germany.[7] Skripov remained in Britain for a further six years after his first approach to Mr van Straubenzee. He was subsequently promoted to the rank of First Secretary and in 1963 was expelled from Australia for espionage.

In Canberra, Skripov had taken control of a woman member of the British High Commission staff who had recently been transferred from New Zealand, where she had been extensively entertained and wooed by another Soviet 'diplomat', Evily Lutsky, Press Attaché at the Soviet Embassy in Wellington. Lutsky conveniently discovered that he shared a love of classical music with the woman, took her to concerts, gave her presents and after a six months' friendship during which he proposed marriage to her, asked her to obtain, first, unclassified and, then, top secret material. Lutsky left New Zealand and the woman, whose loyalty to Britain was unshaken, was moved to the High Commission in Australia. There Skripov took charge of her, and, believing her to be a Soviet agent, gave her £A200 and a radio transmitter. But all the time his dealings with the Englishwoman were being monitored and he was duly told to leave the country. The woman eventually settled quietly in Suffolk and, as a still unnamed 'Miss X', told her story only in 1971.[8]

The social contacts which the Foreign Office welcomed in 1953 set a pattern in Soviet methods which was to be repeated in various guises in the years ahead. Soviet representatives in London tried to present a more affable and reasonable face. They hoped both to disarm their critics and win some measure of influence in the centres of politics and government. Besides developing links with relevant officials, they opened up lines of communication to members of whichever party was in office; this applied to periods of Conservative and Labour rule throughout the 1950s and 1960s. Most contacts were made officially and constituted the routine stuff of diplomacy as practised by any major power. But the technique was adopted also by the KGB, and when contacts were established on a social, personal basis outside formal channels the dangers became very real. Where junior officials were the target of Soviet advances, entrapment and espionage were the ultimate aims; Miss 'X' resisted, but the infinitely more vulnerable Admiralty clerk, John Vassall, for example, succumbed to flattery and was soon trapped by sexual blackmail of a very different sort.

With politicians, the Soviet Union's objectives were more complex. Influence and political intelligence were widely sought. Espionage and blackmail were constant threats for the incautious. A country house swimming party on a summer's afternoon in 1961 brought together the Minister for War, John Profumo, a GRU officer, Eugene Ivanov, otherwise the Soviet Assistant Naval Attaché in London, and a call girl, Christine Keeler. The occasion led to a Soviet attempt to obtain defence secrets, and one of the most notorious scandals of the decade, which combined sex, power and spying, and contributed greatly to the demise of the Tory government. The very same year as Profumo's fateful encounter with Ivanov and Keeler, a Conservative MP, Commander Anthony Courtney, was photographed in bed with a Russian woman in Moscow; four years later the pictures were circulated in London and Courtney's whole life was shattered.[9]

On the Labour side, the Soviet Union made repeated approaches to a variety of MPs and trade unionists. They included some who were likely to be sympathetic to communism, while others who were targeted appeared to stand on the right of the party. Again many of the contacts were on a social level. Others occurred on visits by groups and individuals to the Soviet Union and Eastern Europe; the number of such trips increased markedly as the years passed and cold war gave way to *détente*. In the case of Labour members, where the Soviet advances exceeded the diplomatic, their object was to recruit agents to provide political intelligence, particularly on the unending battles between left and right in the party, to seek out channels for the dissemination of Moscow-approved propaganda, and, increasingly, to try to influence it as it entered government. In one instance, a Labour MP is alleged to have put his name to a pamphlet published in 1961, the material for which was researched by the KGB.[10] In other, more widely publicised cases, Czech intelligence succeeded in persuading Labour members to impart information on internal party matters over a period of years, and approached others. Looking both to public figures and backroom workers, the Czechs became intensely active in these muddy waters in the mid-1960s. The extent of their, and the

KGB's, operations in the political arena will be examined further in due course, in the context of the developments which made them possible.

What was first noticed as a relaxed 'new look' made its appearance at a time of turbulence in Moscow, in the power struggles after the death of Stalin. With his mentor gone, the security supremo, Beria, moved swiftly to seize the reins of power for himself. He sacked Ignatiev and Kruglov and merged the MVD and MGB into one organisation under his own control. But within three months he was himself deposed and arrested, and towards the end of the year was tried, with suitably gruesome irony, as an enemy agent and shot.

The immediate sequel to this ruthless Kremlin in-fighting was the reorganisation of the Soviet security and intelligence machinery. In March 1954 the KGB, the Committee for State Security, was created. The new body, the latest, and the last, in the long line of 'organs' which descended from the Cheka, was separated from the Ministry of the Interior and made responsible for internal political police functions, protecting the national border and for all secret operations abroad, except for those carried out by the GRU. The latter had regained some of its independence after the abolition of the Committee of Information in 1951.

At the head of the KGB was Ivan Serov, deputy chief of the NKGB and MGB since 1941. In March 1956 he became the only serving head of the Soviet security or intelligence services to visit Britain, when he came to London to supervise the arrangements for the visit the following month by Mr Khrushchev and Marshal Bulganin. Such was the public outcry that Serov himself was not readmitted for the visit itself and had to remain offshore on a Soviet ship while his leaders held their talks with the host government. However, the visit was clouded by the mysterious death of a British diver, Commander Crabb, who was hired by MI6 to inspect the hull of the Soviet vessel as it stood off Portsmouth.[11]

When Nikita Khrushchev emerged as the leading figure among the clutch of contenders for supreme power after the death of Stalin, further changes took place in Soviet intelligence and foreign affairs organisations. The Cominform was dissolved in 1956; the next year the Foreign Affairs Department, set up after the abolition of the Comintern in 1943, was divided into three branches, one to handle relations with ruling Communist parties of Eastern Europe, another for Cadres Abroad, which worked closely with the KGB and was responsible for cells inside foreign missions and for supervising party discipline, and a third, called the International Department (ID). Under the one-time Comintern official, Boris Ponomarev, the International Department became the most important of the three sections. It coordinated the various bodies involved in the making of Soviet foreign policy, including the KGB, the Ministry of Foreign Affairs and several academic and research institutes which studied developments in different parts of the world under the aegis of the Soviet Academy of Sciences. The ID also supervised the affairs of non-ruling foreign Communist parties, directed the activities of the whole range of 'front' organisations, and took responsibility for a monthly magazine, *Problems of Peace and Socialism*, the English language version of which is still published, under the title of the *World Marxist Review*.[12]

These moves were intended to serve the longer-term aims, foreign and domestic, defined by Khrushchev from 1956 onwards. The attack on the 'cult of personality' and the revelations of some of Stalin's misdeeds he made at the Twentieth Party Congress in February 1956 ushered in a period of modest liberalisation. Censorship was relaxed and the KGB's internal powers were trimmed. Major initiatives were launched to improve agricultural production and decentralise industry. By the middle of 1957, after the defeat of his leading opponents at home – the so-called 'Anti-Party Group,' which included Malenkov, Molotov and others – Khrushchev's standing was at its height. The following March he became Premier in place of Bulganin, as well as party General Secretary. At the Twenty-Second Party Congress in 1961 Khrushchev felt confident enough, or was rash enough, to predict that within ten years the Soviet Union's levels of production and consumption would surpass those of the USA, and that by 1980, complete communism would have arrived in the Soviet Union.

In the theoretical sphere, Khrushchev developed the doctrine of 'peaceful coexistence', which envisaged the continuation of the class struggle without the inevitability of war between capitalist and socialist camps, so that the transition to socialism in the West could proceed peacefully through a variety of means. This reinterpretation of Soviet ideology, in response to the evolving balance of social and political forces around the world, appeared to offer the opportunity of some easing of East–West tensions, while justifying unrelenting political attacks on the West by the Soviet Union and its supporters, which they believed increased the prospect of the final triumph of communism. It underpinned Khrushchev's handling of foreign affairs, which swung between the conciliatory and the bellicose. He travelled widely, visiting China, Yugoslavia, India, and the USA, as well as

Britain, before the end of the decade. The formation of the Warsaw Pact in 1956 had confirmed Soviet domination of Eastern Europe and when serious dissension emerged in Hungary in 1956, it was crushed by force. Under Khrushchev the Soviet Union also attached renewed importance to the emerging states of Africa and Asia, which he saw as natural allies, or future clients, of the Soviet Union against the old colonial powers.

But his conduct of international relations became increasingly erratic. The flamboyant gestures that were a hallmark of Khrushchev's style were much in evidence at his appearance at the United Nations in 1959 and at the summit conferences in Paris and Vienna in the following two years. Both those meetings were overshadowed by crises in East–West relations: the first the shooting down of an American U2 reconnaissance plane over the Soviet Union, and the second the beginnings of a new Berlin crisis and the building of the wall to confirm the separation of the two halves of the city. Arguably, his major legacy in world affairs was the break-up of the global unity of communism, and the split with China, which became public in 1960. Khrushchev did, however, attempt some *rapprochement* with the USA, while building up Soviet nuclear strength, but miscalculated badly when he overplayed his hand in the Cuba missile crisis of 1962. By then his economic policy was in tatters and more cautious figures in the Kremlin were growing weary of his unpredictability.

Confronted by these shifts in Soviet policy after 1953, British governments made numerous efforts to improve relations with the Kremlin. Following the death of Stalin, the arch cold-war warrior, Churchill, twice proposed the idea of an Anglo-Soviet summit conference to Molotov. The subsequent Eden and Macmillan governments continued to explore ways of reducing tensions and promoting disarmament. After the visit of Khrushchev and Bulganin in 1956, and despite the setback of the Hungarian invasion, the British worked for the Geneva talks, which opened in 1958 and culminated in the nuclear test ban treaty of 1963. In February 1959 Prime Minister Macmillan visited Moscow for discussions with Soviet leaders on a wide range of issues, including disarmament. Macmillan's independent enterprise was not, however, altogether popular with the USA and some European countries.

Although the detail of foreign policy is outside the scope of this book, recently released Cabinet papers for 1958, when Khrushchev was at his most secure in the Soviet leadership, throw some interesting light on British concerns about Soviet tactics and propaganda. Britain's main aims were defined by Foreign Secretary Selwyn Lloyd as the desire to preserve peace, to maintain international stability and defend free institutions where they existed, working closely with the USA, the Commonwealth and various treaty partners.[13] But there was also some anxiety about the effect of Soviet propaganda on public opinion. The Foreign Secretary told his Cabinet colleagues that:

> the Soviet government are playing a clever game in appealing over the heads of governments to public opinion in the Western countries and in the uncommitted countries. In the past, Soviet misdeeds in Czechoslovakia, in Korea, and in Hungary, the unattractiveness of the Soviet leaders (Stalin, Molotov, Vyshinsky), together with the unpleasantness of many Western fellow-travellers, has enabled us to retain the full support of the majority of the public for our attitude to the Soviet Union. But the new Soviet methods have a greater appeal.[14]

Dealing with letters from Bulganin proposing a summit conference in 1958, Lloyd told the Cabinet that despite his public declarations of willingness to talk to the Russians, they showed no signs of a willingness to negotiate themselves. In June 1958 he also drew the Cabinet's attention to a forthcoming World Youth Festival, which would be supported by the World Federation of Democratic Youth and the International Union of Students. Lloyd said that their policy was

> to campaign for 'united action' to disguise the control from Moscow as far as possible and to acquire respectability by associating as many non-Communists as possible with their activities ... At the present time these organisations are a particular danger in their ability to confuse and exploit the desire of people for peace and understanding ....[15]

But there was also evidence of some British irritation with American attitudes on trade with the Soviet Union. The President of the Board of Trade, for example, wanted a more liberal trading policy, with an embargo only on items that were strictly for military uses. He believed that the advent of the H-bomb had made war less likely and that the struggle between communism and the free world had switched to the economic field. His reasoning was that 'a fat Communist is less likely to make war than a thin communist.'[16] But the USA refused to reduce the lists of strategic goods which could not be exported to the Soviet Union, resistance the Board of Trade considered to be 'futile'. The Foreign Office backed the restriction of the strategic list to purely military items, 'provided that it is understood to include items which would significantly help the Soviet Union to mount a nuclear offensive, or defend itself against a nuclear counter-offensive.'[17]

During this period, when Anglo-Soviet diplomatic and trade relations indicated a tentative thawing of cold-war suspicions, some of the KGB's attitudes to the West remained as belligerent as ever. In a speech on the 40th anniversary of the foundation of the Cheka in December 1957, Serov declared that '... at the present time the whole work of the state security organs is directed towards exposing and checking subversive activity by foreign intelligence services and other enemies of socialism.'[18] The 'American imperialists' were portrayed as the leading force among these various enemies, for their ring of military bases aimed at the Soviet Union, their intelligence schools and centres, especially in West Germany, and their radio stations, which 'pour out filthy streams of lies and slander'.

Serov then went over the history of the 'organs' since the revolution, recalling the exposure of the Lockhart plot and the Metro-Vickers 'spy ring'. He attacked the 'vile traitor and adventurer', Beria, and concluded with some ominous comments for the present 'age of science and technology'. Not all scientific workers in the Soviet Union realised, warned Serov, that 'hostile agents are hunting out secrets', and he promised to punish the 'chatterers' who let slip confidential information.

In a report for the Foreign Office on the 40th anniversary celebrations, the British Ambassador to the Soviet Union, Sir Patrick Reilly, noted that attempts were being made to popularise the police forces in the Soviet Union and that past repression was being presented as a temporary aberration. The political police appeared to be demanding the cooperation of the population to carry out its functions, including countering hostile foreign, and particularly American, activity in the Soviet Union. Sir Patrick felt that 'recent months have seen an enhancement of the power of the KGB within the regime',[19] and that Khrushchev might be preparing for further moves against his opponents.

During 1958 further changes occurred at the top of the Soviet intelligence services, though not quite as Sir Patrick expected. In December Serov was placed in charge of the GRU and Aleksandr Shelepin, a vice-chairman of the World Federation of Democratic Youth for the previous five years, and secretary of the party youth organisation, the Komsomol, became Chairman of the KGB at the early age of 40. He immediately moved younger personnel into the KGB from the Komsomol, at the expense of officers with a Stalinist or military background, changes which may have had some adverse effect on operational efficency.

By comparison the GRU was facing an undeniable crisis of

confidence. Serov had been put in charge of military intelligence after the discovery that a GRU officer, Colonel Popov, was an American agent. But Serov himself was removed in disgrace three years later following the more serious case of Oleg Penkovsky, the GRU Colonel who, between 1960 and 1962, passed many secrets to the British, mainly through the businessman, Greville Wynne.[20] After that episode the GRU lost its remaining status in the Soviet hierarchy and was henceforth the junior partner in Soviet intelligence activity.

Shelepin presided over the KGB for only three years, until he was succeeded by another Komsomol official, Vladimir Semichastny. But during his brief reign Shelepin launched one of the major initiatives of the post-war period at a conference for senior KGB officers and other officials in May 1959. This meeting formalised some of the strands of policy which had developed since the death of Stalin and turned them into a plan that defined new priorities and strategies for the KGB. Shelepin's paper to the conference identified the 'main enemies' of the Soviet Union – the USA was the supreme enemy, followed by Britain, France, West Germany, Japan, and other member countries of NATO and other Western-supported military alliances. Soviet and East European intelligence agencies were to be mobilised in support of the Soviet Union's 'long-range policy', to destabilise the main enemies and weaken the alliances between them.[21]

The essence of this 'long-range policy' appears to be a recognition that Western Europe would not fall to communism via military invasion nor through a proletarian revolution of the old style. A prolonged period of ideological struggle lay ahead while the Soviet Union advanced economically and militarily. Espionage would become increasingly geared to providing the technical data to accelerate Soviet progress. At the same time, what were effectively forms of psychological warfare would be deployed to weaken and divide Western institutions and to spread ideas to promote the Soviet interest.

To explore ways of putting these ideas into effect,the KGB set up a section known as 'Department D'. Staffed by fifty to sixty officers under Colonel Agayants, it analysed Western weaknesses, and developed a range of overt and covert techniques to exploit them, including the spreading of 'disinformation', forgeries, and the planting of agents not only for espionage but to influence public and political opinion in directions favourable to the Soviet Union. In the early 1960s similar Disinformation Departments were established in East Germany, Czechoslovakia, Hungary, Bulgaria and Poland.[22] When they were first created, however, their scope for achieving the intended results must have been reduced by the inconsistencies of Khrushchev's foreign policies. The climax of this strategy was to come later in the Brezhnev and Andropov eras.

Espionage against Western military and governmental targets continued, however. To understand its development since Stalin's death, some retracing of steps is necessary. After the breakup of the Cambridge spy network in 1951, Soviet intelligence set about finding a new generation of agents. Over the next ten years it recruited at least twelve spies in Britain, together with an indeterminate number of individuals who did not become fully operational agents or who provided information to the KGB or its East European counterparts without committing any criminal offence. The stories of many of these cases have entered popular mythology as examples of Britain's continuing susceptibility to infiltration by Communist spies: the tales of the best known of them, such as George Blake, John Vassall and the Portland spy ring, have been told many times and will not be repeated here in detail.[23] Together, however, they do highlight some of the main themes in modern Soviet espionage.

Over half of the dozen or so agents recruited between 1951 and 1961 were low level individuals – government clerks, for example, who had access to high grade, classified information. At least four were first compromised outside Britain, while serving in embassies or other official establishments. Many of them lacked the sophistication of the pre-war recruits; they did not rise so high nor generally last as long. Although an ideological commitment to communism was a factor in a perhaps four of the cases, personal weaknesses alone – money, sexual blackmail and feelings of inadequacy – were the determining factors in a majority of the others. With many of the Cambridge spies, by contrast, human failings were masked by an emotional and intellectual attachment to the Communist cause. The misplaced idealism of the atomic scientists who wished, like Fuchs, to 'serve the whole of humanity' did not seem to have motivated the later breed of agent. Of the Communist sympathisers, two were self-selecting, 'walk-ins' in intelligence jargon, who literally strolled through the front doors of Soviet missions and offered to spy. They needed no recruitment.

The vulnerability of members of British establishments abroad – first noted before the war – increased as the Communists stepped up the pressure in the cold-war years. One of the first cases to come to light was that of William Marshall, a former soldier in the Royal Signals, who joined the diplomatic wireless service in 1948 at the age of 21. His recruitment as a Soviet agent took place in 1951 when he was serving in the British Embassy in Moscow. On his return to England a year later, he was approached by Pavel Kuznetzov, a Second Secretary at the Soviet Embassy. One of their meetings took place at a gathering of the British–Soviet Friendship Society, but on seven other occasions in the first half of 1952, Kuznetzov dined the impressionable Marshall at expensive hotels and restaurants in London, such as the Berkeley and Royal Court, the Criterion and the Pigalle.[24] In June 1952 Marshall was arrested after the chance sighting of Kuznetzov by an off-duty member of MI5 and he was sentenced to five years' imprisonment for breaches of the Official Secrets Acts.

Several of the more serious and well-known espionage cases which did not become public until the 1960s began abroad a decade earlier. In 1951 Harry Houghton, who became one of the members of the Portland spy ring, was compromised as a result of black market activities while working as a cipher clerk at the British Embassy in Warsaw. Three years later the homosexual clerk, John Vassall was trapped by the KGB when he was on the staff of the British Embassy in Moscow. The former RAF officer and Aviation Ministry official, Frank Bossard who actively spied for the Soviet Union between 1961 and 1965, was probably talent spotted while attached to the British Embassy in Bonn in 1956. He had money and marital problems which were the main factors that laid him open to exploitation.

The espionage career of the MI6 spy, the half Dutch, half Egyptian, George Blake, also had its origins outside Britain, though in somewhat direr circumstances. In 1950, as a member of the British mission in Seoul he was captured by the invading North Koreans and subjected to exhaustive indoctrination at the hands of an MGB officer. By the time of his return to freedom in April 1953, he was a committed Communist, and began to supply all he could about MI6 to his Soviet controllers, who included the Embassy's First Secretary, Sergei Kondrashev. For the next nine years Blake gave away secrets of many MI6 and CIA operations, including some in Berlin and in East Germany. After a defector's testimony led to his arrest, the 42-year prison sentence he received reflected one year for the life of each British agent he had betrayed.

Not all the difficulties experienced by its Embassy staff overseas had such adverse consequences for the British. An earlier example occurred in January 1949, when Robert Daglish, the assistant editor of an official government sponsored magazine called *British Ally*, which was produced from the Embassy in Moscow for distribution inside the Soviet Union, formed an attachment to the Russian-born former wife of a British subject working in the Embassy. He was told to return home by the Ambassador, who sensed danger, but Daglish left his job and took work outside as a translator. Within a year he announced his intention to return home, and an article over his name appeared in *Pravda*, in which he declared that he wanted to go back to Britain to work for peace. Foreign Office papers on the case show a concern that Daglish might have been of more than propaganda value to the Soviet Union: it wanted to get him back as he had some knowledge and experience of RAF signals work.[25]

Information on military matters remained the Soviet Union's main requirement, embracing material from service intelligence branches, or relating to communications procedures, force deployment and war planning, and weapon research and development. In May 1954 two Assistant Military Attachés at the Soviet Embassy were expelled for trying to obtain the designs of four military aircraft.[26] The recruited agents covered a wide span of departments and projects. Admiralty clerk John Vassall moved from the Naval Attaché's office in Moscow, to naval intelligence in London, and the private office of the Civil Lord of the Admiralty. Harry Houghton worked in naval intelligence and as part of the Portland ring focused on underwater naval weaponry. Frank Bossard had various military intelligence jobs and from 1960 worked in the Directorate of Guided Weapons in the Ministry of Aviation. Douglas Britten, who was recruited by the Soviet Union in 1962, was an RAF chief technician at a secret signals establishment in Lincolnshire.

The two 'walk-ins' of the 1950s had military backgrounds. John Clarence was a petty criminal who had served in the Royal Signals from 1947 until he was diagnosed as a schizophrenic four years later and discharged.[27] Also a member of the Young Communist League, he went to the Soviet Consulate in London during 1952 to offer his services as a spy. He was first asked to sell Soviet literature at Speakers' Corner and to spy on *émigré* organisations. Their activities were being monitored by the Soviet Union as it attempted to eliminate all potential sources of opposition to its rule in Eastern Europe. During 1952 questions were asked in parliament and the press about the alleged harassment by Soviet diplomats of *émigrés* from the Baltic states, the Ukraine and Poland, and particularly of members of the 6,000 strong *émigré* community in Bradford.[28]

Clarence's activities came to the attention of the Special Branch who interviewed him the next year. Up to that point he had committed no offence but shortly afterwards he obtained a clerical job in an anti-aircraft unit in Northumberland, which he used to achieve his ambition of spying for the Soviet Union. In 1954 a mislaid notebook containing details of some of the information he passed to the Soviet Embassy was traced back to him and he was arrested and received a five-year prison sentence.

The second military man to volunteer his services to the Soviet Union was a 22-year-old Flying Officer in the RAF, Anthony Wraight. Although he had trained as a pilot he had been taken off flying duties because of eyesight problems. After writing to the Society for Cultural Relations and getting in touch with the Soviet film agency, he called at the Soviet Embassy in March 1956. His actions were observed and he was interviewed twice by the RAF Provost Marshal branch and by MI5, and warned about his contact with Soviet officials. But he was placed under no restrictions and in December that year flew to East Germany. Wraight did not return to Britain until the end of 1959, when he was arrested and sentenced to three years' imprisonment.[29]

The vast majority of the spies recruited at this time were run by KGB officers under 'legal' cover at the Soviet Embassy in London. As noted earlier, Sergei Kondrashev ran Blake and the Admiralty scientist, Alister Watson. From 1957, the KGB Resident was Nikolai Korovin, one of five diplomats in the senior rank of Counsellors at the Embassy. He was responsible for Watson and Vassall. In 1957 he tried to get information on torpedoes from Harry Houghton, who until then had been handled by Polish intelligence after his return from Warsaw. When Houghton and the other members of the Portland ring were arrested at the begining of 1961, Korovin quickly left the country. For a time, activity by other agents, including Vassall, was suspended until the climate was more favourable for a resumption of spying. The new Resident, known to some of his agents as 'Nicky', was Nikolai Karpekov, a First Secretary at the Embassy from 1958, who had been Korovin's deputy. But Karpekov himself fled the country in September 1962 when Vassall was arrested. The main GRU officer to attract attention in Britain at this time was Captain Eugene Ivanov, the Assistant Naval Attaché who befriended John Profumo and others of the 'Cliveden' set. Through the intermediary agency of the society osteopath, Stephen Ward, he attempted to discover details of the implementation of the US decision to equip West Germany with atomic weaponry. Ivanov was able to operate in Britain for nearly three years, from March 1960 until January 1963, when he left, some three months after the 'Profumo Affair' became public.

The arrangements made by the KGB 'diplomats' for contacting their British agents were traditionally elaborate. To meet Korovin, Vassall was told to wear a Tyrolean hat with a feather on the side and to carry a newspaper under his arm. Korovin would approach him and ask the directions to Belsize Park, to which Vassall would answer that it was a long way and he would be better to take a taxi. Meetings were scheduled in various locations around London for Monday evenings at 7.30. If they were cancelled, signs were left in selected telephone boxes. When contact was safely established, Vassall handed over classified documents which Korovin copied and returned within the hour. Telephone booths were used as dead-letter boxes, and, according to Vassall, all locations were scrutinised by KGB men to make sure that they were suitable for use.[30]

'Dead-letter boxes' were widely used by Frank Bossard, whose direct contacts with Soviet officers was kept to a minimum. The Aviation Ministry official left information on guided weapons at sites in Esher and East Clandon in Surrey, near his home at Stoke D'Abernon, for later collection by KGB men. He was also told to listen to Moscow Radio at specified times for messages indicated in the playing of certain familar Russian tunes such as Kalinka, the Volga boat song and Moscow Nights, each of which signified a different meaning concerning the security of his operations. Any meetings took place in a variety of pubs around London and Surrey. Bossard booked into hotels in the Bloomsbury area of London, close to the British Museum, to photograph documents in his lunch hour. He kept his cameras and other equipment in a left-luggage locker at Waterloo station. After being put under surveillance, Bossard was arrested in March 1965 at the Ivanhoe Hotel in the middle of a document copying session, and was subsequently gaoled for twenty-one years.[31]

In 1952 the movements of Soviet diplomats around Britain were severely restricted when the NATO powers retaliated against curbs imposed on Western officials in the Soviet Union. In future any Soviet official who wished to travel more than thirty-five miles from central London had to give forty-eight hours' notice of his intentions. With some slight variations, similar restrictions were placed on members of East European missions, though they were eased at the end of 1956.[32] The distances within which unrestricted travel is permitted, and the notification periods for journeys, have been varied from time to time, between 35 and 25 miles and from 48 to 24 hours, but they have remained in force since. Although the restrictions offer some measure of control over movements of the representatives of Communist states they have proved of limited effectiveness in countering espionage activities. And any intelligence officer operating as an 'illegal', compensates for the loss of protection against the law afforded by diplomatic status, with the freedom to move around the country without reporting every movement.

Since the war only one 'illegal' Soviet spy controller has been uncovered in Britain. He was Konon Molody, who ran the Portland spy ring under the name of Gordon Lonsdale, a Canadian born in Cobalt, Ontario in 1924. Even in his autobiography, published in 1965, Molody insisted he was Lonsdale the Canadian.[33] But four years earlier the FBI had discovered his true identity: that he was born and brought up in Russia and prepared over many years for a career as a spy. The fullest available account of his life was, however, put together by the British Security Service, one of whose officers interrogated him in prison after his arrest in January 1961. It illustrates the careful weaving together of fact and fiction by the KGB, in order to provide one of its 'illegal' operatives with a convincing cover story.

The MI5 man's history of the life and times of Konon Molody appeared in a police service journal in 1971.[34] The article revealed that Molody was born in Moscow on 17 January 1922, the son of Trofim Konovich Molody, a prominent scientifc writer and editor, who came from a town on the north-eastern coast of Siberia. Molody senior travelled west in 1908 to study at the universities of St Petersburg and Moscow, where he later became a lecturer. In 1914 he married Evdokia Naumova, a doctor who practised for many years in Moscow. Konon was the second of their two children. Trofim died of a brain haemorrhage in October 1929, leaving Evdokia and the children in some difficulty. But help was on hand from Tatyana, one of her sisters who had settled in America following the Bolshevik revolution, after wanderings which had taken her and other members of her family to Estonia, China and Japan.

When Konon was 11 Tatyana returned to Russia, and seeing the privations of the Molody family invited the young boy to live with her in the USA. After using connections which led to the mistress of the NKVD boss Beria, Tatyana obtained an exit visa for Konon, and then, telling the American authorities that he was her son by an earlier marriage, she took him to America in November 1933. For the next five years the future spy who was to become known to the world as Gordon Lonsdale learnt his English and his knowledge of capitalist America in the company of his aunts and relations in California.

In 1938 the 16-year-old Konon toured Europe with another aunt and two English friends, with whom he obtained his first glimpse of the country he was to work against in the future. But with war looming over Europe, he decided to return to the Soviet Union, where he joined the Red Army and served with partisan units in Byelorussia. He found his way into Soviet intelligence and his post-war career remains shrouded in mystery until he surfaced in Vancouver, Canada in 1954.

From there he made his way to London, via the USA. On arrival in Britain he enrolled for studies lasting eighteen months at the School of Oriental Studies at London Universtity, where he met the very MI5 officer who was later to question him and to compile the story of his life. On completing his studies Molody, now well-established as Lonsdale, set himself up in a vending machine business.

It was not until 1958 that he took over Harry Houghton from the 'legal' controllers at the Soviet Embassy and began his main espionage activities. The question about what else Molody was doing before, and indeed after, he came into contact with Houghton, remains unanswered. His superiors were probably anxious that he should get himself properly set up in Britain, with a job and social credentials, before launching into any major spying enterprise, but it is possible that he was running other agents in Britain who have not been discovered.

Under Molody's direction Houghton recruited his mistress, Ethel Gee, who was a clerk at the Portland base. Houghton first introduced Molody to her as an American naval officer, Commander Alex Johnston. Molody also enlisted an American couple, Morris and Lona Cohen, who lived in Ruislip and ran a antiquarian bookshop in the Strand, under the name of Kroger. The Cohens had obtained new passports in Paris, from a member of the New Zealand consulate there, Paddy Costello, who later became Professor of Russian at Manchester University and was an associate of Blunt. The connections with other Soviet spy rings were also emphasised by the fact that the Krogers' names were found in 1957 in the New York flat of the leading Soviet 'illegal' in the USA, Colonel Abel.[35]

The Krogers provided the communications facilities for Molody, and in their suburban house the police found one of the most extensive collections of Soviet espionage equipment ever discovered. The haul included photographic paper for microdots, a microscope for mounting them and, in a talcum powder tin, a microdot reader. Several miniature cameras were recovered, together with one-time code pads, a radio tranmsitter, details of radio call signs, false Canadian passports and 6,000 US dollars. At Molody's London apartment at the White House near Regent's Park, another transmitter, code pads, and more photographic material were found.[36]

In his summing-up of Molody's career, the MI5 officer who met and interviewed him paid professional tribute to the Russian. In selecting people for the 'difficult and dangerous job of an illegal intelligence officer', the Soviet Union looked for 'a rare combination of qualities', which Molody seemed to possess. The work demamded that an 'illegal' must have:

courage in the face of the continual risk of exposure and severe punishment,
endurance to withstand long periods of loneliness and isolation from family,
friends and colleagues, the capacity not only to live a cover story
convincingly, but to live one which would be useful in Western Europe or
the USA, an ability to dominate and command the respect and confidence of
his agents, a knowledge of the matters on which he is directed to obtain
intelligence, and enough technical competence to enable him to operate the
complicated communications system on which the success of his mission,
and perhaps his life, would depend. But quite apart from, and above all
these qualities, the Russian Intelligence Service must be absolutely
confident in the loyalty of an illegal intelligence officer, whose opportunities
for defection and betrayal are much greater than those of his comrades who
work under supervision and within the framework of a Soviet official
organisation, either at home or abroad ... In K. T. Molody, the Russian
Intelligence Service found a man with all the qualities needed for an
intelligence officer.[37]

Molody served only three years of his twenty-five-year sentence: in
April 1964 he was exchanged for Greville Wynne, the British
businessman who had been held in Moscow after the Penkovsky affair.
Molody's arrest at the beginning of 1961 was followed in the next
twenty months by the discovery of Blake and Vassall as well as some
lesser agents. The spy networks built up by Soviet intelligence since
1951 were finally being unwound.

These cases, and the security implications of the Profumo scandal,
had a devastating effect on British public opinion, which became
increasingly sceptical about the effectiveness of the country's defences
against Communist penetration. A series of commissions and
enquiries looked into the background of each case and made
recommendations for improved protection in the future. One of them,
the Radcliffe Committee on Security Procedures in the Public Service
declared in 1962 that

the most serious source of danger lies in the intelligence services of the
Soviet bloc ... These services must be envisaged as steadily at work in this
country collecting information ... they are prepared to employ all the most
up-to-date resources of espionage and they look for useful agents or
instruments wherever skill or occasion present an opportunity.[38]

Inside the security and intelligence services, old files on the Cambridge
spies were reopened after 1963, and a host of new allegations of
Soviet-inspired infiltration was examined, each more sensational

than the last. The source of many of these fresh revelations was a succession of former members of Soviet, Polish and Czech secret services, who had succumbed to the temptations that Molody had resisted, and defected to the West.

DEFECTORS AND THE CZECH CONNECTION

In a little under three years, from April 1960 to December 1962, ten people were tried and sent to prison in Britain for spying for the Soviet Union or East European countries. Indications of the continuing struggle between British and Soviet intelligence services became ever more obvious. Between 1965 and 1972, a further twelve people received gaol sentences for espionage offences. And from 1960 to 1971 more than 130 Soviet diplomats and officials were expelled from Britain for their activities – including some 105 in a single purge in September 1971 – and over forty were refused visas to enter the country. Much of this action was made possible on the basis of information received from defectors from the KGB and East European agencies, who sometimes were able to give specific names and targets. But those same defectors also offered many imprecise and generalised allegations which could not be substantiated. And these unproven assertions have been the source of some of the major controversies that haunt the British intelligence and security services still, and have provoked further public criticism of their record.

Since the Gouzenko affair in Canada in 1946 the successes of Soviet intelligence had been undermined – and the knowledge of Western agencies enormously enlarged – by its continual loss of individual members who preferred life in the West. Averaging out figures from Western intelligence souces, Richard Deacon arrives at a figure of 806 defectors from Soviet and satellite countries to the West between 1953 and 1969, with only 93 going the other way.[39] In many of the known cases a fundamental disillusion with communism is, not surprisingly, the overriding reason for changing sides, although career and personal worries have also played a part in persuading individuals to abandon their homes, and often their families, and seek a new life elsewhere. Not all defectors have been genuine and from time to time, British, American and other security services have been thrown into confusion by deliberately planted false defectors, some of whom find their way back to the bosom of Moscow or East Berlin, and by defectors whose ingenuity and capacity for invention outmatches their direct, personal experience.

Several of the leading defectors in the 1950s and 1960s played a major part in revealing the extent of Soviet espionage in Britain, and in the USA, France, West Germany, and elsewhere. In April 1954 Vladimir Shorokhov, better known as Vladimir Petrov, left his post as the KGB Resident in Australia, followed by his wife, Evdokia, who made a dramatic escape from the clutches of Soviet security men at Darwin airport. Their defection led to the setting up of a Royal Commission along the lines of the Canadian enquiry eight years earlier. It found evidence going back more than ten years of 'legal' GRU and KGB residencies in Australia run by officers based at the Soviet Embassy in Canberra. Their targets embraced the Australian parliament, the Department of External Affairs, security organisations, journalists, scientists, and émigré communities. And similarly to the Canadian experience, the Commission's report, which was published in Sydney in August 1955, found that among the agents recruited to spy for the Soviet Union: 'all the persons whose acts were directly or indirectly connected with espionage were either members of the [Australian] Communist Party or ex-members or pretending to be ex-members thereof or sympathisers with Communism.'[40]

Of particular interest to Britain at the time was further information from Petrov concerning the flight of Burgess and Maclean. Petrov's deputy in Canberra was Filip Kislytsin, who had been at the Soviet Embassy in London after the war and had worked in Moscow on the material provided by the two Foreign Office men. He told Petrov that they had been recruited while undergraduates at Cambridge, and that their escape, and that of Maclean's wife, had been planned in advance by the KGB. Petrov's revelations came as a severe embarrassment for the British government, appearing in a Sunday newspaper just five days before its bland White Paper on the Burgess and Maclean case, which contained its own references to Petrov's testimony.[41]

Later defectors, too, brought mixed blessings for Western governments. A Polish intelligence officer known as Michal Goleniewski provided information to the CIA before defecting in December 1960. He helped the British uncover Houghton and Blake, gave further information on Philby and, some three years later, asserted that there was a middle-ranking spy in MI5. But by that stage Goleniewski had decided that he was the son of Tsar Nicholas II, and his sanity and his sincerity were placed in doubt.[42]

A year after Goleniewski's flight to the West came the most controversial defector of all: Anatoliy Golitsyn. Born in the Ukraine in 1926, Golitsyn joined the Komsomol, the Young Communist League, when he was 15. In 1945, while a student at the artillery school at

Odessa, he became a member of the CPSU and joined military counter-intelligence. From there he transferred to the MGB, attended several 'high-flying' courses, and in 1952–3 was involved in drawing up proposals for the reorganisation of Soviet intelligence. Golitsyn was stationed in Vienna for nearly two years and on his return to Moscow took a law degree at the KGB Academy, before serving as a senior analyst in the NATO section of the KGB Information Department. He was then transferred to Helsinki, under cover of the Vice-Consul's post at the Soviet Embassy. It was from there that Golitsyn defected in December 1961, a man with a brilliant career in the intelligence world but totally disenchanted with the Communist system.

In his extensive debriefings with Western intelligence experts, Golitsyn provided several hundred leads. He pointed to an espionage network in France, and to the treachery of a Canadian diplomat, Herbert Norman, who committed suicide in Cairo. In Britain, MI5 compiled a set of 'ten serials' provided by Golitsyn, specific instances of the Soviet penetration of Whitehall, and in particular of military and intelligence departments. Golitsyn partly corroborated some of the charges made by Goleniewski, and his evidence incriminated Vassall, Blake, Watson, and Barbara Fell, a senior official in the Ministry of Information, who was the mistress of a Yugoslav diplomat and to whom she passed classified documents. Golitsyn named Sergei Kondrashev and Nikolai Korovin as spy controllers, and also spoke of a Ring of Five, recruited in Britain in the 1930s, and run at one stage by Yuri Modin. Although he could identify none of its members directly, MI5 drew up a list which included Blunt, Burgess, Maclean and Philby, with the identity of the fifth remaining in dispute.[43]

Golitsyn's disclosures did not end there. In the course of his exile he formulated increasingly complex theories about Soviet disinformation strategy. He claimed, for example, that the Sino-Soviet split was part of a grand scheme of deception to fool the West into believing that communism was divided and therefore weakened. The scheme, according to Golitsyn, was central to the 'long-range policy' launched in 1959, which meant that the Soviet Union was feeding the West with a ceaseless stream of lies and fabrications about its foreign intentions, the state of its military preparedness, its economic condition and the handling of its internal affairs. He also fuelled suspicions that a Soviet spy still existed in MI5, and that Soviet interference in British politics extended to the assassination of the Labour leader, Hugh Gaitskell in 1963, to open the way for a more left-wing leadership to take over. Such allegations divided intelligence communities on both sides of the Atlantic. In the end Golitsyn's detractors outnumbered his supporters.

Even Peter Wright, whose belief that MI5 was still penetrated corresponded with some of Golitsyn's charges, counted among his critics. By 1967, said Wright, Golitsyn had been 'allowed to think himself too important'.[44]

At that time fresh material was emerging from the first of a new wave of defectors, not from the Soviet Union but the country it had ranked as one of its staunchest allies in the Warsaw Pact – Czechoslovakia. Since the purges of 1952 the Czechs had been governed by a regime of unbending Stalinists. Until, that is, the short-lived reforms of Mr Dubcek in the 'Prague Spring', which ended with the Soviet-led invasion of August 1968. Prior to that, the Soviet Union had entrusted the Czechs with an increasing amount of spying and subversive activity in Britain and other Western countries. Probably the first Czech to be expelled from Britain after the Communist coup in 1948 was Frank Hampel, the secretary of the British–Czechoslovakian Friendship League. He was ordered out of the country in July 1948, despite protests from the League's Chairman, the Labour MP Barnett Stross and several of his colleagues.[45]

During the 1950s the Czechs increased their diplomatic strength in London from a handful to more than twenty-five officials at the end of the decade. Faced with less stringent restrictions than the Soviet Union they were able to extend their covert operations. Between 1957 and 1961 they recruited at least four agents in Britain. In 1957 Colonel Oldrych Prybyl, the Czech Military Attaché, enlisted the services of Brian Linney, an electronics engineer who worked for a company in Sussex which had confidential contracts with the RAF. His identity was revealed the next year by a Czech defector in Washington, and Linney was sentenced to fourteen years in prison, while Prybyl was expelled from the country. At about the same time the Czechs also acquired the services of Nicholas Prager, a Czech-born RAF radar technician. After leaving the air force in 1961, he worked for the English Electric company for ten years on secret defence contracts before his espionage activities were discovered.[46] And in 1963 another Czech diplomat, Premsyl Holan, was told to leave Britain because of his involvement in spying.

But the Czechs were not only interested in technical and military data. In 1957 they recruited two members of the Labour Party to provide political intelligence and information on internal party matters: Will Owen, the MP for Morpeth in Northumberland, who was approached on a visit to Czechoslovakia, and Arthur Bax, head of the party's press relations department. Bax was exposed by the Labour politician, (Lord) George Brown in 1961.[47] Owen and Prager, however, were among several people only identified in 1969–70, on the evidence of Czech military and intelligence officers who had left their homeland shortly before or after the Soviet invasion of August 1968.

These latest defectors included Major-General Jan Sejna, the Czech Deputy Defence Minister, who fled to the USA in December 1967, Major Ladislav Bittman, a Czech intelligence 'disinformation' specialist, and Major Frantisek August and Josef Frolik, who had both been on the staff of the Czech Embassy in London. Between them, they and others like them, unfolded details of the KGB's strategic aims for Western Europe and described its relationship with the services of satellite countries, as well as providing leads to currently active agents. In West Germany the effects were dramatic: at least five military and intelligence officers committed suicide or were found dead in suspicious circumstances following defections by Czechs.

According to Jan Sejna, the Soviet Union had developed a global strategic plan which set out their strategy for the subjugation of the entire non-Communist world.[48] The section for Britain envisaged campaigns to compromise and discredit prominent political leaders such as Harold Wilson and Edward Heath by spreading false information about their sexual, financial or other aspects of their lives. The Czechs, said Sejna, had a special responsibility for carrying out the smear campaigns. As Britain's economic decline gathered pace, the mainstream of politicians would be incapable of commanding public respect and an alternative source of power would be built around the Labour left, the trade unions and the Communist Party (although the Soviet Union had little faith in the British Communist Party as an independent force). Sejna claimed, however, that in 1967 twelve CPGB members received two months' political and military training in Czechoslovakia, including sabotage techniques. They were followed by smaller numbers in subsequent years. The take-over of the trade union movement, and the promotion of closer links between British unions and those in Eastern Europe, was another high priority of the first stage of the plan.

In his account of the strategic plan and its associated preliminary measures, which was published in 1982, Sejna also stated that British Communists contributed to the drawing up of a list of enemies of a future left-wing government. This list, compiled in 1964, consisted of the names of several hundred leaders in politics, industry, the army and the police. To deal with them, the imaginary Soviet-supported regime would then dispense its own form of justice, either through detention without trial, assassination, or, in the case of more senior figures such as Mr Wilson, Mr Heath and Sir Alec Douglas Home, in show trials before execution.

Many of Sejna's claims sound like the ingredients for a fiction thriller rather than as a description of the serious political strategy of a major power. The plan will have certainly been rewritten since Sejna's day, not least to take account of changes in Britain's economic fortunes. But evidence from other Czech defectors goes some way to corroborating Sejna's assertions that in the 1960s and 1970s Soviet and East European intelligence services were focusing on political and industrial subversion as much as military or state espionage.

A series of allegations came from the two intelligence officers who before their defection served at the Czech Embassy in London. Major Joseph Frolik was a member of Czech intelligence for seventeen years before he crossed to the West in August 1969. For two years, from 1964–6, he was a Labour Attaché in London. In July 1973 he reportedly submitted a 500-page document to the CIA detailing Czechoslovakia's covert operations in the West. Among the agents of Czech intelligence were three British MPs.[49] Two of them were recruited in the 1950s by diplomats Jan Paclik and Vaclav Taborsky. Paclik had indeed come to the attention of the British authorities at the time: Foreign Office files show that in 1956 he was warned for 'molesting émigres'.[50]

In 1976 Frolik gave evidence in Washington to a Senate Committee which was investigating Communist bloc intelligence activities in the USA. He told the committee that both the HSR, the Czech equivalent of the KGB, and the military intelligence agency, the GST, maintained Residencies at the London Embassy.[51] This was confirmed by Frantisek August, an intelligence officer of fifteen years' experience, who defected in the same year as Frolik. He also appeared before the committee and said the GST also worked under the cover of the Czech Travel Agency in London. At the hearings Frolik also named the former Labour Postmaster-General, the late John Stonehouse as one of Czech's MP agents. His case officers in London had been Robert Husak and Josef Kalina or Karhan, who also controlled Will Owen MP, who was known only to Frolik as 'Lee'. Among other Czech-run agents in Britain were a member of the Treasury, a former member of MI6 who had died in 1961, a Metropolitan police officer and the ex-RAF man, Nicholas Prager.

In his published autobiography, which had appeared in 1975, Frolik was less specific about individuals, but described activities that extended more widely. He wrote of smear campaigns against politicians, approaches to several leading trade unionists by Communist intelligence agencies and the existence of several other, unnamed, MPs who satisfied the Czechs by passing on information.

Altogether, Frolik claimed that an eighteen-strong Czech intelligence team in London was running some thirty agents in London in the mid-1960s and were maintaining a couple of hundred other contacts.[52] Although these included individuals in the political and trade union spheres, Frolik makes it clear, however, that the Soviet Union took the lead in targeting Labour politicians and union leaders, while his main task – not always adhered to – was the acquisition of military and NATO secrets.

At the Washington hearings August described the two years he had spent in London, from 1961–3, as an intelligence officer under the guise of an attaché in the Embassy consular section. His main targets were MI5 and MI6. He ran Prager, and was in contact with three 'illegal' agents. One of his colleagues, Jan Koshka, controlled an Iraqi Communist who was a secretary to the peace campaigner and philosopher, Bertrand Russell.[53]

Not all the contacts mentioned by Frolik and August ultimately proved beneficial to the Czechs. Some of the trade union leaders and MPs, such as John Stonehouse, were almost certainly approached by Czech intelligence officers and attempts were made to recruit them as informants or 'agents of influence', or to compromise them. But these efforts did not always succeed. Activity centred on the Labour Party was not, however, confined to the Czechs. The KGB had its own designs on some of the party's most influential figures.

A defector from the KGB London Residency in 1971, Oleg Lyalin, revealed that Soviet intelligence officers had targeted close associates of the Prime Minister for their attention. In particular he claimed that the head of the Embassy's Consular Section, Richardas Vaigauskas, a KGB man who had previously served at the United Nations in New York and in Canada, was cultivating Joseph (later Lord) Kagan, the Lithuanian-born manufacturer of 'Gannex' raincoats and one of Harold Wilson's closest confidants. The allegations were investigated by MI5, and Vaigauskas was among the 105 Soviet officials expelled from Britain in September 1971.[54] The names of a number of other members of the Labour leader's entourage also figured in the enquiries, including the late Rudy Sternberg, later Lord Plurenden, who had business connections in East Germany, a Hungarian scrap metal magnate, Sir Sigmund Sternberg, and the late Stephen Swingler MP, a one-time junior minister with East European connections.[55]

Several reasons lay behind increased Soviet interest in the Labour Party. Historically, the Soviet Union had supported its client, the British Communist Party, as its chosen vehicle for the creation of a socialist Britain. But after repeated failures, crises and missed opportunities over the years, it had become abundantly clear that the CPGB would never fulfil Soviet ambitions. Despite its remaining influence in some important sections of the trade union movement and opinion-forming pressure groups, the party had failed to adapt to post-war conditions, and was neither the vanguard of a revolution nor a mass party at the heart of the country's political life. Any residual Soviet desire to reach the bulk of the British proletariat therefore had to be conducted through the Labour Party, the only serious party of the working class, and the trade unions affiliated to it.

By the mid-1960s the arguments for focusing attention on the Labour Party had acquired additional, and more urgent, dimensions. Labour was not merely a broad working-class movement, part of which wanted to transform society in a socialist direction. For the first time since the death of Stalin it was a party of government. A Soviet wish to influence Labour's policies and decisions when it was in office after 1964 was entirely consistent with its strategy throughout the post-Stalin period. This could be partly realised by using conventional diplomatic and propaganda channels on specific issues.

But there was one major obstacle to the extension of Soviet influence on the Labour Party. Although Labour's ranks had always included a small number of members who were sympathetic to communism and to the policies of the Soviet Union, the party was dominated by social democrats, some of whom were bitter opponents of communism in any shape or form. This problem could only be completely addressed by the use of covert methods.

More formal and open contacts could be supplemented by personal approaches to selected individuals undertaken by officers experienced in political intelligence work. Beyond that the Soviet Union could take appropriate steps to boost those elements in the Labour Party who were sympathetic to it, or at least were anti-American and anti-Western, and to reduce the power of the Antlanticist, pro-Western centre and right of the party. This would have been especially true, even before 1964, when questions of defence and disarmament and Britain's future role in the world were such explosive issues in the party. Intelligence sources would have also been expected to obtain information on personalities and on internal developments in the party, encourage the left, and carry out any discrediting of 'right-wingers', ultimately hoping to destroy them and so help overturn the traditional balance of power in the party.

The existence of a ban on recruiting local Communist Party members as intelligence agents, first recorded by Agabekov in 1929, was confirmed by Frolik and August. But there was no such limitation regarding Labour members. If one of the principal Soviet objectives was to gain influence and the covert elements of that policy included obtaining the services of informants and individuals who would spread the Soviet line, the logical place to find them and to plant them in the 1960s was where real influence was located, in the ruling Labour Party, not in the peripheral Communist Party.

Such are the arguments which might have led to intensified Soviet activity aimed at the Labour Party in the 1960s. The testimony of defectors on the detail of what was done and achieved has proved unreliable. But there remains sufficient material to suggest that the Soviet Union, supported in particular by the Czechs, did mount such a campaign, and that it included covert measures of agent recruitment in one section of the party, and the simultaneous smearing and compromising of members of other sections.

By a series of twists that original KGB offensive has provided much of the ammunition for a more recent controversy: the charge that MI5's investigations into the defectors' allegations of Soviet-inspired machinations in the 1960s contributed towards, and became part of, an attempt to undermine the Labour government elected in 1974. Peter Wright eventually scaled down his own version of a 'plot' from thirty MI5 officers to himself and one other.[56] But his disclosures have in turn, become the raw material for a left-wing campaign against the British intelligence and security services in the 1980s. All that is another story. So far, what looks like the first and indeed the only substantive intelligence plot against the Labour Party was the one instigated by the KGB and its allies in the 1960s.

Soviet and East European interest in the affairs of Britain's main political parties features prominently throughout the modern period. Attention was drawn to it by Sir Martin Furnival Jones, the Director-General of MI5, when he gave evidence to the Franks Committee on the reform of the official Secrets Act in 1971. He said that Soviet bloc intelligence services were 'very active in the press world in Fleet Street, and ... among political parties around the Palace of Westminster'.[57] Legitimate or otherwise, the probing and the approaches continue. Where the aim is to influence or obtain intelligence about the government of the day they are not confined to the Labour Party. At the beginning of the present decade, for example, shortly after the Conservatives had been re-elected, it was known to this author that at least two members of the party's Research Department were being individually cultivated and entertained by Soviet or East European diplomats. Beyond that, the Labour Party and the trade unions have a special attraction for Soviet intelligence: they represent the working class in both the political and industrial spheres, include strong socialist elements, and are useful channels for covert propaganda and for 'agents of influence'.

But circumstances and methods alter. By the time the Labour Party returned to office in 1974, the position of the KGB and its Czech allies in London had changed. The staff levels at the embassies of both countries had been drastically cut, MI5 had carried out its own enquiries, and the stories of illicit activity in the previous decade were beginning to emerge publicly. And in Moscow the KGB had been reorganised by Yuri Andropov to create a modern organisation capable of serving the policies of Leonid Brezhnev in the age of 'détente'.

7 The Making of the Modern KGB

THE MACHINERY OF 'ACTIVE MEASURES'

On 20 December 1967 the KGB celebrated the fiftieth anniversary of the foundation of the Cheka, the Extraordinary Commmission set up by Lenin under Felix Dzerzhinsky. In a speech to mark the occasion, the KGB's new Chairman, Yuri Andropov, emphasised the threads of continuity which linked his own organisation to the body which had so effectively dealt with the forces of counter-revolution half a century before. Andropov declared that:

> Lenin clearly defined the fundamental principles of the Cheka's work: utter dedication to the revolutionary cause, close links with the people, unshakeable loyalty to the Party and Soviet government, staunchness in the struggle against the class enemies, and lofty proletarian humanism. These democratic principles have always been and remain the basis of the activities of the Soviet state security services.[1]

Yuri Andropov was the architect of the contemporary Soviet intelligence and security system but never forgot the legacy of the early Bolsheviks and the fundamentals of Marxist-Leninist doctrine. This duality, revolutionary tradition invoked in the name of the modern state, was an essential feature of the new-model KGB he moulded. It provided his expanding organisation with a legitimacy rooted in the revolution of 1917 and a frame of reference for its activities which would be understood by the Soviet people. Andropov idealised Dzerzhinsky for his 'exceptional single-mindedness of character', and his particular interest 'in the struggle against the problem of homeless children'.[2] Such references were also a device to distance himself and the KGB from the atrocities perpetrated by Stalin's secret policemen. In his 1967 speech for example, he attacked the 'political adventurers' who 'committed acts of lawlessness' in the 1930s.

In his speeches and writings Andropov also extended to the international arena the classic themes of struggle against the 'class enemies' and the defence of the revolution. In 1976, he said that 'Soviet

147

foreign policy is a class policy ... because the Party, while pursuing persistently a consistent and sincere policy of peace, firmly adheres to the principles of proletarian internationalism and solidarity with the people's struggle for freedom and social progress.'[3]

For the KGB the intelligence services of the West were enemies of the first rank. In 1967 Andropov stated that Western governments used them

> not only for espionage, sabotage and acts of terrorism but also for attaining their political objectives. The secret services are instructed to do whatever they can to weaken the power of the socialist countries, to undermine their unity and their solidarity with the working class and national liberation movements. The Soviet state security service, jointly with the relevant agencies in the fraternal socialist countries, is giving a condign rebuff to these hostile operations.[4]

Andropov's view of Western intrigue did not mellow during the years of *détente*. At a KGB conference in 1979, under the title, 'Ideological Subversion – the Poisoned Weapon of Imperialism', he said that the 'imperialists' were using subversion 'to weaken and unhinge the socialist system. It ... often amounts to direct interference in the internal affairs of socialist countries.'[5]

Andropov became Chairman of the KGB on 19 May 1967. He replaced the ineffectual Semichastny, who had held the post for the previous six years. Andropov's earlier career had been mainly spent in party and diplomatic posts. Born the son of a railway worker in south east Russia, he first worked as a boatman on the Volga and as a telegraph operator. In 1937, when he was 23, Andropov joined the party youth wing, the Komsomol and took his first step up the long ladder of power by becoming a regional secretary. Like many Soviet leaders, his wartime career is shrouded in myth-making clouds. Andropov's official biography stated that he served with the partisan movement in Karelia.[6] He was certainly part of the Komsomol organisation in the Karelo-Finnish Republic which had been created in 1940, and was probably in charge of a forced labour battalion responsible for timber production.[7]

After the war Andropov entered the Soviet foreign service. He was a Counsellor at the Soviet mission in Budapest from 1953–7, during which time he was intimately involved in the planning and execution of the Soviet invasion of Hungary. When he returned to Moscow he became head of the new Central Committee department handling relations between Communist parties in socialist countries. Over the next ten years he made numerous visits to Eastern Europe and further afield, including three trips to North Vietnam, as well as to North Korea and Cuba, and held the same position until he took charge of security and intelligence. In June 1967, just a month after his appointment to head the KGB, and a week following his fifty-third birthday, Andropov's arrival at the apex of the Soviet power structure was signified by his elevation to the Politburo, albeit at first as a candidate (non-voting) member.[8]

Initially, his principal tasks were to build a more efficient organisation that was commensurate with the Soviet Union's status as an emerging world power and, on the domestic scene, to find ways of containing dissent without resorting to the arbitrary repression which had characterised earlier crackdowns on deviationists and minorities.

After the overthrow of Khrushchev in October 1964, a triumvirate, consisting of Kosygin as Prime Minister, Podgorny as President and Leonid Brezhnev as party General Secretary had assumed power. By the end of the decade the latter had established himself as the paramount figure. Under Brezhnev the Soviet Union sought – and in 1969 achieved – strategic nuclear parity with the USA. The security which that afforded opened the way for the beginning of the Strategic Arms Limitation Talks (SALT) and a policy of 'peace' and '*détente*'. Brezhnev proceeded cautiously in his relations with the USA and its Western allies. Above all he wished to avoid the risks and adventurism associated with Khrushchev. American policy in Vietnam was condemned, and in the Middle East at the time of the Arab–Israeli war of 1967, while the Soviet Union tried to extend its own influence in the region. Trade with the West grew, despite continuing American resistance to easing the limitations on deals involving strategic materials and the latest technology. A Nuclear Non-Proliferation Treaty had been signed by the USA, Britain and the Soviet Union in 1968, and two years later Moscow reached an accord with West Germany – a major landmark in the history of post-war Europe. The easing of East–West tensions helped Brezhnev confront some of his other problems.

Relations with other Communist nations were in a state of turmoil in the late 1960s. The dispute with China assumed threatening proportions and led to border skirmishes, while the path of reform struck by Dubcek in Czechoslovakia ended in August 1968 to the roar of Warsaw Pact tanks. Soviet policy in Czechoslovakia was criticised by some Western Communist parties, who gave voice to their concerns at the gathering of world parties held in Moscow in 1969. Their independence only increased in the decade ahead, particularly in the

Italian and Spanish parties, with the advent of the phenomenon –
incomplete and short-lived though it turned out to be – of
'Eurocommunism'.[9]

Brezhnev was also concerned to prevent the spread of liberalisation
inside the Soviet Union, and to quash any false hopes that 'détente'
would lead to any internal relaxation. The trial in 1966 of the writers
Andrei Sinyavsky and Yuli Daniel for sending their work to the West
for publication provoked an international outcry and signalled the
early onset of a new wave of repression. Pressures for reform which
had their origins outside the Soviet Union may have prompted the
intensification of stricter domestic controls but they were not the cause
of them.

Andropov's job as incoming head of the KGB was to contain dissent
in a less crude manner than had been the custom in the past. And
indeed, as noted earlier, he was critical of what was done in the 1930s.
His methods did, however, include the full range of police powers of
arrest and imprisonment, censorship, internal exile or deportation, the
refusal of exit visas to Jews especially, the suppression of dissenting
groups and journals, and the extended use of psychiatric hospitals as
places of detention. In his 1979 speech at a KGB Conference, after
more than ten years' experience in controlling dissidents, Andropov
described this aspect of the KGB's responsibilities in benign,
avuncular terms:

> The state security men are called on to fight for every Soviet citizen
> whenever he has made a slip or strayed from the path, so as to help him
> return to the right track again. This in one of the major aspects of the
> activity of the state security agencies. It is of great political significance,
> ensues from the human essence of our system, and meets the requirements
> of the Party's ideological work. With their special means ... the state
> security men are fighting against everything that is alien to our ideology
> and morality, and making their contribution to the great cause of moulding
> the new man.[10]

Throughout his fifteen years as head of the KGB Andropov made
extensive changes in its methods and structure. The organisation he
bequeathed to his successors in 1982 consisted of five Chief
Directorates, which were divided into subsidiary sections known as
Directorates, Services or Departments. Western estimates of the
strength of the KGB suggest in the region of 90–100,000 officers and
another 300–400,000 troops in the Border Guards, who are also under
KGB control.[11] At any one time during Andropov's rule, up to 15,000

officers were stationed abroad, including those under diplomatic cover, or serving in trade delegations and commercial concerns, on the staffs of magazines and news agencies or in international organisations. Altogether, the KGB may have accounted for up to 35 per cent of all Soviet officials around the world.[12]

Many of the reforms introduced by Andropov were intended to improve the efficiency of the KGB's activities abroad, which were the responsibility of the First Chief Directorate. In 1968 and again two years later, Andropov upgraded the Disinformation Department, as greater emphasis was placed on 'active measures', which meant the use of covert propaganda and campaigns of political influence, as distinct from pure espionage. It became known as Service A and had a headquarters staff of some 200 people.[13] In 1969 a Planning Directorate was set up to analyse and distribute the fruits of foreign intelligence to other departments. And in 1971, after the defection in London of Oleg Lyalin, a member of Department V, responsible for assassinations and sabotage, the whole area of KGB 'wet-operations' was overhauled and brought under the control of the Service which dealt with 'illegals'. The Soviet Union had for some years been moving away from its earlier practices of hunting down and murdering its enemies, following the adverse publicity which resulted from defection to the West in 1962 of Bogdan Staschinsky, a KGB officer who had murdered two Ukrainian exiles in West Germany.[14] In future the Soviet Union covered its tracks in any 'wet-operations', or as in the case of Georgi Markov, the Bulgarian journalist murdered in London in 1978 by his fellow countrymen, delegated the business to a satellite organisation.[15]

By the early 1980s, the First Chief Directorate had become a substantial bureaucracy itself, with approximately 20,000 officers.[16] They were deployed in three Directorates: A, controlling 'illegal' officers; T, which collected scientific and technological intelligence; and K, which was charged with the penetration of foreign intelligence services and maintaining discipline among Soviet missions abroad. In addition there were three Services: I, for analysis and planning; A, for planning and coordinating Active Measures operations; and R, which scrutinised and learned from recent and current KGB operations. Actual operations and the running of agents were carried out by one of the eleven geographical departments: the Third covered Britain, Australia, New Zealand and Scandinavia. Finally, the First Chief Directorate under Andropov had six other autonomous departments, responsible for technical equipment, ciphers and communications, and liaison with Eastern European intelligence agencies.[17]

Other Chief Directorates included the Second, which looked after internal security functions, the Fifth, which Andropov greatly enlarged, to monitor dissident activity, and the Eighth, concerned with ciphers and the interception of foreign communications. The Border Guards were run by their own Directorate and other separate Directorates included the Third, which watched over the armed forces, and the Seventh, for surveillance operations inside the Soviet Union.

Such is the breadth of the work carried out by the modern KGB, and the growing importance of propaganda-related activity through 'active measures', that its role cannot be considered in isolation from other parts of the Soviet government machine. Under Andropov the KGB established a voice on the Politburo, which determines all major strategic decisions on all aspects of Soviet policy, including the main thrust of the KGB's contribution.

The KGB also works closely with the International Department (ID), which for the past thirty years has been central to the the formulation and execution of Soviet foreign policy. The department is separate from the Ministry of Foreign Affairs, which provides the country's professional diplomatic service, and is one of over twenty departments of the party Central Committee, under the direction of the General Secretary and the Secretariat. With a staff of some 300, the ID serves the Politburo by reviewing and coordinating policy submissions and prepares briefs for its discussions. Its founding head, Boris Ponomarev, became a candidate member of the Politburo in 1972 and remained in charge of the department until 1986 when – at the age of 80 – he had been in the post for twenty-nine years. In the autumn of 1976, he made a controversial visit to Britain as the guest of the Labour Party, and visited other Western European countries and the USA. On the revival of the Western 'peace' movements at the end of the 1970s Ponomarev became more directly involved in the World Peace Council, and in 1979 attended the first meeting of its Presidential Commission to be held in the USA.[18]

Besides its contacts with the Politburo, the KGB and the Ministry of Foreign Affairs, the ID has developed close working relationships with the military establishment and the academic institutes which operate under the aegis of the USSR Academy of Sciences. Established in 1957, the same year as the ID, these institutes brought together economists and social scientists and specialists in particular countries or regions: the Institute of the USA and Canada, for example, which is headed by a party Central Committee member, Georgi Arbatov, a frequent broadcaster on Western media; and the Institute for the World Economy and International Relations (IMEMO). Andropov was said to take a close interest in their activity and encouraged their expansion. By 1974 the IMEMO had 572 research associates and a further 725 in connected institutes covering Africa, Latin America, the USA and Canada and the International Workers' Movement.[19]

Prominent among the ID's responsibilities from its inception were the maintenance of close links between Moscow and non-ruling Communist parties and supervision of the 'front' organisations. The rise of 'Eurocommunism' became a source of some irritation to Moscow by the mid-1970s. *Détente* was at its height – the Helsinki Final Act arising from the Conference on Security and Cooperation in Europe had been signed the previous August and a new round of SALT talks was in the offing. In this somewhat more relaxed environment, the European parties, led by the Italians, the French and the Spanish, believed that the time had come for them to assert a degree of doctrinal independence.

At a conference of forty-five European Communist parties in Berlin in June 1976, Ponomarev failed to win support for the Moscow line that progress towards socialism in Europe was due to Soviet policy and in particular to *détente*. The Soviet Union insisted that *détente* opened the way for the intensification of 'class struggle' but that its own interests could not be sacrificed to the ambitions of any Western party. The result was that the conference's final communiqué made no mention of the traditional Soviet formula of 'proletarian internationalism,' nor paid any of the usual tributes to Soviet wisdom and leadership.[20]

Problems with Western Communists contributed to a renewed emphasis on the role of the 'front' organisations. In 1977 for example, the World Peace Council served Soviet interests in a major campaign against the neutron bomb. This was followed two years later with an effort of far greater magnitude. It was prompted by the collapse of *détente* after the Soviet invasion of Afghanistan in December 1979 and the decision by NATO earlier that same month to modernise its theatre nuclear forces by deploying Cruise and Pershing missiles in Europe. In Britain, the local representatives of the fronts had for long languished in obscurity. But in 1973 the Labour Party abolished its list of proscribed organisations and the World Peace Council and the World Federation of Trade Unions began to seek out fresh support. In 1980, in reponse to the changed circumstances, the WPC's affiliate, the clumsily-titled, All-Britain Peace Liaison Group, became the British Peace Assembly, with support from Labour MPs and leading trade unionists as well as members of the much divided and ailing Communist Party. In the new-wave 'peace movement' of the 1980s, however, the supporters of the WPC had to compete with neutralists, with radical feminists, churchmen and the 'greens'.[21]

These diverse political developments added to the ID's role in opening up informal channels of communication between Soviet leaders and selected non-Communist politicians, parties and organisations in the West. To facilitate this a number of Soviet Embassies in major Western countries included an International Department representative on their staff. And as Leonard Schapiro pointed out, ID members in Soviet Embassies also performed an intelligence function, probably in conjunction with the KGB, and enjoyed 'a virtually independent status in the embassy ... in their clandestine pursuits'.[22]

Coordination of propaganda in the later Brezhnev-Andropov years was vested in a new International Information Department (IID), which was set up in 1978. Its head was a Central Committee member, and former director of the TASS news agency, Leonid Zamyatin. The establishment of the IID was the latest in a number of attempts by the Politburo to achieve greater effectiveness in the disseminaton of its propaganda message. From 1947 until his death in 1982, Mikhail Suslov held overall responsibility, as head of the Agitation and Propaganda Department, and was the Soviet Union's foremost ideologist. The short-lived Committee of Information and the Cominform contributed in their respective areas to the development of a concerted propaganda output. And in the middle of the 1960s, after the fall of Khrushchev, an Information Department was formed but appears to have lapsed by the end of the decade. Zamyatin's department suffered much the same fate as these earlier efforts. The intention was that it should coordinate material emanating from the TASS and Novosti news agencies, from major publications such as *Pravda*, and the external broadcasts of Radio Moscow and Embassy information services. But its exact duties do not seem to have been very clearly defined and in 1986 Mr Gorbachev disbanded it. Its remaining functions were absorbed by the Propaganda Department. Zamyatin, meanwhile, became the Soviet Ambassador in London.

Throughout the entire lifespan of 'détente', the Soviet Union devoted an increasing amount of resources to the development of what are known as 'active measures', in Russian 'aktivniye meropriyatiya'. There is no exact equivalent in Western terminology to describe them. 'Active measures' involve the use of overt and covert propaganda techniques to obtain political influence in non-Communist countries. They were first adopted in any systematic way at the end of the 1950s, when the Soviet leadership reviewed its 'long-range' policies and the uses of its intelligence services. But it was only during Andropov's reign that the techniques were refined and given greater priority. The vehicles for 'active measures' may be Soviet Embassies, trade, scientific and commercial organisations, official Soviet publications or broadcasts, international bodies in which the Soviet Union is represented, or individual academics and journalists, and 'front' organisations. The International Department and relevant propaganda departments each have a part to play in carrying out 'active measures'. Service A of the KGB's First Chief Directorate performs a key role in developing themes and ideas for campaigns of 'active measures', and oversees the implementation of those which entail the adoption of clandestine methods. The KGB also coordinates and directs particular operations carried out by East European intelligence agencies.

One of the main components of 'active measures' is 'disinformation', which is defined in the Soviet Shorter Political Dictionary as the 'dissemination of false and provocative information'. According to a KGB training manual which was quoted in a CIA study published in 1980:

> Strategic disinformation assists in the execution of State tasks, and is directed at misleading the enemy concerning the basic questions of State policy, the military–economic status, and the scientific–technical achievement of the Soviet Union; the policy of certain imperialist States with respect to each other and to other countries; and the specific counter-intelligence tasks of the organs of State security ....[23]

Much of the available knowledge about Soviet 'disinformation' practices comes from American sources, including reports by Congressional committees, studies and publications issued by the US government, and the work of academic specialists and former members of Soviet and East European intelligence who have defected.[24] They describe a continual flow of material from the Soviet Union and its allies intended to undermine alliances such as NATO by sowing dissension between member nations, misleading Western opinion about Soviet intentions and actions, and to discredit or weaken opponents of Soviet policy. The techniques employed range from the use of forged documents, to placing articles in selected publications, spreading rumours, and the use of agents of influence to create a more favourable environment for Soviet aims. Targets may be specific government or political circles, a particular group or minority in society, or public opinion in general. Some 'disinformation' statements or campaigns may be directly attributable to Soviet sources, while covert initiatives involving the KGB attempt to conceal the true origins of any action.

American intelligence sources state that forgeries, one of the characteristic 'disinformation' ploys, first began to appear in any quantity in the late 1950s. But they were of poor quality and readily identifiable as bogus. After a lull between 1972 and 1976, new forgeries appeared, and were executed with much greater sophistication. Altogether, according to a senior CIA officer in 1980, about 150 Soviet forgeries had been identified since the end of the war.[25] Although they are more common in Africa and Asia than in Europe, forgeries have appeared in most NATO countries at some time. One bogus US Army Field Manual appeared in more than twenty countries in the late 1970s and was quoted as evidence of American support for terrorism in Italy and elsewhere.[26] In 1980, when the revival of the 'peace' movement was beginning, a series of forged NATO documents was reportedly circulated in Britain by an unknown group, under the title 'Holocaust Again in Europe'.[27]

Sometimes 'disinformation' simply means the spreading of lies. A recent Soviet inspired campaign alleged that the AIDS virus had been created in 1977 by American scientists working on the development of new biological weapons. From a letter which appeared in an Indian newspaper in 1983, Soviet radio, newspapers, magazines and news agencies proceeded to repeat the charge. A retired East German biophysicist, Professor Jacob Segal, became the main spokesman in the campaign, and was quoted worldwide, despite rejections of his theory by scientists in both Western and Communist countries. In Britain the allegation appeared in publications as diverse as the *Sunday Express*, which interviewed Segal, and the newsletter of the British Peace Assembly.[28]

The media are of cardinal importance in the execution of 'disinformation' campaigns, not only as a means of disseminating false information, but as a channel for 'agents of influence' and as a cover for the KGB's own officers. The category of 'agent of influence', one who informs and guides a section of opinion along a desired line, is difficult to define. This is partly because, unlike espionage agents, 'agents of influence' steal no secrets, are not necessarily blackmailed or motivated by financial gain and, finally, as influence itself is not easy to measure, the effects of their work are not always visible or its genesis traceable. At the beginning of the present decade, however, two such agents who were under the undisputed direction of the KGB, were discovered.

In 1980 Pierre-Charles Pathé, a French journalist, was sentenced to five years' imprisonment for having been a Soviet agent for the previous twenty-one years. The son of the film maker, he was controlled by a succession of KGB officers attached to the Soviet Embassy in Paris or to UNESCO offices. Pathé was a well-known journalist who wrote for a range of publications, under his own name and a pseudonym. He also produced a confidential newsletter which was distributed to Embassies and French politicians and newspapers, and provided the KGB with assessments of political developments.[29] The year after the unmasking of Pathé, a Danish journalist was exposed as a Soviet 'agent of influence'. Arne Herlov Petersen had put his name to pamphlets attacking Western leaders, including in 1980 one in English entitled 'True Blues: the Thatcher that couldn't mend her own roof', the text of which was provided by his Soviet controller. He also obtained the signatures of 150 Danish artists endorsing Soviet proposals for a northern European nuclear-free zone; the petition's expenses were partly met by the Soviet Embassy. Over several years Petersen acted as a conduit for the distribution of funds to Danish 'peace' groups, circulated forgeries, and gave the KGB information on political and journalistic figures. His last controller, Vladimir Merkulov, a KGB officer at the Soviet Embassy in Copenhagen was expelled from Denmark in November 1981.[30]

Media appointments also came to represent an important cover for 'legal' KGB officers outside Embassies or trade missions. According to Ilya Dzhirkvelov, a former KGB officer and deputy secretary of the Union of Soviet Journalists, there were many countries in which the TASS offices 'were staffed entirely by KGB and GRU officers ... In countries where there are two TASS correspondents, one of them is usually a KGB or GRU officer.'[31] He claimed that Leonid Zamyatin, the then head of TASS, currently the Soviet Ambassador to Britain, 'readily handed over' TASS jobs to KGB men, including those in London and Dublin. And another former KGB officer, Stanislav Levchenko, ran 'agents of influence' and other 'active measures' campaigns in Tokyo while masquerading as a correspondent of the magazine, *New Times*. He stated that in the mid-1970s, all but two of the twelve *New Times* correspondents were KGB officers.[32]

By 1980 the US government estimated that the Soviet Union was spending some $3,363 million dollars a year on propaganda and covert activity, including $150 million by the KGB's active measures branch, Service A, and its foreign residencies. Over half the total was accounted for by Radio Moscow foreign service ($700 million), and the two news agencies, TASS ($550 million), and Novosti ($500 million).[33]

The expansion of Soviet propaganda and 'active measures' during the period of 'détente' was paralleled by a rapid growth in the regime's technological and military requirements. Military strength underpinned the whole strategy of détente: without nuclear parity and without strong conventional forces, which the Soviet Union had shown', in Angola in 1975 and in Afghanistan four years later, it was prepared to use, it could not lay claim to be a world power and challenge American supremacy.

From this position of strength détente had brought the Soviet Union several advantages: it meant a reduction in some of the historic tensions in Europe, and a consequent decrease in the dangers of nuclear war. But it had not led to any diminution of the ideology of the 'class struggle' or rivalry with the West in the Third World and, although the Soviet leadership was not prepared to risk any of its strategic gains, it expected that it would be able to push forward (as in Angola and Afghanistan), and that the 'correlation of forces' around the world would move decisively in favour of socialism in the foreseeable future.

Détente also enabled the Soviet Union to acquire from the West the very goods, technology and capital that it needed to advance militarily and economically. Like all aspects of Soviet policy, this had its covert dimension: alongside the expansion in East–West trade during the 1970s came a rise in espionage to obtain military, economic and technological data.

The collection and analysis of highly complex technical information demands special skills. Besides the KGB, which has extended its capabilities in this area, various sectors of the Soviet military–industrial establishment became involved in the total effort, as consumers and collectors. They included a host of ministries, commissions and committees which identified requirements, contributed to the task of intelligence gathering and assessed and circulated the results.

Foremost among the customers were the armed forces themselves. Throughout the 1970s defence spending consumed in the region of 13 per cent of the country's gross national product. The army's voice in policy matters increased throughout the Brezhnev period, and markedly so after 1976 when Dmitri Ustinov became Defence Minister after the death of Marshal Grechko. Soviet leaders encouraged the military to expect the fulfilment of its wishes: Andropov was no exception and when he became General Secretary in November 1982, promised to 'provide the army and navy with everything necessary'.[34]

Under General Pyotr Ivashutin, its chief since the disasters of the early 1960s, the army's own service, the GRU, re-emerged as an important element in the Soviet intelligence apparatus. It remained much smaller than the KGB: in 1976 it had an estimated 2,000 officers at its headquarters.[35] The GRU was responsible for electronic signals intelligence (sigint), for scientific and technological data with military applications and it also trained selected groups of Third World insurgents. Operations are directed through four geographical departments, one of which covers North and South America and the UK.

The extent of the Soviet Union's drive to acquire the latest technology from the West became clear as a result of an operation by French intelligence. In 1981 and 1982 the French received some 4,000 highly classified documents from an agent – known as Farewell – inside the KGB's science and technology directorate. He had access to details of the KGB's current activities in that field, the names of its officers and some of its agents, their main targets, and passed on details of the way the Soviet Union organises the business of gathering and analysing technological intelligence.[36] As a result of Farewell's information, the French government expelled forty-seven Soviet diplomats in 1983, and arrests were made in France and West Germany of scientists and engineers who had spied for the Soviet Union.

At the centre of the Soviet military–industrial complex in the early 1980s was the Commission for Military Industry (VPK) on which the the heads of twelve ministries were represented. It managed that sector of the economy and served as the processing centre for its requirements and for those of various interested ministries and commissions. The VPK worked closely with the State Commmittee for Science and Technology (GKNT), which initiated and controlled the Soviet Union's trade and commercial agreements with the industrial world. Also involved in the collection of material at this time were the Ministry of Foreign Trade and the Academy of Sciences. The fruits of intelligence were passed to various institutes and commissions for relevant industries and research projects.

It appears a highly centralised system, but according to French intelligence it functioned very effectively. Through it, in the words of a French intelligence officer, the Soviet Union had established 'a vast network ... tasked with the aggressive collection of state-of-the-art and advanced technology, all intended for use in their military industry. The Soviets have, in fact, decided to use the West as their data bank for their new technology.'[37]

In recent times the Soviet Union has explored numerous avenues to obtain the materials and the data it requires to keep in touch with the pace of 'hi-tech' progress. Up to 90 per cent of the material collected by the Soviet Union is believed to come from open sources,[38] – legitimate business operations or scientific or trade delegations, or from technical journals, conferences, and exhibitions. Western countries combine to try to prevent the export of computer and other advanced or sensitive items to Communist countries, but their controls have constantly been circumvented and whole sections of Soviet science and industry have depended on Western know-how or Western parts.

But there is much that can only be obtained illegally. And the KGB's Directorate T 'holds a unique and essential place at the centre of the organisation for obtaining scientific, technical and technological information'.[39] Its targets have included items relating to nuclear research, missile and space technology, lasers and computers. Gains made by the Soviet Union as a result of their success in obtaining secret military technology from the West, include the guidance system of the SS20 missile, the Antonov 72 transport plane, the Blackjack bomber, torpedo systems and thermal shields for inter-continental missiles.[40] For more general commercial information, the KGB has used the Soviet Chamber of Commerce and Industry, exploiting its contacts with foreign firms, and operated at trade fairs and exhibitions. According to CIA estimates, approximately one-third of the Chamber's known staff of 140 at the beginning of 1987 were KGB officers.[41]

A great deal of what is known about Soviet technological espionage and the organisation which lies behind it comes from official French and American sources, and is supplemented by evidence that has emerged from cases in other Western countries, notably West Germany.[42] Combined with the testimony from the USA and from defectors on covert propaganda, a wide-ranging, if uneven, picture emerges of the scale of clandestine Soviet activity during the Brezhnev and Andropov years. In Britain, the unevenness is more pronounced, and any examination of how the Soviet Union deployed its undoubted resources during this period raises some questions which cannot be answered.

ANDROPOV'S MISSING AGENTS

When Yuri Andropov reviewed the state of his world-wide assets after becoming head of the KGB in 1967, he must have quickly put a question mark against their recent performance in Britain. It does not appear, for instance, that they could take credit for the release from Wormwood Scrubs of George Blake in October 1966, which was carried out by an Irishman with the help of members of the anti-nuclear Committee of 100. This infamous event has attracted renewed interest following the exposure in 1987 of the identities of the two 'ban-the-bombers' concerned, Michael Randle and Pat Pottle, a former private secretary to Bertrand Russell. The claim that Blake was freed by political activists with a background of involvement in the 'peace' movement was, however, not new: in 1976, in a book about revolutionary groups in Britain, this author quoted from a now defunct, anarchist-edited magazine, which had revealed in 1973 that the spy's escape was assisted by people associated with a group called the 'Spies for Peace'. This small, loosely-knit body was set up by members of the London Committee of 100 early in 1963. Over the next three to four years they engaged in a series of protest actions. The best known of these were their raids on secret government establishments intended for use in wartime, the whereabouts of which they revealed in a widely-distributed pamphlet. The details, which included much classified material, were, interestingly, broadcast on Prague Radio in April 1963.[43]

In the first year of Andropov's rule as KGB chief, four spies were arrested in Britain and between 1968 and 1972 a further six. A month after he took charge an East German agent named Peter Dorschel was arrested after he had recruited a Scottish bookmaker, William McAffer, in an attempt to target the nuclear submarine base at Holy Loch.[44] Three months later the KGB became entangled in a diplomatic row when they tried to force a Russian physicist studying at Birmingham University to return to the Soviet Union. The man, Vladimir Kachenko, was pursued by car, and bundled by the KGB aboard an aircraft which was surrounded by police cars on the runway at Heathrow Airport. But, after being removed and examined by British doctors, he decided after all that he wanted to return to Moscow and was allowed to leave.[45]

The KGB's embarrassments continued in 1968. In May two members of a Soviet trade delegation were expelled after they were arrested by police outside the MI5's garage in Battersea, complete with cameras and wireless receivers. Three months after that, a Royal Navy able seaman, Robin Cloude was sentenced to five years in prison for trying to sell information to the Soviet Naval Attaché. And in September 1968 the RAF chief technician, Douglas Britten was arrested after six years of spying, while his controller, Aleksandr Boriskenko, a First Secretary at the Soviet Embassy, promptly left the country.[46] The McAffer, Cloude and Britten cases confirmed continuing Soviet interest in military matters and they were followed by the allegations from the succession of Czech defectors concerning widespread spying and subversion earlier in the decade.

One of the British responses to the wave of incidents and arrests was to limit the size of the Soviet Embassy in London to eighty diplomats. But the numbers of Russians in trade and other bodies outside the Embassy continued to grow. The total more than doubled between 1960 and 1970, during which time the British had expelled twenty-seven Soviet officials and refused visas to another forty. By 1971 there were approximately 550 Soviet representatives in Britain, 300 more than in 1960 and more than in any other Western country, including the USA; of those some 280 had diplomatic status.[47] The Conservative government which came to power in June 1970 was determined to address the problem of espionage presented by such large numbers, and to redress the imbalance with the much smaller British representation in the Soviet Union – there were about forty British diplomats in Moscow. The Foreign Secretary, Sir Alec Douglas Home, raised the issue with his Soviet counterpart, Mr Gromyko, when he visited London in October 1970 and by letter at the beginning of December, but to no avail.

Matters came to a head in August 1971 when Oleg Lyalin, ostensibly a member of the Trade Delegation, was arrested for drunken driving. He was, however, an officer of the KGB's Section V, which specialised in sabotage and assassination and for several months had been passing information to British counter-intelligence.[48] He gave details of Soviet plans to disrupt communications, military installations and essential services in the event of war, and revealed the names of KGB officers in London as well as some of their agents. Rather than face punishment in Moscow, the 34-year-old Lyalin decided to defect. The repercussions were immediate and worldwide. Section V officers were recalled from their posts and their department reorganised. On 24 September 1971, three and a half weeks after Lyalin's arrest, the British instigated the largest purge of a Soviet mission ever carried out by a Western government.

A total of some 90 officials were expelled from Britain and the readmission of another fifteen who were out of the country at the time was refused. No replacements were allowed for the expellees and a new ceiling of 445 was put on the total of Soviet representatives permitted in Britain at any one time. Approximately half of those ordered out were diplomats on the staff of the Embassy, and this included seven of the eleven officers at the senior rank of Counsellor. Among the others were members of the Trade Delegation and Soviet companies in Britain, such as the Moscow Narodny Bank, UMO Plant, dealing in construction plant hire, and the Soviet Film Agency. Only one of the ten service attachés at the Embassy was told to leave. He was Captain (Second Class) Lory Kuzmin, an Assistant Naval Attaché, who had run a spy in the Royal Navy, Sub-Lieutentant David Bingham, since early 1970. Shortly after the expulsions, Bingham voluntarily confessed and in March 1972 was sentenced to twenty-one years' imprisonment.

Bingham's admission of guilt was folowed by another, that of Leonard Hinchcliffe, a diplomatic service administrator. He had been blackmailed into giving information to a Soviet agent while stationed in Khartoum, as a result of a relationship he had formed with the wife of a colleague – the latest in the long series of British government servants compromised and recruited by Soviet intelligence while serving abroad. He received a ten year sentence.[49] Several other cases resulted from Lyalin's evidence. They included two Greek tailors in London, Kyriacos Costi and his brother-in-law, Costantinos Martianou, who had been recruited by the KGB in 1961 when they were both members of the Young Communist League, and the son of a Malayan lawyer, Sirioj Abdoolcader. Abdoolcader worked as a clerk in the motor licensing department of the Greater London Council and had given Lyalin the numbers of Special Branch and MI5 vehicles.[50]

The expulsions and subsequent arrests came as a serious blow to the operations of the KGB in Britain, but they did not end them completely. And any damage to the prestige of Andropov's intelligence service or to the international standing of the Soviet Union generally was short-lived. The additional resources of the East European and Cuban Embassies in London remained available, with over 100 diplomats between them. The Czechs, however, suffered further problems at the end of 1973, when Pavel Siska, a personal assistant to the Czech Ambassador in London, defected. In the next three months the Ambassador, Dr Miroslav Zemya, was recalled to Prague and at least seven out of eighteen Czech diplomats returned home.[51]

Throughout this whole period the Soviet Union's main agent in Britain continued his activity, undisturbed. Geoffrey Prime offered his services to Soviet intelligence in January 1968, at the age of 29, when he was stationed in Berlin with the RAF. Later in the year he resigned from the air force and joined the signals intelligence department, the Government Communications Headquarters (GCHQ). He worked at the GCHQ for nine years, in London and at its base in Cheltenham. The material that Prime was able to hand on to his Soviet controllers on developments such as the American 'Rhyolite' reconnaissance satellite made him one of the more significant spies of the technological age.[52] After leaving the GCHQ in 1977 he found work as a taxi driver and wine salesman, but twice met KGB officers, in Vienna and in April 1980 in East Berlin. His arrest in 1982 only came about as a result of local police enquiries into assaults on young girls. When he admitted to the espionage offences he was tried and was gaoled for thirty-five years, the longest prison term for a Soviet spy since the Blake case.

Prime's career as a spy spanned almost the entire duration of Andropov's fifteen years as chairman of the KGB. He was one of only three agents identified to date, who were recruited in Britain during that time, from the middle of 1967 to mid-1982. The others were Cloude, who was active for a matter of a few months, and Bingham. All the other cases which came to light during that time had their origins before May 1967. No case has yet become public of any British subject who was recruited by Soviet intelligence or any of its allies between 1970 and the summer of 1982. Then, a 19-year-old Lance Corporal in the Intelligence Corps, Philip Aldridge, offered secret documents to the Russians.[53] But by that time Andropov had ceased to be in charge of the KGB.

There are a number of explanations for this possible dearth of spies. One is that none has been discovered because there weren't any. In the light of all that happened in the previous half century, it would seem improbable that the Soviet Union had suddenly abandoned Britain as a target for espionage, or given up its searches for willing or exploitable individuals. It was true that the USA, West Germany, NATO establishments on the continent, and to an extent, France and Japan, were regarded as more important, and were more vulnerable, in the 1970s. But even allowing for some slippage in the KGB's league table of countries to be penetrated, Britain still ranked in the top half-dozen. If, however, agents were found by the KGB during that period, some of them are probably still active, up to twenty years later. In the absence of more cases, one could conclude that either Andropov was the least successful of all Soviet secret service heads in planting his agents in Britain, or he was one of the supreme spymasters of all.

Evidence that has recently come to light of a Czech operation suggests that Eastern bloc intelligence services may have reverted to the use of 'illegal' operatives after the reduction in the early 1970s of the number of posts available to them under diplomatic cover. In March 1989 a man known as Erwin van Haarlem was sentenced to ten years' imprisonment for offences under the Official Secrets Acts. Supposedly born in Holland in 1944, 'van Haarlem' was a highly trained Czech intelligence officer who had been in Britain since 1975 – less than two years after the cuts in Czech representation in London, and four years following the mass expulsions of Soviet officials. The extent of his spying is not yet known but, according to reports of his trial (see for example *The Times*, 28 February and 4 March 1989), it involved infiltrating the Jewish community in Britain and gathering information about British interests concerned in research for the 'Star Wars' project.

Another explanation is that given the changes in method Andropov instituted, Soviet aims were being accomplished not only by conventional espionage, but in covert propaganda and 'influence' operations and in the gathering of technological data through means that fell short of actual spying. If that were so, then, as in the past, British counter-measures have lagged behind current Soviet practice.

The prospects for the 'legal' KGB controllers at the Embassy in Kensington Palace Gardens or the Trade Delegation in Highgate were certainly more limited after 1971. Their position was made worse in 1985 with the defection of Oleg Gordievsky, the KGB's London Resident for the previous three years, and an agent of the British Secret Intelligence Service since 1971. Gordievsky identified the MI5 officer, Michael Bettaney, who in 1983 wrote to a KGB man at the Soviet Embassy with top secret information about the workings of British counter-intelligence and its assessment of KGB and GRU operations in Britain. Bettaney was imprisoned for twenty-three years and the KGB officer he contacted, a First Secretary named Arkadi Gouk, was told to leave the country.[54]

Information from Gordievsky also contributed to a fresh round of multiple expulsions of Soviet officials. Between 1981 and 1985 a further forty-five were removed, including thirty in September 1985 alone. They included diplomats, service attachés, embassy ancillary staff, members of the Trade Delegation and commercial companies, staff attached to international organisations and media correspondents.[55] New limits were set by the British government for the numbers of diplomats and other officials: by 1985 the Soviet Union was allowed only thirty-nine diplomats in Britain, to be counted among a total of 205 for all officials.[56] British action was paralleled in many Western countries. In the four years 1982–5, 160 Russians were expelled by Western European governments, including the forty-seven told to leave France by President Mitterrand in 1983. This compared with 163 for the whole of the years 1970–80, which also included the 105 from Britain.[57]

Overall around a half of those declared *persona non grata* in Britain after 1971 were connected with trading activities, either through the Trade Delegation or individual Soviet-owned firms. From the late 1960s onwards the Soviet and East European trading presence had grown enormously. According to a recent academic study, by 1979 there were eight Soviet companies established in the country, fourteen Polish, eleven East German, ten Czech, five Hungarian, four Rumanian and four Bulgarian.[58] Over two-thirds of them had been set up since the 1960s.

Between them they covered the full breadth of business and financial activity, ranging from banking, reinsurance, transport, and shipping, to travel agencies, textiles and clothing, food, chemicals, and general import and export firms. Most were engaged in servicing or marketing activity, or acted as purchasing agents for their domestic industries. Some of these concerns, mainly the Soviet, East German and Czech ones were wholly owned by their respective governments, while some of the others were set up on a joint basis with Western interests. All, however, are directed by their appropriate Ministries of Foreign Trade. The turnover for thirty-four companies on whom information was available in 1980 was £1.13 billion. Besides these companies, the Soviet Union was able to send inspectors to British firms following a trade agreement with the Labour government in 1975. Within five years there were some 65 Soviet inspectors in Britain, attached to firms such as Rolls Royce, Ferranti, International Computers, Swan Hunter and Vickers.[59]

What proportion of these companies' time and effort is devoted to the conduct of normal business and how much to gathering information, either openly or by other means, is impossible to judge. Their relatively recent expansion offers an additional resource to that of the Trade Delegation, whose record of participation in clandestine activities goes back seventy years. Some of the academic business specialists are sceptical of the extent to which the operating companies themselves are used for espionage.[60] But of those in Britain, staff of the Moscow Narodny Bank, Razno, which markets consumer goods, Anglo Soviet Shipping and Trade Delegation members employed by the parent companies of UMO Plant, together with a manager of the airline, Aeroflot, were among the officials expelled in 1985.

It is even more difficult to assess the degree of Soviet involvement in covert propaganda and 'agent of influence' operations in Britain. The period of their expansion under Andropov coincided with a time of considerable political and social conflict throughout the UK. If Soviet objectives embraced the weakening of capitalism, the NATO alliance or the fabric of Western society generally, existing problems such as industrial unrest, urban violence, and mass 'peace' protests, combined with the polarisation of party politics and the existence of a left-wing intelligentsia might have offered some useful levers, and some worthwhile points of weakness to probe. But as the Soviet Union had learned in its infancy, the exploitation of local discontents and indigenous left-wing movements is less easy to accomplish in practice inside sophisticated Western countries than it appears in a theoretical tract or a strategic master plan.

With those qualifications in mind, the Soviet Union's interest in the affairs of Northern Ireland may serve as a case in point. Soviet sympathy for Irish republicanism can be traced back to the days of Lenin, and to a proposed treaty between the Bolsheviks and the Irish Republic, which involved the supplying of rifles to the IRA.[61] More recently, according to the former Czech General, Jan Sejna, an IRA delegation visited Czechoslovakia in 1963 and, with Soviet approval were given £60,000 in cash, weapons and ammunition, and IRA members subsequently received military and political training.[62]

Throughout the past twenty years of unrest in Ireland, Soviet propaganda has constantly portrayed the British as an occupying, imperialist power while lending its support to 'progressive' republicanism. One of the earliest signs that its interest might assume more active forms came in October 1971 when the Dutch authorities intercepted a large shipment of arms at Amsterdam's Schipol Airport. The weapons had been bought by two IRA members from Omnipol, a Czech trading company with intelligence connections.[63] From that time onwards there were numerous reports of Soviet, East European or Cuban training for IRA terrorists and the provision of weapons. Towards the end of 1971 the Soviet Union secured the upgrading of its mission in Dublin to full embassy status, and augmented its staff with an influx of intelligence officers. In December 1975 the Dublin correspondent of TASS, Vladimir Kozlov, was identified as a member of the KGB's assassination and sabotage department and expelled. Ilya Dzhirkvelov, the former KGB man and Soviet journalist, has also stated that Dublin was one of the stations where TASS offices were entirely given over to KGB and GRU officers.[64] During 1981 a Russian journalist named Boris Shtern claimed that while working on an assignment ten years earlier he had witnessed the transfer of cargo from a Soviet trawler onto two smaller vessels off the Irish coast. Shtern believed the cargo may have been arms and ammunition.[65] And also in 1981, Viktor Lazin, the first Soviet diplomat to be expelled from Britain for ten years, was believed to have had contacts with the IRA.[66]

The experience of the past two decades suggests that the Soviet Union has found secret operations in Britain less easy than in earlier periods. But it also indicates that Soviet sponsored covert activity became broader in scope during this time, extending from the acquisition of state secrets and military espionage to a massively resourced, but less easily defined, battery of 'active measures' and the collection of technological and commercial data.

Under Yuri Andropov, the KGB enhanced its status in Soviet society and it became a major force in policy-making. Its members formed an educated elite at the heart of the Soviet system, honoured as 'Chekisty', after the secret police of the revolution, and as the 'Sword and Shield of the Party', a force which had learned to contain dissent without mass repression. Andropov's achievements were confirmed when, in 1982, he first took charge of ideology and propaganda after the death of Suslov and then, in November became party General Secretary in succession to Brezhnev. But his victory was short-lived. *Détente* had collapsed and a new 'cold war' was taking shape. The Soviet economy was faltering and corruption was rife. Andropov began to tackle some of the enormous problems but within two years he too was dead. After a brief and regressive interlude under Konstantin Chernenko, an era of radical reappraisal beckoned, complete with its own uncertanties and enigmas.

8 A New Beginning?

The policies of Mikhail Gorbachev raise a multitude of questions for the Soviet Union and the world. They embrace every aspect of Soviet affairs, the country's economic performance, its constitution,and its defence and foreign policies. For the KGB and all the associated elements of the intelligence and 'active measures' apparatus, the impact of the present changes is no less real than it is for other parts of the bureaucracy. At some future stage the evolution of a less closed society could weaken the assumptions and the traditions on which the KGB's power is built. Equally, an increased Soviet demand for the technology that is so vital to its rapid economic development, coupled with a greater efficiency, could bring about the further refinement and sharpening of its intelligence effort. A less restrictive internal regime does not preclude the existence, and the use, of a more assertive organisation for external operations.

No final verdict can yet be returned on any part of the Gorbachev experiment. The programmes of 'glasnost' and 'perestroika' which Mikhail Gorbachev has launched since he became General Secretary in March 1985 are treading in uncharted territory, beyond the limited reforms carried out by Khrushchev, or the New Economic Policy and the intra-party debates of Lenin's day. The legacy of centuries of despotism and totalitarianism hangs heavily over attempts to devolve responsibility, in workplaces or in the local Soviets. The bureaucrats, military officers and managers whose status depends on maintaining the old ways are not confined to a few faces on, or off, the Politburo. Their resistance or even inertia can undermine the entire strategy. Added to this, developments in the Baltic states, Armenia and elsewhere, point to an increase in the burdens and strains of holding together a land empire, as national minorities develop an appetite for greater freedom. And the inefficiencies of a centralised economy have repaid the hopes of the masses with a further fall in living standards.

Abroad, few modern leaders have made such an immediate impression on world affairs as Gorbachev. In the first steps towards nuclear disarmament taken with President Reagan: the destruction of chemical weapon stocks, withdrawal from Afghanistan, and the scaling down of Soviet ground forces in East Europe, new terms are being set for great power relationships. But it is premature to pronounce the cold war dead. Although active hostility between East and West may be diminishing, to the benefit of everyone, that does not mean the end of all distinction between socialist and capitalist systems, nor of the continuation of a certain rivalry between them. If the cold war is fading, it is because Soviet style socialism has failed to satisfy human wants and aspirations and because its expansion has been resisted. But if President Gorbachev were to succeed in reviving the fortunes of socialism, the ideological competition between communism and capitalism could revive also.

As commentators have often remarked, for all his radicalism President Gorbachev is no closet liberal, edging, even ever so slowly, towards the installation of Western-style democracy and the breaking down of all barriers. He is a Marxist and a Leninist, who can, when the occasion demands, turn on the anti-capitalist rhetoric, and not only to keep his conservative sceptics happy. For President Gorbachev, Leninism may signify toleration of debate and discussion, within the confines of the Communist Party, and denote a willingness to permit economic flexibility. It is also a symbolic means for him to renounce the repression of the Stalin era and the stagnation and corruption associated with Brezhnev. But for the West there are other ingredients of Leninism which are less welcome; in Western eyes, Leninism stands for revolution, and its spread across the world.

Like all new Soviet leaders President Gorbachev has made as many changes as politically possible in the composition of the Politburo, the Central Committee, and in key party and ministerial posts in the republics as well as at the centre. These reached their peak at the end of September 1988 when Gorbachev became President in place of Gromyko, who was also removed from the Politburo, picked a new KGB chief, demoted several of his opponents, set up six Central Committee commissions, and promised elections in 1989 for a new Congress of Deputies. At that point, nine of the twelve-member Politburo could be described as supporters of reform, with three generally described as 'hard-liners', who opposed the pace and style of change, if not the substance.

Before these dramatic moves, numerous steps over the previous three-and-a-half years had brought fresh faces to the fore. Many of them affected the conduct of Soviet policy abroad and its intelligence agencies. At the top, the veteran Andrei Gromyko had been earlier succeeded by Eduard Shevardnadze, the former head of the Georgian MVD, as Foreign Minister. The party International Department has undergone some reorganisation since the removal in 1986 of the octogenarian Ponomarev in favour of Anatoli Dobrynin, the long-serving Ambassador to the United States. Continuity was maintained through Vadim Zagladin, a Western specialist and former Brezhnev speechwriter, who retained the post of first deputy head in the department which he had held since 1975. Also in 1986 the International Information Department was wound up and its functions for the coordination of information transferred to the Propaganda and Agitation Department, which was itself placed under new direction. The new head of propaganda was the 60-year-old former Ambassador to Canada, Alexandr Yakovlev. Early in 1987 the World Peace Council was restructured with the installation of a Finnish Communist as General Secretary and the strengthening of the Council's secretariat, and the presidential committee. A Novosti journalist, Genrikh Bovorik, was made President of the Soviet Peace Committee. In his late fifties Bovorik had earlier worked for the KGB and is the brother-in-law of the new head of the KGB, Vladimir Kryuchkov.[1]

At first the KGB prospered under Gorbachev. He had been an ally of Yuri Andropov, and supported his attack on corruption and mismanagement. In return, Andropov had furthered Gorbachev's career. The result was that within a year of Gorbachev coming to power, all fourteen Soviet republics included the local KGB chairman on their equivalent of the Politburo, compared with only seven before.[2]

But any hopes that the chairman of the KGB, Viktor Chebrikov, may have entertained about the enlargement of his own personal power were short-lived. In the changes of September 1988 he was placed in charge of a new Central Committee department for legal policy. His successor as chairman of state security was Vladimir Kryuchkov, a lawyer by training, and a KGB man of over twenty years' experience. Aged 64, he had been head of the First Chief Directorate, responsible for espionage abroad and disinformation, for over ten years and ranked as one of the KGB's four deputy heads. Unlike Chebrikov, and indeed Andropov who promoted him, the new KGB Chairman was at the time of his appointment only a member of the several hundred-strong Central Committee and not the Politburo.

This may signify some reduction in the influence of the KGB, but on the basis of recent reports there are no indications of any curtailing of espionage and other hostile measures against the West. In March 1988 six alleged Soviet agents were arrested in West Germany for passing on secret documents about the Tornado and Jaguar 90 aircraft to the KGB.[3] In June the Canadian government expelled seventeen Soviet diplomats, who were, according to the Canadian External Affairs Minister, 'engaged in a wide-ranging espionage operation which sought to obtain classified information for commercial and miltary purposes'.[4] The spies had also attempted to penetrate the Canadian Security Intelligence Service and the Royal Canadian Mounted Police.

Nor have satellite intelligence agencies in Eastern Europe relaxed their efforts. In August 1988 a Hungarian spy ring was uncovered in West Germany and Sweden. NATO secrets obtained from US servicemen in Germany were passed to Hungarian agents through couriers based in Gothenburg. Eight people were arrested, including a retired US army sergeant and two Hungarian-born brothers, both physicians, who emigrated to Sweden in the 1960s. Reports at the time described it as 'one of the most successful Eastern bloc spy rings of modern times'.[5] The following month three Czech diplomats, believed to be members of military intelligence, were expelled from Britain.[6]

It comes as little surprise therefore that Western governments remain unconvinced of any significant shift in the Soviets' use of covert methods. In the spring of 1988 a strongly-worded report by the US Information Service, on active measures in the era of glasnost, noted that at least twelve major Soviet disinformation campaigns were proceeding, including the story that the AIDS virus was manufactured by American military scientists, and allegations that the CIA had carried out a series of assassinations, including those of the Swedish Premier, Olaf Palme, Mrs Ghandi, Samora Machel of Mozambique, and the attempt on the life of the Pope. The report also argued that the propaganda of the Soviet Peace Council had become more subtle, and was calculated to reinforce Western assumptions about the improvement of Soviet behaviour under Gorbachev, and the reasonableness of its peace proposals which might appeal to a wide audience in Western countries.[7]

The West has also renewed its endeavours to enforce bans on the export of certain computer items to Communist countries. In November 1987, in one of a number of cases, a British businessman was sentenced for selling computer equipment to the Bulgarian State Procurement Agency for use in Bulgaria, Poland and Czechoslovakia in defiance of export controls.[8] Twelve months later the Minister of State at the British Foreign Office, Mr William Waldegrave, told the House of Commons Select Committee on Foreign Affairs that 'there is no evidence of a diminution in covert activities of a traditional kind by the KGB abroad. There is some evidence of an increased drive to steal other people's technology.'[9]

For over seventy years East and West have been locked in ideological conflict, reinforced since the war by military confrontation and economic rivalry. One of the most intense manifestations of that shared hostility has been the relentless struggle between secret services. From the Soviet side the use of covert agencies has assumed new significance, for the present day KGB represents not merely an executive tool for the use of policy-makers but is a central pillar of the Soviet system, in domestic and foreign affairs. The values of the Committee of State Security today are those of Dzerzhinsky's Chekists in 1917 and are the bedrock of Soviet communism, as Yuri Andropov was fond of reminding his audiences. The KGB is therefore not just an intelligence service but a political institution and a power in its own right.

Likewise, the totality of covert Soviet activity abroad has extended beyond espionage to embrace a range of clandestine activities with political objectives. In pursuit of clearly understood goals, secret Soviet enterprises in the West have continually adapted to changing cicumstances. In the initial post-revolutionary fervour, illicit methods were employed to finance and prepare Western countries for their own upheavals. It rarely worked as Moscow envisaged, and as the Soviet state began to reach out for trade and diplomatic recognition, its missions became vehicles for spying and more specifically targeted subversion. This continued, wherever it was practical throughout the 1920s and 1930s, including in Britain following the resumption of relations after the breach of 1927. But the pre-war years saw the development of new techniques, the use of 'illegal' officers to seek out and persuade young intelligentsia to devote their lives in secret to the cause of world fraternity. The sequel was the infiltration of the heart of government, during the wartime alliance and afterwards. When ideological appeal was not enough, the Soviet Union fed its growing appetite for Western military and technological data by securing agents and information through blackmail and exploiting personal weakness. And it used its secret agencies, too, in the political and propaganda dimensions of the East–West struggle to a degree and with effects that remain still unknown.

These are the phases through which secret Soviet activity in Britain has passed. Its experience has been shared to greater or lesser extent by all the Western countries. Indeed present day operations against Britain are just one strand of the total Soviet strategy for the whole of NATO and other democratic countries around the world.

It would be foolish to expect any major nation to concede the right to spy on other states. That is part of international affairs. To that extent, the KGB will continue to mount offensives for the gathering of economically and militarily desirable intelligence. And if President Gorbachev's drive for reform moves into a higher gear the role of the KGB may increase. A more efficient KGB in pursuit of greater amounts of technological and industrial intelligence will make for a keener, rather than a less menacing adversary. As the guardian of the party and the revolutionary spirit, it will also no doubt find ways of accommodating itself to his revolution as it has done to those of the past. But the Soviet Union is coming to terms, politically and psychologically, with the grim legacies of its own history. If President Gorbachev wishes to present the Soviet Union in a new light to the world, he must surely recognise that crimes and errors have been committed, too, in Soviet dealings with other states. However, these are not confined to the past. It remains to be seen whether he can open an era of complete trust and confidence betwen the Communist and non-Communist world, which would involve the repudiation of those aspects of Soviet behaviour represented by the modern-day KGB with its paraphernalia of 'active measures', so accurately characterised by the British goverment, nearly seventy years ago, as 'hostile action'.

Appendix I: Soviet Security and Intelligence Organisations

CHEKA or VCHEKA (Vserossiiskaia Chrezvychainaia Komissiia po borbe s kontrrevoliutsiei i sabotazhem)

All-Russian Extraordinary Commission for Combating Counter-Revolution and Sabotage

Duration: December 1917 – February 1922

Chairman: Felix Dzerzhinsky

GPU (Gosudarstvennoe Politicheskoe Upravlenie)

State Political Administration

Duration: February 1922 – July 1923

Chairman: Felix Dzerzhinsky

OGPU (Obedinennoe Gosudarstvennoe Politicheskoe Upravlenie)

Unified State Political Administration

Duration: July 1923 – July 1934

Chairmen: Felix Dzerzhinsky (1923–6)
Vyacheslav Menzhinsky (1926–34)
Genrikh Yagoda (1934)

NKVD (Narodny Komissariat Vnutrennik Del)

People's Commissariat for Internal Affairs

Duration: July 1934 – March 1946

Chairmen: Genrikh Yagoda (1934–6)
Nikolai Yezhov (1936–8)
Lavrenti Beria (1938–45)
Sergei Kruglov (1945–6)

NKGB (Narodny Kommissariat Gosudarstvennoe Bezopasnosti)

People's Commissariat for State Security

Duration: February 1941 – June 1941 and April 1943 – March 1946
    (detached from NKVD)

Chairman: Vsevolod Merkulov

MVD (Ministerstvo Vnutennikh Del)

Ministry of Internal Affairs

Duration: March 1946 – March 1954

Chairmen: Sergei Kruglov (1946–53 and 1953–4)
         Lavrenti Beria (1953)

MGB (Ministerstvo Gosudarstvennoe Bezopasnosti)

Ministry for State Security

Duration: March 1946 – March 1953 then merged with MVD

Chairmen: Vsevolod Merkulov (1946)
         Viktor Abakumov (1946–51)
         Semen Ignatiev (1951–3)

KI (Komitet Informatsii)

Committee for Information

Duration: 1947–51, then abolished

Chairmen: Vyacheslav Molotov
         Valerian Zorian
         Andrei Vyshinsky

KGB (Komitet Gosudarstvennoe Bezopasnosti)

Committee for State Security

Duration: March 1954 – present

Chairmen: Ivan Serov (1954–8)
         Alexandr Shelepin (1958–61)
         Vladimir Semichastny (1961–7)
         Yuri Andropov (1967–82)
         Vitali Fedorchuk (1982)

Viktor Chebrikov (1982–8)
Vladimir Kryuchkov (1988–)

GRU (Glavnoe Razvedyvatelnoe Upravlenie)

Chief Intelligence Directorate (of the Soviet General Staff)

Duration: 1918 – present

Heads include: Jan Berzin (1924–35)
Solomon Uritsky (1935–7)
Ivan Proskurov (1938–40)
Filipp Golikov (1940–1)
Alexi Panfilov (1941–2)
Fedor Kuznetsov (1943–6)
Sergei Shtemyenko (1946–9)
Vladimir Kurasov (1949–51)
Miikhail Shalin (1951–6 and 1957–8)
Ivan Serov (1958–62)
Pyotr Ivashutin (1963–)

Appendix II: An MI5 Report on the Communist Party

The report was prepared in the autumn of 1941 by MI5 for submission to the War Cabinet through the Security Executive and the Home Secretary. Among the MI5 officers involved in its preparation was Roger Hollis. The paper is discussed in Chapter 4.

SECRET
THE COMMUNIST PARTY OF GREAT BRITAIN

Policy and Tactics

1. A careful study of the history of the Communist movement both here and abroad shows that, whatever surface changes there may be in tactics, the fundamental concept which never changes is the revolutionary overthrow of capitalism. This is one of the basic themes of all Communist classics from Marx onwards. Stalin himself in his book on Leninism, the most recent edition of which appeared since the outbreak of the present war, quotes Lenin's own words: 'The liberation of the oppressed class is impossible, not only without a violent revolution, but also without the destruction of the apparatus of State power which was created by the ruling class.' So long as this remains an axiom in Communist teaching, it is clear that the Third International, to which the Communist Party of Great Britain is affiliated, cannot exist without this revolutionary aim.

2. The surface changes in tactics are nevertheless such – particularly in a time of 'Popular Front' like the present – that it is easy to lose sight of the underlying continuity of plan. It is, therefore, of the utmost importance that the Government should be in a position to appraise rightly the policy, aims and methods of the Communist Party now and in the future.

Changing methods
3. In the twenty-two years of its existence the Third International

178

has employed various means of approaching its goal of revolution. Its two main methods have been to attack from outside when the Party has been in open opposition to all established authority, and to penetrate from within in times when Popular Front tactics have been in operation. These lines of approach have been laid down by Moscow from time to time and have in general been universal directions applying to all national Communist Parties affiliated to the Third International. A very obvious example of this was the speech of Dimitrov at the 7th World Congress of the Communist International held in Moscow in 1935 at which he launched the programme of the Popular Front. The Popular Front campaign failed to prosper in this country and consequently five leading members of the Communist Party of Great Britain – Pollitt, Dutt, Gallacher, Kerrigan and Stewart – were summoned to Moscow in August 1937, where the Party's methods were thoroughly overhauled. In addition to this comparatively open control of the broad lines of policy, information from most secret sources has revealed, during the periods in which it has been available, the complete subservience of the Communist Party of Great Britain to Moscow even in matters of merely domestic importance.

Britain at War

The outbreak of war
4.   The Communist Party had represented itself for so long as the only consistent opponent of Fascism that it was not surprising that Harry Pollitt and the Party generally should have been carried away into support of the war against Germany when it broke out in September 1939. Even so the Party's opposition to the Chamberlain Government had been so strong that it was felt necessary to qualify this support, and the Party declared that they were fighting a war on two fronts – against Hitler abroad and against the 'pro-Fascist Chamberlain Government' at home.

Comintern instructions
5.   The Executive Committee of the Communist International Moscow saw the fallacy of this line, and both Dimitrov, the Secretary General, and André Marty, a member of the Executive, laid down the correct procedure to a leading member of the British Communist Party who happened to be in Moscow at the time. These verbal instructions were followed by peremptory written orders from Moscow to the British Party, copies of which have come into the possession of the investigating authorities. These instructions reached the Communist

Party in this country in the last days of September 1939, and read in part: 'The present war is an imperialist and unjust war for which the bourgeoisie of all the belligerent states bear equal responsibility. In no country can the working class or the Communist Party support the war ... The Communist Parties which acted contrary to these tactics must now immediately correct their policy.'

6.   As a result of these instructions, the British Communist Party made its first volte-face, and issued on 7 October a new Manifesto saying that its original appreciation of the war had been entirely wrong. From that moment the Party followed the policy of revolutionary defeatism, which by Lenin's definition carried with it the duty that every revolutionary party of the working class in all the belligerent countries should work for the defeat of its own imperialist Government. The aim of this policy was so to weaken each 'imperialist' government that it would be faced with the alternatives of accepting defeat at the hands of its 'imperialist' opponent, or resigning and handing over power to a 'Workers' Government', which in the Communist view would be synonymous with the Communist Party.

Attack on government
7.   The technique followed by the Communist Party here was to launch a general attack upon the Government, and all authority through all papers – such as the *Daily Worker, World News & Views, Challenge, The Labour Monthly, The New Propellor*, etc. – under its control. Pamphlets and leaflets were directed to the same purpose, as were the addresses of Party speakers whose material is regularly supplied to them from Party headquarters in the form of speakers' notes. These attacks were maintained just as actively against the present National Government as against its predecessor.

Industrial unrest
8.   This general campaign was designed to spread dissatisfaction and distrust of the Government, and served as a basis for the more direct attack upon production in the factories. Here the Party representatives within the Trade Unions set themselves up as the champions of the workers' rights, which had been won after years of struggle, and were about to be betrayed by Trade Union leaders, who had sold themselves to the Government. In effect this policy resulted in the opposition to every attempt to increase production by working overtime, by dilution, or procedure. Every petty grievance was magnified into a major wrong, and every attempt at conciliation was opposed. One Party leader even

stated that there was not a factory in which there was no grievance and there was not a grievance which could not be turned into a strike.

Shop stewards
9. The Communist Party had realised for a number of years that the most effective method of penetrating industry was through the Shop Stewards. The Party, therefore, set out to establish its industrial members as Shop Stewards, and as a result the Communist representation among Shop Stewards is out of all proportion to the total number of Communists in industry. In order to make full use of its hold upon the Shop Stewards movement the Communist Party formed a body named the Engineering and Allied Trades Shop Stewards National Council, which is entirely under Communist control, the chief organiser being a prominent Party member, Peter Zinkin, who is also editor of the Council's paper, the *New Propellor*. This Shop Stewards National Council directs not only the Party members but many other extremists amongst Shop Stewards in industry. Through this body the Party has created for the Shop Stewards a new function as leaders of the rank and file of Trade Unionists in matters outside the immediate problems of their shop, and in this way hopes to bring it about that Trade Union members will look for leadership to the Shop Stewards, and thus to the Communist Party, and not to the Trade Union leaders. This policy of 'dual unionism' is designed in effect to establish a parasite political union within the present Trade Union structure.

Exploitation of grievances
10. Though much of the Party's energy was devoted to making trouble in industry, it was also prepared to exploit any other grievance, which would meet with popular support. It was with this aim in view that the Party started its campaigns for deep shelters, increased pensions, equal food distribution, better army pay, and in particular, the mischievous campaign against the use of soldiers for clearing away air raid debris. In this instance the Party represented that the soldiers, many of whom were good Trade Unionists, were acting as blacklegs and were robbing their fellow Trade Unionists of their proper work and their proper wages. They also put forward a demand to 'arm the workers in the factories', which was probably designed to encourage class bitterness by luring the Government into some hasty statement that the workers could not be trusted with arms.

Subsidiary bodies
11. The technique of penetration carried on in industry through the

Engineering and Allied Trades Shop Stewards National Council has long been practised by the Communist Party in other spheres. They have established secret groups of Party members among journalists and such other professional workers as doctors and lawyers, and they have set up or gained control of a number of bodies which operate without any direct connection with the Communist Party. Such bodies established by the Party include the Labour Research Department, the Russia Today Society, the Society for Cultural Relations with the Soviet Union, and Tenants' Defence Leagues, Peoples Vigilance Committees, ARP Coordinating Committees and Shelter Committees, which have sprung up with Communist encouragement all over the country. Party members have also been urged to obtain positions upon such bodies as Trades Councils, while professional members have established groups in the Haldane Society, on the legal side, and have obtained a measure of control of such bodies as the Association of Architects, Surveyors and Technical Assistants. Many of those who have followed the lead of the Communist Party in these bodies are not themselves Party members and would certainly not subscribe to the full revolutionary programme of the Party. They are, nevertheless, sympathetic towards various items in the Party's programme and are regarded by the Party not only as possible recruits, but as a protective cover if the Government should move against the Party. The Peoples' Convention, held in January 1941, is the greatest example of the organisation of support for the Communist Party largely from non-Party sources.

Russia at war

A 'people's war'
12.   The attack by Hitler upon the Soviet Union found the Communist Party of Great Britain unprepared. The inclination of the leaders at first was to see in this new aggression the consequence of the Hess visit, and to prophesy that the British Government would 'switch the war' and join with Hitler in the attack upon the Soviet Union. Mr Churchill's promise of aid for the Soviet Union gave these leaders cause for thought, and Stalin's warm welcome to this promise in his speech on 3 July acted as a clear instruction to Communists in this country and elsewhere that the policy of the Communist Parties must now change, and that all Parties must campaign for the maximum aid to the Socialist fatherland. The Communists, therefore, proclaimed that the war had now become a genuine people's war, and that it was their duty to see that government inefficiency, or 'friends of Fascism' in

the Government, did not deprive the Soviet Union of the maximum aid which she had demanded and must receive.

New technique
13. Even this apparent cooperation in the war effort did not prevent the Communist Party from making mischievous suggestions that there were pro-Fascist reactionaries in high places, who were more anxious to see the downfall of the Soviet Union than the defeat of Hitler. The Party demanded the public trial of Hess and the publication of alleged recent secret negotiations. It continued its agitation for deep shelters and better provisions for ARP, and it attacked the corruption, waste and disorganisation in industry.

14. This last point is of interest as an example of its new technique of penetration from within in the place of attack from outside. Previously managements had been represented as grasping capitalists interested only in obtaining from their men maximum output at minimum wages in the interest of profit. The Communist Party had therefore opposed the managements, and had represented themselves to be the champions of the workers. Since the attack on Russia, managements are represented to be delaying production owing to their inefficiency and thus to be robbing the Soviet Union of the assistance which she needs. The London Shop Stewards' Conference on production held on 23 August this year under the presidency of a well-known Communist, Joe Goss, produced a very clear illustration of this tendency, for Goss in his opening address said:

> a few employers were guilty, not only through their inefficiencies and their desire to accumulate profits, but by virtue of their hatred of the Soviet Union and their admiration of Hitler's methods of dealing with the working class, of deliberately sabotaging the greatest possible output.

The Communist Party has already called for the establishment of production committees, which will be in the control of the shop stewards and will thus eliminate not only managements but also the present Trade Union organisation.

Basic aims unchanged
15. Information received from most secret sources, which have proved reliable in the past, reveals that various leaders of the Communist Party have stated that the basic aims of the Party are still revolutionary. 'The Party must at all times strive towards such means and such activities as will best prepare the way for revolution.'

Another Party leader addressing a secret meeting of local Party representatives said:

> The basic aims and long term strategy of the Party are unchanged but the immediate tactics must be altered to utilise the present situation to the full ... The Communists have no illusions that Churchill's aims and theirs are likely to coincide for long but meanwhile he is putting their policy in force and they must pretend to back him up completely – they do back him in support for Russia ... If the Communists rally popular support for this, when the time comes and Churchill and Eden want to alter their policy, popular opinion will be too strong to allow it ... They must convince the British Government of the genuineness of their support, so nothing must be said to imply that this is a short-term policy and that their long-term aims are not changed. This is one of the reasons for our giving such publicity to having 'changed the line'.

Attacks on management

16.   Yet another Party leader admitted that accusations of 'ca canny' and absenteeism against Communist workers had been true in the past 'when the Party line was not to help the national effort'. This must be changed now as it was essential that managements should not be able to blame faults of production upon the workers. He continued:

> In the past the Communist Party has attacked and opposed the managements. Now they want joint committees with the workers and managements. They believe they can more effectively gain control and undermine the managements from within once they have achieved joint committees ... The Party did mean to try to speed up production but at the same time they mean to use the campaign also to undermine the managements – discrediting the managements and achieving additional administrative power for the workers.

17.   The admission that 'ca canny' methods had been used in the past was openly confirmed by a shop steward speaking at the recent London Shop Stewards Conference. According to the report in the Communist paper *New Propeller*, this man said: 'No longer can we say in the factory or section: 'automatic opposition to the gaffer' (foreman). That's out. We want increased production.' Here we have a shop steward who, according to the Communist Party, is a responsible representative of the workers, admitting that he has automatically opposed authority, and has only attempted to obtain increased production after his country has been at war for almost two years.

Factory meetings
18.   The Communist Party has devoted itself energetically to obtaining recognition as a responsible leader of labour, engaged in furthering the war effort. It has therefore made a number of attempts to hold meetings in Government establishments and factories, ostensibly to stimulate production. It is known that the Party attaches great importance to establishing itself in this way. It is probably for this reason that the speeches actually delivered at the few meetings which have been held in works have been unexceptionable, because the Party speakers are anxious at the moment to establish their right to address these meetings. It is nevertheless known that Pollitt, following a meeting in Whitehall, expressed scornful astonishment that the authorities were so blind as to allow him to speak, and this suggests that the Party itself intends that the present innocuous phase should only be a temporary one. It will be shown later that the communist press is already attacking the government, and it is reasonable to assume that, if the Party is once allowed to establish that its members may address factory meetings, their speeches will soon follow suit.

Undermining trade unions
19.   These new and more subtle methods of attack have been intensified also in the case of the Trade Unions. The Communist Party has continued to give the greatest publicity to the work of the Shop Stewards not only as the champions of the workers' rights but also as the leaders in the drive for increased production. In this latter capacity the Engineering and Allied Trades Shop Stewards National Council has recently appeared as an independent leader of labour, and is thus a direct threat to the authority of the Trades Union Congress itself. A typical example of this occurred recently, when a request was addressed by a member of the Select Committee on National Expenditure to W. Swanson, convenor of Shop Stewards at Napiers, to furnish evidence of delays in production. Swanson is a member of the Communist Party and Vice-Chairman of the Shop Stewards National Council. The Council seized the opportunity of taking this request as addressed to itself. This has caused considerable jubilation in the offices of the Council, where it is felt that this to some extent offsets the refusal of the Trades Union Congress to grant affiliation or have any dealings with the Council.

Subsidiary bodies
20. Similar attempts to obtain official recognition have been made in the case of other subsidiary organisations of the Communist Party. A new venture, called the Anglo-Soviet Youth Friendship Committee, has also been launched under the control of an astute secret member of the Young Communist League, who is also responsible for the Communist inspired International Youth Rally, to be held in the Albert Hall on 11 October. This Rally has already attracted some popular and official support.

21. Apart from this the Popular Front has not given rise to any great number of new bodies, but there has been an intensified use of those apparently non-Communist organisations over which the Party nevertheless exercises control. The Russia Today Society has shown greatly increased activity and Soviet exhibitions and Anglo-Soviet committees under Communist direction are being organised in many parts of the country.

Press attacks
22. While the Party speakers and organisers are still moving carefully in official contacts, the Communist press is already beginning to come out into the open in its new attempts to discredit the Government. This is well illustrated by the following quotation from a recent issue of *World News and Views*, to which members of the party were instructed to look for guidance on matters of policy after the suppression of the *Daily Worker*.

> Mr Churchill's statement of policy made on 9 September completely failed to satisfy public disquiet ... The biggest and most alarming fact that emerged, a fact that will undoubtedly encourage Hitler, is that the organisation of a Second Front is not contemplated at this stage.
> Taken in conjunction with the statements of Lord Moyne and Mr. Attlee on behalf of the Government, we have here a declaration of a definite policy which can be summed up as limited assistance to Russia, rejection of military action, 'ceaseless study of the whole problem' – after 12 weeks of the most bloody battles of history – continued postponement of any announcement of a date for the Three-Power Conference, and waiting until next year.
> It is in this context that Colonel Moore-Brabazon's statement takes on the greatest importance. It becomes, not an isolated episode or 'indiscretion', but a test of Government policy. The fact that his statement was not repudiated emphasises that what Moore-Brabazon said, and what the

Government explained as its policy, may have been differently phrased, but from the point of view of practical effect they were not very far removed.

It is of interest to note that this extract is taken from the report of a speech of Harry Pollitt, who, when speaking with another voice, has been accepted as a whole-hearted and valuable ally in the war effort.

Escape from difficulties
23.   Throughout the period of revolutionary defeatism the Communist Party of Great Britain applied the instructions laid down by Lenin for the last war so slavishly that they did not realise that the Russian situation then and the British situation in this war were not analogous. As a result the Party had to meet a great deal of criticism both from its own members and from possible supporters, who saw clearly that its policy was defeatist, even if they failed to realise the full implications of revolutionary defeatism.

24.   The attack by Hitler upon the Soviet Union enabled the Communist Party to escape from the embarrassing situation into which revolutionary defeatism had landed them, and to carry on their revolutionary activities under a banner of increased production and resistance to Hitler. From this point of view the Communist menace may be considered even more dangerous now than in the past because so many more people are likely to be attracted by its present popular front policy, which the Party itself represents as the only method of obtaining a quick and successful end to the war.

25.   This new line is, however, a change in tactics only, and not in the basic revolutionary policy, as has been already pointed out in the secret reports quoted in paragraphs 15, 16 and 17. The aim and technique remain the same, but the Communists are now operating in conditions much more favourable to the Party.

The present programme
26.   The Party's present programme can briefly be summarised as follows:

1. the winning of mass support and recognition by specious offers of co-operation in the war effort.
2. the attack on the Government for failing to meet the irresponsible demands foisted upon the public by the Party's publicity machine.
3. the attack on management, skilfully camouflaged under the demand for Production Committees.
4. the undermining of established Trade Unions by Shop Stewards

arrogating to themselves functions independent of the Unions, and by the creation of the parallel organisation, the Shop Stewards National Council.

5. the exploitation of other bodies, either captured or created by the Party, to spread Communist teaching and win new adherents.

27.   In this appreciation the endeavour has been made only to use published material or information coming from secret sources, which are unimpeachable or have been proved to be reliable in the past. It is in the light of these facts that policy should be determined.

Appendix III: Senior Soviet Representatives in Britain 1918–89

Provisional Plenipotentiary (unofficial)
January to September 1918 Maxim Litvinov

Heads of Trade Delegation
1920–3 Leonid Krasin
1923–4 Christian Rakovsky

Chargés d'Affaires
1924–5 Christian Rakovsky
1925–6 Leonid Krasin
1926–7 Arkady Rosengolz

Ambassadors
1929–32 Gregory Sokolnikov
1932–43 Ivan Maisky
1943–7 Feodor Gousev
1947–52 Georgi Zarubin
1952–3 Andrei Gromyko
1953–60 Yakov Malik
1960–6 Aleksandr Soldatov
1966–73 Mikhail Smirnovsky
1973–80 Nikolai Lunkov
1980–6 Victor Popov
1986– Leonid Zamyatin

Appendix IV: Soviet Officials Expelled from Britain 1968–89

June 1968
Yuri A. Dushkin and Vladimir A. Loginon, members of trade delegation

August 1970
Leonid Tvukhin, Third Secretary, scientific and technical department since October 1968; post-graduate student Birmingham University 1967–8

June 1971
Lev N. Shertsnev, First Secretary
Valery S. Chousovitin, Third Secretary

September 1971
(a) Embassy Diplomatic staff
Anatoli I. Akimov, Counsellor
Ivan P. Azarov, First Secretary
Igor D. Biryukov, Counsellor
Nikolai B. Bobarykin, Third Secretary
Yuri S. Cheremukhin, Third Secretary
Vladimir N. Dyudin, Attaché
Vladimir G. Filatov, Counsellor
Prokopi I. Gamov, First Secretary
Anatoli S. Golyakov, Attaché
Aleksandr A. Gresko, Third Secretary
Vladislav B. Karelin, Third Secretary
Viktor V. Karyagin, Counsellor and Cultural Attaché
Yuri B. Kashlev, Counsellor
Vasili P. Khmyz, Attaché
Igor K. Klimov, Second Secretary
Boris G. Kolodyazhny, Counsellor
Yuri A. Kondratenko, First Secretary
Vladimir U. Korobov, Third Secretary
Aleksandr I. Kotusov, Attaché
Nikolai K. Krikunov, Second Secretary
Evgeny I. Kutuzov, Second Secretary
Captain Lory T. Kuzmin, Assistant Naval Attaché
Georgi A. Kuznetsov, Counsellor
Anatoli I. Lapshin, Second Secretary
Leonid A. Leontiev, Attaché
Boris V. Makarenko, Second Secretary

Vladimir I. Melnik, Attaché
Boris P. Meshkov, Third
Secretary
Yuri V. Morozov, Third Secretary
Anatoli P. Orobinsky, Third
Secretary
Viktor M. Pankovsky, Third
Secretary
Leonid Y. Petrovichev, Attaché
Lyudmila A. Postnikova, Attaché
Vasili I. Pronin, Second Secretary
Leonid A. Rogov, First Secretary
Stanislav N. Semenenko, First
Secretary
Yuri F. Sepelev, Counsellor
Yuri V. Skoptsov, First Secretary
Ivo-Aat A. Soidra, Second

Secretary
Eduard V. Ustenko, Second
Secretary
Richardas K. Vaygauskas, Second
Secretary and Head of Consu-
lar Section
Viktor T. Veklenko, Third
Secretary
Yuri N. Voronin, Counsellor
Viacheslav A. Yasakov, Third
Secretary
Anatoli A. Yashchenko, Third
Secretary
Gennady A. Zhuravlev, Second
Secretary
Konstantin I. Zotov, Second
Secretary

(b) Trade and non-diplomatic personnel:

Aleksandr P. Akesnov
Nikolai F. Aleksandrov
Yevgenni I. Artishevsky
Eduard Aykazyan
Vasili F. Barynin
Mikhail F. Breytigam
Viktor G. Budanov
Vladislav Bunin
Yuri Y. Chernetsov
Aleksandr Chetvertukhin
Aleksei N. Deniskin
Anatoli V. Filipov
Viktor Filoenko
Vsevolod N. Generalov
Sergei M. Golubov
Yevgenni Y. Gorlenko
Anatoli N. Ivanov
Yuri B. Kabatov
Yuri K. Kolychev
Fedor P. Komarovsky
Yuri T. Khodajaev, Head, Soviet
Film Export Agency
Igor K. Konstantinov

Gannadi N. Kopoykin
Yuri F. Korniyenko
Ivan A. Kulikov
Yevgenni F. Kuzin
Yuri A. Kuznetsov
A.P. Kvardakov
Igor K. Laptev
Yuri I. Lavkovsky
Valeri A. Lavrov
Oleg B. Lazarev
Vladimir A. Leonov
Igor V. Makarevich
Yuri I. Panin
Lev A. Pavlov
Boris D. Perebillo
Emilya A. Petrovicheva
Dmitri Proshin
Vladimir A. Pushkin
Ivan P. Ragozkhin
Aleksandr Runkov
Igor P. Samarin
Ludmila S. Simburtseva
Sergei N. Sokolov

Dmitri I. Sorokin	Viktor V. Yurasov
Yuri M. Ter-Sarkisov	Ivan P. Zavorin
Anatoli P. Troitsky	Vladimir A. Zelenev
Nikolai Tsutskov	Leonid A. Zhernov
Gennadi N. Vasichev	Artur Zolotarev
Y.N. Viskov	Viktor N. Zotov

August 1981
Viktor Lazin, Second Secretary since 1977

February 1982
Vadim F. Zadneprovsky, member Trade Delegation

December 1982
Captain Anatoli Zotov, Naval Attaché

January 1983
Vladimir A. Chernov, translator International Wheat Council since
    September 1978; age 31; not formally a Soviet official

April 1983
Sergei V. Ivanov, Second Secretary since August 1981
Colonel Gennadiy A. Primakov, Assistant Air Attaché since June 1980
Igor V. Titov, *New Times* correspondent since 1982
Anatoly Chernyayev, Third Secretary and Labour Attaché since
    September 1979

September 1983
Vasily Ionov, member Trade Delegation since April 1981

May 1984
Arkadi V. Gouk, First Secretary

April 1985
Captain Third Rank Oleg A. Los, Assistant Naval Attaché; age 44
Vyacheslav Grigorov, Charter Manager, Aeroflot; age 37
Captain Viktor Zaikin, Assistant Naval Attaché since May 1983
Lt.-Col. Vadim Cherksov, Assistant Military Attaché since November
    1982; age 40
Oleg Belaventsev, Third Secretary since July 1982: age 36

September 1985
(25 officials were ordered out of the country on 12 September and another five on 16 September)

Mikhail Y. Boghdanov, Correspondent *Socialist Industry* since September 1980; age 43; non-diplomat

Sergei A. Bolovets, Correspondent Novosti news agency since February 1983; age 47

Viktor Daranov, Embassy clerk since October 1983; age 40; non-diplomat

Yuri Ejov, First Secretary

Aleksandr T. Gorelov, Embassy driver since January 1985; age 34; non-diplomat

Valery P. Ipatov, Moscow Narodny Bank since October 1983; age 36; non-diplomat

Vyacheslav I. Kalitin, First Secretary, Licence and Technical Department since June 1985; age 46

Igor F. Khomutov, Technical and Maintenance Department since July 1985; age 38; non-diplomat

Aleksandr A. Kodintsev, Correspondent, Novosti news agency since June 1985; age 30, non-diplomat

Yuri P. Komov, Trade representative, Mezhdunarodnaya Kniga since August 1984; age 36; non-diplomat

Boris A. Korchagin, First Secretary, Cultural Department since April 1985; age 45

Valery A. Kotov, Deputy managing director, Razno since February 1981; age 39; non-diplomat

Oleg P. Krasakov, Trade representative, Avtopromimort since April 1984; age 37; non-diplomat

Yuri A. Kudimov, Correspondent *Komsomolskaya Pravda* since December 1983; age 32; non-diplomat

Viktor O. Logush, Trade representative, Elektronorytechnika since January 1985; age 38; non-diplomat

Vladimir I. Lyubenko, Trade representative, Avtoexport Traktoroexport Zapchastexport since 1982; age 37; non-diplomat

Anatoly N. Meretikov, Third Secretary, Soviet Consulate since January 1985; age 34

Colonel Viktor A. Mishin, Assistant Air Attaché since August 1984; age 42

Yvacheslav D. Mishustin, Embassy security guard since September 1982; age 35; non-diplomat

Viktor I. Muzalev, Correspondent TASS; age 38; non-diplomat

Eduard V. Perepelkin, Trade representative, import machinery department, trade delegation since January 1982; age 36; non-diplomat

Valery V. Prokopchik, Representative, export machinery department, trade delegation since September 1981; age 43; non-diplomat

Yuri P. Rozhkov, Translator, International Cocoa Organisation since February 1985; age 37; non-diplomat

Yevgenny I. Safronov, First Secretary since August 1980; age 37

Mikhail D. Savvateyev, Translator, International Wheat Council since June 1984; age 33; non-diplomat

Sergei I. Sayenko, Correspondent Radio Moscow since June 1984; age 34; non-diplomat

Viktor V. Timofeyev, Representative, Sudoimport department, trade delegation since March 1984; age 40; non-diplomat

Valery G. Tokar, Second Secretary, Soviet Consulate since September 1983; age 40

Dmitry M. Vasileyv, Attaché, Technical and Maintenance Department since February 1985; age 39

Ivan I. Vikulov, Director Anglo Soviet Shipping since September 1984; age 47; non-diplomat

Alexsandr I. Yerokhin, clerk Service Attachés' office since December 1984; age 40; non-diplomat

Urly V. Yezhov, First Secretary Soviet Embassy since December 1982; age 48

Notes

CHAPTER 1: A 'SWARM OF INTRIGUERS'

1. Quoted in E. H. Carr: *The Bolshevik Revolution 1917–23*, vol. 3, p. 30.
2. Quoted in John Reed: *Ten Days That Shook the World*, p. 131; also Jane Degras (ed.): *Soviet Documents on Foreign Policy*, vol. 1, pp. 1–3.
3. Reed, p. 132.
4. A Statement of Bolshevik Policy, dated 3 November 1917, quoted in David Lloyd George: *War Memoirs*, vol. 2, p. 1559.
5. Richard H. Ullman: *Anglo-Soviet Relations 1917–21*, vol. 1, p. 28.
6. Robert Payne: *The Life And Death of Lenin*, p. 167. Lenin said after one meeting: 'There are many revolutionary and socialist elements among the English proletariat, but they are all mixed up with conservatism, religion and prejudice, and somehow the socialist and revolutionary elements never break through the surface and unite.'
7. David Shub: *Lenin*, p. 79.
8. Isaac Deutscher: *Stalin*, p. 102.
9. Ullman, pp. 59–61.
10. Graham Leggett: *The Cheka*, pp. 267–9; Richard Deacon: *A History of the Russian Secret Service*, pp. 167–8.
11. George Bilainkin: *Maisky*, pp. 14–16.
12. Walter Kendall: *The Revolutionary Movement in Britain 1900–21*, p. 328
13. Bogomolov's career illustrates some of the difficulties attached to tracking the careers of Soviet figures. In 1952 another Russian diplomat, Alexandr E. Bogomolov, was appointed Soviet Ambassador in Prague, but the Soviet authorities and, consequently, some of the Western media, including *The Times* and the *Daily Worker* confused his biography with that of D. V. Bogomolov. The British Foreign Office checked their own records and discovered there were two Soviet diplomats called Bogolomov: D. V. Bogolomov, who was British born, was not being sent to Prague and in fact had not been heard of since his post in China. A. E. Bogomolov was born in 1900 and joined the Diplomatic Service in 1939. From 1941–3 he was Soviet Ambassador to the Allied Powers in London. See Public Record Office (PRO): FO 371 100919
14. See Harry Rositzke: *The KGB*, p. 54. Edward van der Roehr: *The Shadow Network*, pp. 70ff, and Robert Lamphere and Tom Shachtman: *The FBI–KGB War*, p. 278. for Abel's English connection. Colonel Abel was betrayed by a drunken member of his own network and his cover as a photographer was blown. He was sentenced to thirty years' imprisonment in 1957 but was exchanged five years later for the American U2 spy plane

pilot, Gary Powers. On his return to the Soviet Union Abel was treated as a hero and permitted to write his life-story. According to this, he was born in Russia in 1902. Deacon follows the Soviet version of Abel's life in his *History of the Russian Secret Service*, p. 319.
15. See Kendall, chapters 5 and 13. for the Russian *émigrés* and their influence on the British left.
16. *The Times*, 4 December 1917.
17. ibid.
18. *The Times*, 28 November 1917.
19. PRO: CAB 23/4, Cabinet meetings on 29 and 30 November and 4 December 1917.
20. Lloyd George, p. 1546.
21. PRO: CAB 24/41 3587. Edward Troup to J. Gregory, 9 February 1918.
22. *The Times*, 3 January 1918
23. Leon Trotsky: *My Life*, p. 351; also quoted in Carr, vol. 3, p. 28.
24. Degras, vol. 1, p. 8.
25. Lloyd George, p. 1546.
26. ibid., p. 1541.
27. ibid., p. 1555. Lloyd George used the same words at a Cabinet meeting on 7 February 1918 (PRO: CAB 23/5 WC 340).
28. Lloyd George, p. 1553; PRO: CAB 23/5 WC 327, 21 January 1918.
29. Kenneth Young (ed.): *The Diaries of Sir Robert Bruce Lockhart*, vol. 1, p. 32
30. PRO: CAB 23/5 WC 342.
31. PRO: CAB 23/5 WC 353.
32. ibid.
33. Leggett. p. 111. But as he points out this did not take into account the execution of 400 prisoners in a single night at Kronstadt fortress and even a total of 1,300 was very probably an underestimate.
34. PRO: CAB 24/66 GT 5923.
35. Leggett, p. 299.
36. Ullman, vol. 3, p. 97
37. Christopher Andrew: *Secret Service*, pp. 341–2.
38. ibid., pp. 342–3; Kendall, p. 248.
39. *The Times*, 15 August 1919; see also Kendall and Andrew.
40. Kendall, pp. 246–7; Andrew, pp. 389–90.
41. PRO: CAB 24/114 CP 2067.
42. Andrew, p. 390.
43. PRO: CAB 24/117 CP 2316.
44. Kendall, pp. 248 and 426; Andrew Boyle: *The Climate of Treason*, p. 31.
45. Kendall, p. 78.
46. PRO: CAB 24/97 CP 544; CAB 24/99 CP 791; CAB 24/103 CP 1039.
47. Carr, vol. 3, pp. 466–7.
48. Henry Pelling: *The British Communist Party*, p. 6.
49. PRO: CAB 23/10 WC 574 30 May 1919.
50. Ullman, vol. 3, pp. 89–90
51. Francis Meynell: *My Lives*, p. 118
52. ibid., pp. 122–4; accounts of the affair are also given in Andrew, pp. 378–9; Kendall, pp. 253–4; and Boyle, pp. 27–8.
53. PRO: CAB 24/114 CP 2067

54. Quoted in Ullman, vol. 3, p. 93. Beatrice Webb also recalled her first meeting with Kamenev in 1918.
55. PRO: CAB 24/111, 9 September 1920.
56. PRO: CAB 24/111, 2 September 1920
57. Ullman, vol. 3, p. 269.
58. Carr, vol. 3, p. 29; Shub, p. 387.
59. Leggett, p. 17.
60. ibid., pp. 463–8.
61. Quoted in Carr, vol. 3, p. 127.
62. Carr, vol. 3, p. 197; Shub, pp. 398–9.
63. Jane Degras: *The Communist International*, vol. 1, p. 106.
64. Walter Krivitsky: *I Was Stalin's Agent*, p. 69.

CHAPTER 2: TRADE, RAIDS AND PROPAGANDA

1. Trade Agreement, Cmd 1207, 1921.
2. Degras: *The Communist International*, vol. 1, p. 225.
3. ibid., pp. 244–5.
4. PRO: CAB 24/128 CP 3350.
5. PRO: Cab 24/123 CP 2952.
6. PRO: CAB 24/125 CP 3034.
7. A Selection of Papers dealing with the Relations between His Majesty's Government and the Soviet Government, 1921–7. Cmd 2895. 1927; see also Andrew, pp. 398–403.
8. PRO: CAB 24/138 CP 4171 and CP 4173.
9. J. T. Murphy: *New Horizons*, pp. 88–9.
10. Details of individual British Communists working in Moscow from Murphy, p. 242, and Communist Papers, Cmd 2682. 1926.
11. Krivitsky, p. 54.
12. Murphy, pp. 239–40.
13. PRO: CAB 24/131 CP 3600.
14. PRO: CAB 24/134 CP 3854 and CAB 24/138 CP 4183.
15. PRO: CAB 24/138 CP 4171.
16. PRO: CAB 24/135 CP 3917 and 3993; CAB 24/139 CP 4242
17. Pelling, pp. 24–5 and 40–1.
18. Carr, vol. 3, pp. 398–402.
19. Boyle, p. 31.
20. PRO: CAB 24/118 CP 2452.
21. PRO: CAB 24/131 CP 3509.
22. ibid.
23. ibid.
24. PRO: CAB 24/131 CP 3561.
25. PRO: CAB 24/134 CP 3854 and CAB 24/135 CP 3917.
26. PRO: CAB 24/135 CP 3960.
27. Peter Wright: *Spycatcher*, p. 259.
28. ibid., p. 260
29. Deacon, *A History*, p. 174.
30. Andrew Sinclair: *The Red and the Blue*, p. 63. In their life of Anthony Blunt, *Conspiracy of Silence*, Barrie Penrose and Simon Freeman mention

Kapitza's scientific work at Cambridge, but like Sinclair do not identify him as a spy (pp. 134–5).
31. PRO: HO 45 14449
32. Anthony Cave Brown and Charles B. MacDonald: *On a Field of Red*, p. 634.
33. Leggett, p. 233.
34. ibid., p. 355.
35. ibid., p. 299.
36. L. D. Gerson: *The Secret Police in Lenin's Russia*, p. 235.
37. Georges Agabekov: *OGPU – The Russian Secret Terror*, p. 33.
38. PRO: CAB 24/139 CP 4282.
39. Pelling, p. 28.
40. Correspondence between His Majesty's Government and the Soviet Government, Cmd 1869, 1923.
41. Pelling, ibid.
42. Murphy, pp. 286–7. Petrovsky married Rose Cohen and both suffered in the purges of the 1930s when they were accused of Trotskyism; see Noreen Branson: *History of the CPGB*, p. 246.
43. Degras, p. 96.
44. PRO: CAB 24/166 CP 273(24); Andrew, pp. 428–9.
45. PRO: ibid.
46. Pelling, pp. 29–30; A. J. P. Taylor: *English History 1914–45*, p. 225.
47. See summaries of the Zinoviev letter affair in Gabriel Gorodetsky: *The Precarious Truce*, pp. 35–52; Andrew, pp. 430–45.
48. Christopher Farman: *The General Strike*, pp. 54–5; Nigel West: *MI5*, pp. 79–80. West suggests that the government was disappointed not to find evidence of Soviet funding of the CPGB but he seems unaware of the vast amount of information which was already available to the police.
49. Communist Papers, Cmd 2682, 1926.
50. Andrew, pp. 460–1; Pelling, p. 41.
51. Farman, p. 209.
52. ibid., p. 82.
53. Andrew, pp. 445–8, and Deacon, pp. 179ff.
54. PRO: HO 24834.
55. PRO: CA 24/180 CP 236 (26) and CP 244 (26); Andrew. pp. 456–9.
56. PRO: FO 371 12581.
57. Parliamentary Debates, 4 July 1927.
58. PRO: CA 24/158 CP 4(23). Lakey's mother and aunt were employed at Soviet House as charwomen. See chapter 3 for the Narodny Bank case.
59. Note from His Majesty's Government to the Government of the USSR, Cmd 2827, February 1927.
60. *The Times*, 17, 18 and 19 January 1928; see also West, pp. 62–5 and 70–5; Andrew, pp. 467–9, for summaries of the McCartney–Hansen case.
61. Gorodetsky, p. 222.
62. *The Times*, 16 May 1927.
63. Parliamentary Debates, 24 May 1927, col. 1845.
64. ibid., col. 1849.
65. ibid., col. 1843.
66. Documents illustrating the Hostile Activites of the Soviet Government and the Third International against Great Britain, Cmd 2874, 1927.
67. Quoted by Baldwin in his statement, col. 1846.

68. Cmd 2874 and quoted by Baldwin.
69. Cmd 2874; see also West, pp. 69–70.
70. Jan Valtin: *Out of the Night*. Valtin came to England as a Comintern agent at the end of 1931 (see chapter 3).
71. Parliamentary Debates, 23 June 1927, cols 2020–1.
72. Boyle, p. 102.
73. PRO: FO 371 12581.
74. PRO: FO 371 16331.

CHAPTER 3: THE AGE OF THE 'ILLEGALS'

1. Degras (ed.): *Soviet Documents on Foreign Policy*, vol. 2, p. 233
2. Krivitsky, p. 92.
3. The government's findings were published as a White Paper, Russian Banks and Communists Funds, Cmd 3125, 1928. The Home Secretary also made a statement in the House of Commons on 11 June 1928, Parliamentary Debates, cols 635–42.
4. Agabekov, p. 189; see also below.
5. PRO: CAB 24/202, CP 79 (29), 12 March 1929.
6. *The Times*, 6 January 1930.
7. PRO: FO 371 14854.
8. PRO: CAB 24/215, CP 349 (30), 24 Oct 1930.
9. E. H. Carr: *The Twilight of the Comintern, 1930–5*, p. 209.
10. Andrew. p. 512.
11. PRO: CAB 24/261. CP 82 (36). 18 March 1936. See Andrew, pp. 509–20 for a summary of Communist activity against the armed forces in the 1930s; for a Communist account see Branson, pp. 61–8.
12. Murphy, p. 303; see also Pelling, pp. 49–52.
13. Krivitsky, pp. 75–6.
14. *The Times*, 15 March 1938, reporting Glading's trial in the Woolwich Arsenal case; see below.
15. Pelling, p. 59.
16. PRO: FO 371 14854.
17. PRO: FO 371 14853.
18. Carr, *Comintern*, p. 211.
19. Valtin, p. 326.
20. ibid., p. 321.
21. ibid., p. 323. He seems uncertain of her nationality. He says initially she was German and later refers to her as Danish.
22. PRO: FO 371 15614
23. PRO: FO 371 16336.
24. ibid.
25. PRO: FO 371 24856.
26. For example. Valtin, Poretsky and Agabekov.
27. Elizabeth Poretsky: *Our Own People*, pp. 54–5.
28. Agabekov. p. 274; also Krivitsky, pp.73–5 and Alexander Orlov: *Handbook of Intelligence and Guerrilla Warfare*, pp. 42–8.
29. Poretsky, p. 81.
30. Agabekov, p. 274.

31. Charles A. Willoughby: *Sorge: Soviet Master Spy*, p. 122.
32. Agabekov, p. 189.
33. Max Perthus: *Henk Sneevliet*, p. 340; Poretsky, pp. 80–1.
34. Poretsky, p. 84.
35. *Daily Mail*, 14 May 1930.
36. Poretsky, p. 83
37. Krivitsky, p. 275; see also Nigel West: *MI5*, p. 87.
38. W. R. Corson and R. T. Crowley: *The New KGB*, pp. 417–18. They do not, however, name the artist.
39. Gordon Brook-Shepherd: *The Storm Petrels*, p. 175; Corson and Crowley cover the case in detail but refer to Oldham throughout as 'Scott', pp. 140–67; see also Deacon, *A History*, p. 379.
40. Corson and Crowley. p. 165; Brook-Shepherd. pp. 174–9; Deacon, *A History*, pp. 218–20.
41. Wright. p. 328.
42. E. H. Cookridge: *The Third Man*, p. 24.
43. Wright, pp. 325ff. West: *MI6*, p. 243; Pincher: *Too Secret, Too Long*, pp. 567ff; Deacon: *'C': A Biography of Sir Maurice Oldfield*, p. 77.
44. Orlov: pp. 108–9;
45. See for example. Boyle; Sinclair, *The Red*; and Penrose and Freeman among recent accounts.
46. Boyle, pp. 56–7; Patrick Seale and Maureen McConville: *Philby: The Long Road to Moscow*, p. 32.
47. Cookridge, p. 19.
48. See later chapters; also Wright; Pincher; and Penrose and Freeman.
49. Michael Straight: *After Long Silence*, p. 60.
50. Boyle, p. 105. He follows Cookridge on this; see Cookridge. p. 24.
51. Boyle, p. 115 and Cookridge, p. 37. Cookridge states that Springhall was the intermediary in Maclean's as in Philby's case.
52. Hugh Thomas: *John Strachey*, p. 110.
53. ibid., p. 129.
54. George Bilainkin, p. 194.
55. CIA: *The Rote Kapelle*, p. xi.
56. Wright, p. 267.
57. CIA, pp. xii–xiii and 96ff.
58. ibid., pp. 381–3.
59. *The Times*, 22 and 28 October 1937.
60. *The Times*, 3 and 24 September 1937.
61. The Home Office decided that the Council's letter of protest was 'not worded so as to call for any action' and no reply was given, HO 45 15518.
62. CIA, p. 383; Penrose and Freeman, pp. 476–7.
63. CIA, p. 342.
64. Quoted in CIA, p. 96.
65. Cave Brown and MacDonald claim Weiss recruited Burgess, p. 460. Their study draws on the CIA report on *The Rote Kapelle*, which does not make that claim. An earlier study of the Soviet Union's European spy networks at this time, Ronald Seth's *Forty Years of Soviet Spying*, uses several German sources, including Gestapo reports, but makes no references to any British connections on the part of Robinson and does not mention Weiss. Peter Wright mentions Robinson briefly and the handwritten notes

found in his room, which listed forty or fifty names and addresses in Britain; p. 237.
66. CIA, p. 100.
67. Leopold Trepper: *The Great Game*, pp. 137–8.
68. See Wright and Pincher.
69. Brook-Shepherd said, in 1977, that it was widely accepted that Deutsch had recruited and/or controlled Philby, Burgess and Maclean, p. 184. That is not the case; Wright, p. 227 and Pincher, p. 376, mention the incident of the photograph involving Philby.
70. Trepper, p. 128.
71. Seale and McConville, p. 73.
72. Alexander Foote: *Handbook for Spies*, p. 21; See chapter 5 below for Foote's later activities.
73. Ruth Werner: *Sonjas Rapport* is Ursula Kuczynski's autobiography; Pincher and Robert Chadwell Williams: *Klaus Fuchs, Atom Spy*, contains summaries of her career based on it; see also chapter 4, below.
74. Robert Conquest: *The Great Terror*, pp. 699–713.
75. Leonard Schapiro: *The Communist Party of the Soviet Union*, p. 424.
76. Andrew, pp. 593–4.
77. Brook-Shepherd, p. 182.
78. Boyle, p. 216; Wright, p. 228; the suspicious circumstances of the death are also discussed by Pincher, *Too Secret, Too Long*, p. 67; West, *MI5*, p. 87; Corson and Crowley, p. 167; and Deacon, *A History*, p. 250.
79. To describe him as 'Austro–Hungarian' is one way out of the apparent contradiction. He was described specifically as an Austrian in the Russian army by Percy Glading at the Woolwich Arsenal trial, *The Times*, 4 February 1938; this is repeated by Andrew, p. 524 and West, p. 81; But see Poretsky, who knew Maly, p. 128, for his Hungarian and religious conections; Corson and Crowley, p. 418; Brook-Shepherd, p. 176; Pincher, *Too Secret, Too Long*, p. 207; Wright, p. 227; Deacon, *A History*, p. 379; and Boyle, p. 151 follow her view; see also those sources for subsequent references in this paragraph.
80. Poretsky, p. 213.
81. For recent summaries of the case, see Anthony Masters: *The Man Who Was 'M'*, pp. 43–55; Andrew, pp. 520–5; West, pp. 80–7.
82. Pelling, p. 102.
83. Wright, p. 228.
84. Cookridge, p. 50.
85. Chadwell Williams, p. 60; see chapter 4 below.
86. PRO: FO 371 24846.
87. ibid.
88. Pelling, p. 111; Branson, p. 267; see Appendix II below for MI5's view of events.

CHAPTER 4: 'ON A BETTER WICKET'

1. Winston Churchill: *The Second World War*, vol. III, p. 333.
2. Quoted by Churchill, p. 469.
3. Quoted in Graham Ross: *The Foreign Office and the Kremlin – British*

Documents on Anglo–Soviet Relations 1941–5, p. 116.
4. ibid., pp. 127–30.
5. ibid., see also Anthony Glees: *The Secrets of the Service*, chapter 2, for an analysis of British policy towards the Soviet Union during the war.
6. Ross, pp. 157–66.
7. Wright, p. 228; Gromov-Gorski was identified by the American Soviet agent, Elizabeth Bentley at a Congressional Hearing in May 1949, see Corson and Crowley. p. 477; he later resurfaced as Professor Nitkin of the Moscow Institute of History, see John Barron: *The KGB*, p. 167, and Pincher p. 536.
8. Post Office Directory 1942–43; *Who's Who*.
9. Boyle, Penrose and Freeman, and Pincher have further detail.
10. Wright, pp. 182–6.
11. PRO: FO 369 5057 and press reports of the deportation hearings, including *The Daily Telegraph*, 11 August 1954. Nigel West: *A Matter of Trust – MI5 1945–72*, p. 178 and Pincher, p. 575 refer briefly to the Belfrage case.
12. PRO: FO 371 24856; also for the Lazar Ram case.
13. Murray told his version of the story in *A Spy Called Swallow*; official papers are at the PRO in FO 371 24856 and 29532.
14. PRO: FO 371 24856.
15. PRO: FO 371 47709.
16. Harry Sporborg to Christopher Warner, Head of the Northern Department, 24 February 1945, PRO: FO 371 47709.
17. M. R. D. Foot: *SOE 1940–46*, p. 145.
18. ibid.; West: *MI5*, pp. 354–6; Glees, chapter 3, for subversion in MI6.
19. Douglas Hyde: *I Believed*, p. 139.
20. ibid., p. 140.
21. Report of the Canadian Royal Commission, 1946, p. 37. See chapter 5 below for Gouzenko's defection.
22. Hyde, p. 117.
23. See Chadwell Williams, pp. 32–4.
24. Jürgen Kuczynski: *Memoiren*, p. 373.
25. Werner, p. 295; see also Pincher, p. 94.
26. Werner, p. 297.
27. ibid., p. 298.
28. ibid., p. 335. The date she left England is disputed: see chapter 5 below.
29. See Pincher: *Their Trade Is Treachery* and *Too Secret, Too Long*, and Wright, for the case against Hollis; their methods and conclusions are examined by Glees, while West: *Molehunt* suggests Graham Mitchell was the alleged mole in MI5; Chadwell Williams also reviews the evidence. The former FBI officer, Robert Lamphere, also believes Hollis was the 'mole' on the grounds that he is the most likely person to have alerted Philby about the contents of deciphered KGB messages after the war. He devotes only a short paragraph to the question and gives the wrong dates for Hollis's tenure of office as Director-General of the Security Service: it was 1956–65. not 1952–56; see Lamphere and Shachtman, p. 244.
30. See Glees, pp. 172–9 and 333–6.
31. A note by the secretary, William Armstrong, 1 October 1941, PRO: FO 371 29523.

32. A memorandum circulated by Sir Herbert Creedy on 26 October 1942, PRO: FO 371 32583. The responsibilities of the Executive were very wide-ranging. Yet when Viscount Swinton died in 1972 his obituary in *The Times*, even at that distance of time, referred only to one aspect, that the Executive 'was concerned with security measures both in Britain and overseas where British ships or supplies were liable to sabotage'. (*The Times*, 29 July 1972).
33. ibid.
34. ibid.
35. West: *MI5* contains details of the Security Executive senior members and staff, pp. 192–3.
36. Viscount Swinton's comments at the 49th meeting of the Security Executive, 1 October 1941, PRO: 371 29523.
37. PRO: FO 371 32583.
38. West: *MI5*, p. 195 and Andrew pp. 668–9.
39. Viscount Swinton, PRO: FO 371 29523.
40. Memorandum for the War Cabinet. PRO: ibid. The full report is in Appendix II.
41. ibid.
42. ibid.
43. ibid.
44. Viscount Swinton's memo of 2 October 1941, PRO: ibid.
45. ibid.
46. Minutes of 49th Meeting of the Security Executive, 1 October 1941, PRO: ibid.
47. Minutes of 50th Meeting of the Security Executive, 15 October 1941, PRO: ibid.
48. ibid.
49. Churchill. vol. III. p. 319. He gave explicit instructions in August 1940 that Morton should 'be shown everything' so that he could select and submit original intelligence documents, as Churchill did not wish to rely on digests and summaries from the Joint Intelligence Committee; see also Glees, pp. 167–8 for Morton's role during the war.
50. PRO: FO 371 135413.
51. See Pincher: *Too Secret, Too Long*, p. 207 and Glees, pp. 150–2. Smollett had become a naturalised British subject in 1938, when he changed his name from Smolka. At that time he was head of the Foreign Department of Exchange Telegraph. On returning to Austria after the war, he was *The Times* correspondent in Vienna from 1947–9. In 1973 Smollett became the Commercial Adviser to the Austrian President.
52. Extract from Smollett's paper in a note prepared for the Security Executive by William Armstrong, PRO: FO 371 29523.
53. Smollett was asked for a view about a complaint from Moscow about anti-Soviet items in the British press: 'by refusing to give into an exaggerated Soviet demand he avoided appearing pro-Soviet, yet at the same time that exaggerated Soviet demand was used to justify pro-Soviet intervention in other cases.'; Glees, p. 151.
54. Directive by the Ministry of Information, PRO: FO 371 29523.
55. PRO: ibid.; in fact the note gave the wrong date, 1927, instead of 1924, for the formation of the Society. When the Marxist historian, Christopher Hill

was working in the Foreign Office in 1945 he attempted to use the Society in a scheme to promote Russian studies in Britain, despite the fact that MI5 listed it as a Communist-infiltrated organisation; see Glees, p. 283.

56. See Pincher, *Too Secret, Too Long*, p. 61. quoting an earlier work by Glees as his source for his statement that there is no documentation on the Kuczynski family; Glees's reply dealt effectively with it, p. 326.
57. PRO: 371 34416.
58. ibid.
59. ibid.; also Glees, p. 327.
60. PRO: FO 371 24842 N731.
61. PRO: FO 371 29523.
62. PRO: CAB WP (44) 202.
63. PRO: FO 954 24 SOE/44/17.

CHAPTER 5: 'THE THREAT TO WESTERN CIVILISATION'

1. Annex to Report by the Chiefs of Staff, 13 March 1947, PRO: CAB/21 2554, DO(47) 25.
2. This information was contained in a letter from the Crown Estate Office to the Foreign Office on 13 May 1958, when there was some protracted wrangling between the British and Soviet authorities over the renewal of the leases. The British paid twice as much for its Embassy in Moscow and had only a five-year lease. The Soviet Trade Legation also owned a country house. Seacox Heath, near Etchingham in East Sussex, which was used by all Soviet officials as a weekend residence and for a summer school; see PRO: FO 371 135413 and 135414.
3. Paul Falla, PRO: FO 371 86877.
4. Quoted in Robert Payne: *The Rise and Fall of Stalin*, p. 632.
5. Quoted in Hugh Thomas: *Armed Truce*, pp. 38–9.
6. ibid., p. 109.
7. PRO: FO 371 56832.
8. PRO: CAB 129 CP(48) 72.
9. Hyde, p. 201; Hugh Thomas suggests 'there were perhaps twenty "underground" Communist MPs: MPs elected as Labour politicians but secretly Communist members or friendly to the party ...', *Armed Truce*, p. 326.
10. Quoted in Pelling, p. 141.
11. Quoted in Clive Rose: *Campaigns Against Western Defence*, p. 285.
12. Report of the 30th Annual Conference of the Association of Scientific Workers, May 1947.
13. ibid.; see below for the Nunn May case; one of his colleagues, Norman Veall, who was a member of the Young Communist League in England, and a member of the ASW, was actively involved in the setting up of a Canadian branch of the ASW in 1944. His more open Communist sympathies are thought to have precluded his being asked by the Soviet Union to engage in espionage on its behalf; see the Report of the Canadian Royal Commission, p. 516.
14. Pelling, p. 145.
15. Transcript of the meeting by the BBC Russian Section, contained in a Foreign Office file, PRO: FO 371 56924.

16. Review of the British Dock Strikes, 1949, Cmd 7851.

17. Aims of the World Peace Movement, PRO: CAB 130, Gen 341.

18. Meeting of Cabinet sub-committee, Gen 341, 30 October 1950, PRO: ibid.

19. ibid..

20. See Boyle, pp. 289–90; Wright, p. 238 and Pincher: *Too Secret, Too Long*, pp. 265ff.

21. Philby: *My Silent War*, pp. 143–54 for his account of the Volkov affair.

22. Ismail Akhmedov: *In And Out of Stalin's GRU*, p. 190.

23. H. Montgomery Hyde: *The Atom Bomb Spies* contains the fullest account of the Gouzenko case; Gouzenko's own story is told in *This Was My Choice*; Wright, Pincher, *Too Secret, Too Long*, West: *Molehunt*, Glees and Chadwell Williams debate the meaning of Gouzenko's revelation – not given in his own book – that there was a spy serving in a section of 'Five of MI', one of two agents code-named 'Elli'. The case against Hollis, who interviewed Gouzenko in Canada, is circumstantial. It was certainly not Blunt as some people have suggested and Philby seems the most likely candidate. In later years Gouzenko embellished his original story and in the words of Nigel West 'suffered from a colossal, over-inflated ego', see *Molehunt*, pp. 66–82.

24. Quoted in Montgomery Hyde, p 43.

25. PRO: FO 371 56912.

26. Report of the Canadian Royal Commission, pp. 19–29.

27. ibid., p. 79.

28. Alan Moorehead: *The Traitors*, p. 37; three members of Zabotin's staff also disappeared. See also Montgomery Hyde, p. 61 for some possible explanations of Zabotin's fate, either suicide by jumping overboard in the Atlantic or heart attack shortly after arriving back in Moscow.

29. PRO: CAB/21 2554, DO(47) 25.

30. ibid.

31. PRO: CAB/21 2554, DO(47), 9th Meeting, 26 February 1947.

32. ibid.

33. PRO: CAB/21 2554, DO(47), 19th and 21st Meetings, August and September 1947.

34. Montgomery Hyde, p. 133; Moorehead, pp. 116 and 208–9; Chadwell Williams, pp. 100–1.

35. Chadwell Williams, p. 62.

36. ibid., pp. 116–20; also Lamphere and Shachtman, pp. 134–5; Fuchs' name was also found in a notebook belonging to Israel Halperin, a university professor of mathematics in Ontario, who was exposed by Gouzenko.

37. Chadwell Williams, pp. 134–5; Montgomery Hyde, p. 177.

38. Werner, p. 324

39. Foote, pp. 44–8.

40. Reproduced in Deacon: *'C'*:, pp. 83–6.

41. See Chadwell Williams, pp. 53–9 for the view that Foote was a British agent. He also argues that the Swiss network of which Foote was a member was used by the British to pass German 'Ultra' material to Moscow, without revealing its true ultimate source. But the British had no need to do this as they were passing a considerable amount of such material directly to the Soviet Union through the British mission in Moscow, without disclosing the fact that it was from 'Ultra'; see Peter Calvocoressi: *Top Secret Ultra*, pp. 94–5.

42. Lamphere and Shachtman, p. 128; see also Chadwell Williams, pp. 159–60.
43. Quoted in Montgomery Hyde, p. 137.
44. For the final months in Britain and defection of Burgess and Maclean see: John Mather (ed.): *The Great Spy Scandal*; B. Page, D. Leitch and P. Knightley: *Philby – The Spy Who Betrayed a Generation*; Seale and McConville; Douglas Sutherland: *The Fourth Man*; John Fisher: *Burgess and Maclean*; and works quoted by Boyle, Penrose and Freeman, Pincher, *Too Secret, Too Long*, Glees, and West: *Molehunt*.
45. West: *A Matter of Trust*, p. 221; Pincher: *Too Secret, Too Long*, p. 491 and Penrose and Freeman, pp. 407–8.
46. PRO: FO 371 77634.
47. ibid.
48. PRO: FO 371 86761.
49. ibid.

CHAPTER 6: THE KGB AND THE 'LONG RANGE POLICY'

1. Foreign Office to British Embassy, Moscow, 14 December 1953, PRO: FO 371 106535.
2. Memorandum by G. W. Harrison, 12 November 1953, PRO: ibid.
3. The correspondence is on Foreign Office files, PRO: FO 371 106534.
4. Report of the Conservative Party Conference 1953, p. 30.
5. Van Straubenzee's report, forwarded by Peter Smithers to the Foreign Office, 23 November 1953, PRO: FO 371 106535.
6. Nutting's reply to Smithers, 2 December 1953, PRO: ibid.
7. See Wright, p. 257, Pincher: *Too Secret, Too Long*, p. 491, West: *A Matter of Trust*, pp. 199 and 221, and Baron: *The KGB*, p. 391.
8. *The Daily Telegraph*, 29 September 1971.
9. For the Courtney case, see Chapman Pincher: *Inside Story*, pp. 116–17.
10. James Tyson: *Target America*, p. 171, quoting a CIA Report on the Congressional Record, September 1965.
11. See Pincher: *Too Secret, Too Long*, West: *A Matter of Trust* and Wright for accounts of the Crabb case.
12. See Richard H. Shultz and Roy Godson: *Dezinformatsia*, p. 23, and Rose, pp. 78–80.
13. Memorandum by Selwyn Lloyd, Relations with the Soviet Union, 21 January 1958, C(58)9, PRO: CAB 129/91.
14. ibid.
15. Memorandum by Selwyn Lloyd, World Youth Festival, 18 June 1958, C(58)127, PRO: CAB 129/92.
16. Memorandum by the President of the Board of Trade, Trade with the Soviet Union, 23 January 1958, C(58)18, PRO: CAB 129/91.
17. Foreign Office briefing for discussion at Cabinet, 30 January 1958, PRO: FO 371 135307.
18. Summary of *Pravda* article, 21 December 1957 by Serov, contained in Foreign Office files, PRO: FO 371 135363.
19. Report to Foreign Office, 17 January 1958, PRO: ibid.
20. Wynne's own story, *The Man From Moscow* was published in 1967.
21. Anatoliy Golitsyn: *New Lies for Old*, p. 49

22. Ladislav Bittman: *The KGB and Soviet Disinformation*, p. 39.
23. West: *A Matter of Trust* and Pincher: *Too Secret, Too Long* and *Their Trade Is Treachery*, contain summaries of the main post-war espionage and intelligence cases and have been consulted accordingly, together with the published reports of various official bodies and enquiries, which both West and Pincher have used extensively. Peter Wright's *Spycatcher* also looks at most of the principal cases. There are earlier accounts by Norman Lucas: *The Great Spy Ring* and in Seth. Vassall, Molody (Lonsdale), and Houghton have written their own stories, and there are biographies of Blake by E. H. Cookridge and, more recently by H. Montgomery Hyde.
24. *Manchester Guardian*, 10 July 1952.
25. PRO: FO 371 86835.
26. Seth, p. 215
27. West, *A Matter of Trust*, pp. 64–5.
28. Marquess of Reading, Parliamentary Questions, House of Lords, 29 October 1952; and PRO: FO 371 100910. At the beginning of 1956 a Second Secretary at the Czech Embassy, Jan Paclik, was warned by the Foreign Office for 'molesting *émigrés*', PRO: FO 371 122211; see also this chapter below.
29. PRO: FO 371 122895; also West, *A Matter of Trust*, pp. 79–81.
30. John Vassall: *Vassall: the autobiography of a Spy*, and Lucas.
31. See the Report of the Standing Security Commission, June 1965, Cmnd 2722; West, *A Matter of Trust*, pp. 165–6 and Pincher, *Too Secret, Too Long*, pp. 542–6.
32. PRO: FO 371 128441.
33. 'Gordon Lonsdale's' autobiography, *Spy*, was published shortly after his return to Moscow.
34. 'A Russian Intelligence Officer Exposed', *Police Journal*, April–June 1971.
35. See Lamphere and Shachtman, p. 292.
36. Lucas, pp. 163–5. The Krogers each received a twenty year prison sentence, Molody twenty-five years, and Houghton and Gee, fifteen years each.
37. *Police Journal*, op. cit.
38. Security Procedures in the Public Service, April 1962, Cmnd 1681.
39. Richard Deacon: *A History of the Russian Secret Service*, p. 316.
40. Report of the Royal Commission on Espionage, Sydney, August 1955, p. 100.
41. The White Paper published on 23 September 1955 is reproduced in full in West's *Molehunt*; see also Boyle, p. 445, and Penrose and Freeman, pp. 408–9.
42. Deacon, pp. 362ff and Wright, p. 294.
43. There is general agreement that Burgess, Maclean and Philby were members of the 'Ring of Five'. West says that Cairncross was also a member but not Blunt, while Wright, followed by Pincher claims that Blunt was, but certainly not the lesser spy Cairncross. They all agree that Watson was a strong possibility for the fifth man. The case for Cairncross over Blunt does not seem a convincing one, given the latter's seniority, his role in recruiting younger men and the success of his later career, all of which made him a valuable asset to Soviet intelligence.
44. Wright, p. 315.

45. *The Times*, 22 July 1948; an adjournment debate in the House of Commons was initiated by George Wigg on 30 July 1948.

46. West: *A Matter of Trust* pp. 83–4 and 215–17, and Pincher, *Too Secret, Too Long*, pp. 315 and 603. The day after Prybyl left the country a new Czech Ambassador arrived in London. He was Miroslav Galuska, a 36-year-old former *Rude Pravo* journalist and head of the Press Department of the Czech Ministry of Foreign Affairs. British Foreign Office officials believed that Galuska wished to improve relations with Britain and they were keen that a minister should accept the Ambassador's invitation to lunch at his residence. The occasion was to be a 'purely social one' and they suggested John Profumo, the recently-appointed Parliamentary Under-Secretary in the Foreign Office. His office said he would be glad to accept, and an official enquired: 'Would it be a stag lunch?' (PRO: FO 371 134699). In the light of Mr Profumo's later social encounters with Eastern European diplomats, the question has a certain irony.

47. The Arthur Bax case was disclosed to Chapman Pincher: see *Inside Story*, pp. 23ff and *Too Secret, Too Long*, pp. 346–8.

48. Jan Sejna: *We Will Bury You*, pp. 104 and 142–50.

49. *The Times*, 4 January 1974.

50. PRO: FO 371 122211.

51. Transcripts of the hearings were published in Communist Bloc Intelligence Activities in the United States (1976).

52. Josef Frolik: *The Frolik Defection*, p. 93.

53. Communist Bloc Intelligence Activities in the United States.

54. Wright, pp. 364–5.

55. Swingler was a junior minister in the Departments of Transport and Health and Social Security until his death in February 1969 at the age of 53. His brother, Randall Swingler, who died in 1967, was the literary editor of the *Daily Worker* before and during the war and remained a member of the Communist Party until 1956. The names of various members of the Wilson entourage were raised again in a series of articles which appeared in May 1987 in connection with the 'Spycatcher' affair; for example, *Sunday Telegraph* and *The Observer*, 3 May and *The Times*, 4 May 1987.

56. Wright's comments on BBC TV Panorama, reported in *The Times*, 14 October 1987: he said instead of the thirty officers mentioned in *Spycatcher*, only eight or nine talked about it, and only he and one other were serious. Earlier press reports of Wright's revelations had attributed to him statements which he had not made and were not inferred in his published book. *The Times* article of 4 May 1987, mentioned above, said that Wright 'apparently details' in his book some '23 crimes and 12 acts of treason', including allegations of smears and bugging against Labour ministers, and politicians in Northern Ireland. These did not come from Wright but were remarkably similar to naterial being circulated at the time by a former employee of the Ministry of Defence in Northern Ireland. The appending of this extraneous material to the *Spycatcher* affair is further evidence of the way in which Wright's original purpose, to expose Soviet infiltration of the Security Service, has been overtaken by a current campaign against it.

57. Report of the Departmental Enquiry into Section Two of the Official Secrets Act, Cmnd 5104, September 1972, vol 3.

CHAPTER 7: THE MAKING OF THE MODERN KGB

1. From 'Soviet state security services – fifty years' in Y. V. Andropov: *Speeches and Writings*, pp. 99–100.
2. Quoted in Martin Ebon: *The Andropov File*, pp. 42–3.
3. 'Leninism: the science of and art of revolution', Andropov, p. 154.
4. 'Soviet state security services, ibid., p. 105.
5. ibid., pp. 191–2.
6. Ebon, p. 18.
7. Arnold Beichman and Mikhail S. Bernstam: *Andropov*, p. 14.
8. Andropov became a full member of the Politburo in 1973.
9. Leonard Schapiro: 'Soviet attitudes to national communism in Western Europe', in Howard Machin (ed.): *National Communism in Western Europe*.
10. Andropov, p. 197.
11. See John Barron: *KGB Today*, pp. 445–55 for a description of the KGB in the early 1980s. His earlier book: *KGB – The Secret Work of Soviet Secret Agents*, gives the picture ten years earlier. Additional information is contained in various CIA and US government reports and Senate investigations, such as *Foreign Affairs and Military Intelligence* (1976) and *Soviet Covert Action – the Forgery Offensive* (1982).
12. See Ebon, p. 79, and *Soviet Active Measures* (1982).
13. *Soviet Active Measures*.
14. Barron: *The KGB*, p. 306; Bittman, p. 67.
15. See Vladimir Kostov: *The Bulgarian Umbrella* (Harvester 1988).
16. Bittman, p. 18.
17. Barron: *KGB Today*, pp. 448–53; *Foreign and Military Intelligence*.
18. Rose, p. 92.
19. Jonathan Steele: The Limits of Soviet power, p. 89.
20. See Schapiro: *The Communist Party of the Soviet Union*, pp. 53–8, and Rose, p. 89.
21. Accounts of the Soviet role in the 'peace' movement are given in Rose and in depth in Paul Mercer: *The Peace of the Dead*.
22. Schapiro: *The Communist Party of the Soviet Union*, p. 57.
23. Quoted in Covert Action and Propaganda (US 1980); also Bittman, pp. 49–50 and Shultz and Godson, p. 37.
24. These include the US government publications referred to in this chapter and given in full in the bibliography, and works by Shultz and Godson, Bittman, Levchenko and Dzhirkvelov.
25. James Benjamin, Director of Operations, CIA, in *Soviet Covert Action – the Forgery Offensive*.
26. Bittman, pp. 104–7 for forgeries in NATO countries.
27. Shultz and Godson, pp. 153–4.
28. *Sunday Express*, 26 October 1986; *Soviet Influence Activities* (US 1987)
29. *Soviet Active Measures*; Shultz and Godson make a detailed analysis of the newsletter's contents, pp. 133–49; see also Pincher: *The Secret Offensive*, pp. 118–20 and Bittman, pp. 81–2.
30. *Soviet Active Measures*; Pincher, *The Secret Offensive*, pp. 120–1 and Bittman, pp. 86–7.
31. Ilya Dzhirkvelov: *Secret Servant*, p. 179.

32. *Soviet Active Measures*.
33. *Soviet Covert Action – The Forgery Offensive*.
34. Jonathan Steele: *The Limits of Soviet Power*, p. 13.
35. *Foreign Affairs and Military Intelligence*.
36. Thiery Wolton: *Le KGB en France*.
37. Henri Regnard: 'The theft of Western technology', in *The Journal of Defense and Diplomacy*, April 1984; also Wolton, p. 249.
38. Wolton, p. 252.
39. Regnard.
40. Wolton, p. 250.
41. *Intelligence Collection in the USSR Chamber of Commmerce and Industry*. According to this report, the Chamber has representatives in fourteen countries and each year hosts 200 trade exhibitions and 100 Western delegations to the Soviet Union.
42. Jay Tuck: *High-Tech Espionage* investigates some major cases and also considers the West's response through CoCom, the Coordinating Committee for East–West Trade, which has its headquarters in Paris and consists of most NATO members.
43. See my *Revolutionaries in Modern Britain*, pp. 183–5, for the background to the Spies for Peace and the original reference to their involvement in the freeing of Blake. H. Montgomery Hyde's 1987 biography of Blake, *George Blake – Superspy*, referred to the two Committee of 100 men only as 'Reynolds' and 'Potter'. *The Sunday Times* pursued the matter and on 4 October 1987 revealed their true identities. *The Daily Telegraph* of 19 April 1963 reported the Prague Radio broadcast. This, together with Frantisek August's evidence before a senate committee in 1976 that an Iraqi employed as a private secretary to Bertrand Russell was a Czech agent, poses some intriguing questions about the extent of Czech involvement in various aspects of this affair.
44. West: *A Matter of Trust*, p. 206.
45. ibid., pp. 207–9.
46. ibid., pp. 210–12 for the Cloude and Britten cases; Britten was sentenced to twenty-one years' imprisonment.
47. *The Times*, 25 September 1971.
48. Chapman Pincher: *Too Secret, Too Long*, p. 630.
49. West, *A Matter of Trust*, p. 227 for Bingham and Hinchcliffe.
50. Costi was gaoled for six years and Martianon for four years, and Abdoolcader for three; see West, *A Matter of Trust*, pp. 223–5.
51. *The Times*, 5 March 1974.
52. See Corson and Crowley, pp 357–66, West: *GCHQ*, pp. 253–5 and Pincher, *Too Secret, Too Long*, pp. 720–8. The Report of the Security Commission, Cmnd 8876, 1983, outlines Prime's career.
53. Pincher, p. 733.
54. ibid., pp. 735–8. Pincher does not refer to Gordievsky's part in the Bettaney affair; see West: *Molehunt*, pp. 196–201.
55. See Appendix IV for the complete list.
56. *The Times*, 23 April and 19 September 1985.
57. *Foreign Affairs Notes* (US State Department, January 1988)
58. Malcolm Hill: 'Soviet and Eastern European company activity in the United Kingdom and Ireland', in Geoffrey Hamilton (ed.): *Red Multinationals or Red Herrings?*

59. Brian Freemantle: *KGB*, p. 90.
60. For example, Carl McMillan of Carleton University, Canada; see Hamilton, p. 6.
61. The government published the findings in Bolshevism and Sinn Fein (parliamentary paper, Cmd 1326, 1921). This and other events are covered briefly in a report by the Institute for the Study of Terrorism: *IRA, INLA: Foreign Support and International Connections* (1988).
62. Sejna, pp. 147–9.
63. Freemantle, p. 89.
64. Dzhirkvelov, p. 179.
65. *The Times*, 30 April 1981.
66. *The Daily Telegraph*, 7 August 1981.

CHAPTER 8: A NEW BEGINNING?

1. Soviet Influence Activities.
2. Zhores Medvedev: *Gorbachev*, p. 254.
3. *The Times*, 29 and 30 March 1988
4. *The Times*, 23 June 1988.
5. *The Times*, 26 August 1988.
6. *The Times*, 23 September 1988.
7. *Soviet Active Measures in the Era of Glasnost* (United States Information Service, April 1988).
8. *Sunday Telegraph*, 22 November 1987.
9. *The Independent*, 24 November 1988.

Bibliography

OFFICIAL SOURCES AND DOCUMENTS

Unpublished
Files of the British Foreign Office, Cabinet Office and Home Office in the Public Record Office, Kew.

Published
A selection of papers dealing with relations between HMG and the Soviet Government 1921–7 (Cmd 2895, 1927).

Communist papers (Cmd 2682, 1926).

Documents illustrating the hostile activities of the Soviet Government and the Third International against Great Britain (Cmd 2894, 1927).

Lord Denning's Report (Cmd 2152, 1963).

Report of the Security Commission (Cmd 3856, 1968).

Report of the Security Commission (Cmd 8876, 1983).

Report of the Standing Security Commission (Cmd 2722, 1965).

Report of the Tribunal appointed to enquire into the Vassall Case and related matters (Cmd 2009, 1963).

Russian banks and Communist funds (Cmd 3125, 1928).

Security procedures in the Public Service (Cmd 1681, 1962).

Report of the Royal Commission to investigate the facts relating to and the circumstances surrounding the communication by public officials and other persons in positions of trust of secret and confidential information to agents of a foreign power (Ottawa 1946).

Report of the Royal Commission on Espionage (Sydney 1955).

Communist Bloc Intelligence Activities in the United States (Senate Sub-Committee Hearings, US Government Printing Office 1976).

Contemporary Soviet Propaganda and Disinformation (US Department of State 1987).

Foreign Affairs and Military Intelligence (Report of the Senate Select Committee, US Government Printing Office 1976).

Intelligence Collection in the USSR Chamber of Commerce and Industry (US Department of State 1987).

Soviet Active Measures (Senate Committee Hearings, US Government Printing Office 1982).

Soviet Covert Action – The Forgery Offensive (House of Representatives Sub-Committee Hearings, US Government Printing Office 1980).

Soviet Influence Activities: A Report on Active Measures and Propaganda 1986–7 (US Department of State 1987).

The CIA and the Media (House of Representatives Sub-Committee, US Government Printing Office 1978).

The Rote Kapelle: The CIA's History of Soviet Intelligence and Espionage Networks in Western Europe 1936–45 (University Publications of America 1979).

Y. V. Andropov: *Speeches and Writings* (Pergamon Press 1983).

Jane Degras (ed.): *Soviet Documents on Foreign Policy* (Oxford University Press 1951–3).

———: *The Communist International 1919–43, Documents* (Frank Cass 1971).

Graham Ross: *The Foreign Office and the Kremlin – British Documents on Anglo-Soviet Relations 1941–5* (Cambridge University Press 1984).

PUBLISHED WORKS BY FORMER SOVIET AND EAST EUROPEAN INTELLIGENCE OFFICERS AND AGENTS

Georges Agabekov: *OGPU – The Russian Secret Terror* (New York 1931).

Ismail Akhmedov: *In and Out of Stalin's GRU* (Arms and Armour Press 1984).

Ladislav Bittman: *The KGB and Soviet Disinformation* (Pergamon–Brassey's 1985).

Ilya Dzhirkvelov: *Secret Servant* (Collins 1987).

Alexander Foote: *Handbook for Spies* (Museum Press 1948).

Josef Frolik: *The Frolik Defection* (Leo Cooper 1975).

Anatoliy Golitsyn: *New Lies For Old* (The Bodley Head 1984).

Igor Gouzenko: *This Was My Choice* (Eyre & Spottiswoode 1948).

Harry Houghton: *Operation Portland* (Rupert Hart Davis 1972).

W.G. Krivitsky: *I Was Stalin's Agent* (Hamish Hamilton 1939).

Jürgen Kuczynski: *Memoiren* (Cologne 1983).

Stanislav Levchenko: *On the Wrong Side* (Pergamon–Brassey's 1988).

Gordon Lonsdale: *Spy* (Neville Spearman 1965).

Aleksei Myagov: *Inside the KGB* (Foreign Affairs Publishing 1976).

Alexander Orlov: *Handbook of Intelligence and Guerrilla Warfare* (University of Michigan 1963).

Kim Philby: *My Silent War* (MacGibbon and Kee 1968).

Elizabeth Poretsky: *Our Own People* (Oxford University Press 1969).

Jan Sejna: *We Will Bury You* (Sidgwick & Jackson 1982).

Viktor Suvorov: *Soviet Military Intelligence* (Grafton Books 1986).

————: *Spetsnaz* (Hamish Hamilton 1987).

Leopold Trepper: *The Great Game* (Michael Joseph 1977).

Jan Valtin: *Out of the Night* (New York 1941).

John Vassall: *Vassall: Autobiography of a Spy* (Sidgwick & Jackson 1975).

Ruth Werner: *Sonjas Rapport* (East Berlin 1982).

OTHER PUBLISHED WORKS

Christopher Andrew: *Secret Service* (Heinemann 1985).

John Barron: *KGB – The Secret Work of Soviet Secret Agents* (Hodder & Stoughton 1974).

————: *KGB Today – The Hidden Hand* (Hodder & Stoughton 1984).

Arnold Beichman and Mikhail Bernstam: *Andropov* (New York 1983).

George Bilainkin: *Maisky* (Allen & Unwin 1944).

Andrew Boyle: *The Climate of Treason* (Coronet edition 1980).

Noreen Branson: *History of the Communist Party of Great Britain, 1927–41* (Lawrence & Wishart 1985).

Gordon Brook-Shepherd: *The Storm Petrels* (Collins 1977).

E. H. Carr: *The Bolshevik Revolution*; *The Interregnum*; and *Socialism in One Country* in *A History of Soviet Russia* (Macmillan 1950–5).

————: *The Twilight of the Comintern 1930–5* (Macmillan 1982).

David Caute: *The Fellow Travellers* (Weidenfeld & Nicolson 1973).

Anthony Cave Brown and Charles B. MacDonald: *On a Field of Red* (Robert Hale 1982).

Robert Conquest: *The Great Terror* (Macmillan 1968).

E. H. Cookridge: *The Third Man* (Putnam 1968).

————: *George Blake Double Agent* (Hodder 1970).

W. R. Corson and R. T. Crowley: *The New KGB* (Harvester Press 1986).

Edward Crankshaw: *Khrushchev* (Collins 1966).

Richard Deacon: *'C': A Biography of Sir Maurice Oldfield* (Macdonald 1985).

————: *A History of the Russian Secret Service* (Grafton Books 1987).

Isaac Deutscher: *Stalin* (Pelican edition 1966).

Tom Driberg: *Ruling Passions* (Cape 1977).

Allen Dulles: *The Craft of Intelligence* (Weidenfeld & Nicolson 1963).

Martin Ebon: *The Andropov File* (Sidgwick & Jackson 1983).

Robin Edmonds: *Soviet Foreign Policy: The Brezhnev Years* (Oxford University Press 1983).

Christopher Farman: *The General Strike* (Hart-Davis 1972).

John Fisher: *Burgess and Maclean* (Robert Hale 1977).

M.R.D. Foot: *SOE 1940–6* (BBC 1984).

Brian Freemantle: *KGB* (Michael Jospeh 1982).

Leonard D. Gerson: *The Secret Police in Lenin's Russia* (Philadelphia 1976).

Anthony Glees: *The Secrets of the Service* (Cape 1987).

Gabriel Gorodetsky: *The Precarious Truce: Anglo–Soviet Relations 1924–7* (Cambridge University Press 1977).

Geoffrey Hamilton (ed.): *Red Multinationals or Red Herrings?* (Pinter Publishers 1986).

Ronald Hingley: *The Russian Secret Police* (Hutchinson 1970).

————: *The Russian Mind* (The Bodley Head 1977).

R. N. Carew Hunt: *The Theory and Practice of Communism* (Geoffrey Bles 1950).

Douglas Hyde: *I Believed* (Heinemann 1950).

H. Montgomery Hyde: *The Atom Bomb Spies* (Sphere Books 1982).

————: *George Blake – Superspy* (Constable 1987).

Bill Jones: *The Russia Complex* (Manchester University Press 1977).

Walter Kendall: *The Revolutionary Movement in Britain 1900–21* (Weidenfeld & Nicolson 1969).

Lesek Kolakowski: *Main Currents of Marxism* (Oxford University Press 1978).

Robert Lamphere and Tom Shachtman: *The FBI–KGB War* (W. H. Allen 1987).

George Leggett: *The Cheka* (Oxford University Press 1981).

Moshe Lewin: *The Gorbachev Phenomenon* (Century Hutchinson 1988).

David Lloyd George: *War Memoirs* (Odhams 1936).

Norman Lucas: *The Great Spy Ring* (Arthur Barker 1966).

Howard Machin (ed.): *National Communism in Western Europe* (Methuen 1983).

Anthony Masters: *The Man Who Was M* (Basil Blackwell 1984).

John S. Mather (ed.): *The Great Spy Scandal* (Daily Express 1955).

Zhores A. Medvedev: *Andropov* (Basil Blackwell 1983).

————: *Gorbachev* (Basil Blackwell 1988 edition).

Paul Mercer: *The Peace of the Dead* (Policy Research Publications 1986).

Francis Meynell: *My Lives* (The Bodley Head 1971).

Alan Moorehead: *The Traitors* (Hamish Hamilton 1952).

J. T. Murphy: *New Horizons* (The Bodley Head 1941).

John Murray: *A Spy Called Swallow* (W. H. Allen 1978).

F. S. Northedge and Audrey Wells: *Britain and Soviet Communism* (Macmillan 1982).

Alec Nove: *Stalinism And After* (Allen & Unwin 1975).

Bruce Page, David Leitch and Phillip Knightley: *Philby* (André Deutsch 1968).

Robert Payne: *The Life and Death of Lenin* (W. H. Allen 1964)

————: *The Rise and Fall of Stalin* (W. H. Allen 1966).

Henry Pelling: *The British Communist Party* (A. & C. Black 1975 edition).

Barrie Penrose and Simon Freeman: *Conspiracy of Silence* (Grafton Books 1987).

Max Perthus: *Henk Sneevliet* (Amsterdam 1978)

Chapman Pincher: *Inside Story* (Sidgwick & Jackson 1978).

————: *Their Trade Is Treachery* (Sidgwick & Jackson 1981).

————: *Too Secret, Too Long* (Sidgwick & Jackson 1984).

————: *The Secret Offensive* (Sidgwick & Jackson 1986).

John Reed: *Ten Days That Shook the World* (Communist Party of Great Britain 1926, Penguin edition 1966).

Clive Rose: *Campaigns Against Western Defence* (Macmillan 1985).

Harry Rositzke: *The KGB – The Eyes of Soviet Russia* (Sidgwick & Jackson 1982).

Leonard Schapiro: *The Government and Politics of the Soviet Union* (Hutchinson 1968 edition).

————: *The Communist Party of the Soviet Union* (Methuen 1970).

Patrick Seale and Maureen McConville: *Philby: The Long Road to Moscow* (Hamish Hamilton 1973).

Ronald Seth: *Forty Years of Soviet Spying* (Cassell 1965).

David Shub: *Lenin* (Pelican edition 1966).

Richard H. Shultz and Roy Godson: *Dezinformatsia: Active Measures in Soviet Strategy* (Pergamon–Brassey's 1984)

Andrew Sinclair: *The Red and the Blue* (Weidenfeld & Nicolson 1987).

Jonathan Steele: *The Limits of Soviet Power* (Penguin edition 1985).

Jonathan Steele and Eric Abraham: *Andropov in Power* (Martin Robertson 1983).

Michael Straight: *After Long Silence* (Collins 1983)

Douglas Sutherland: *The Fourth Man* (Secker and Warburg 1980).

A. J. P. Taylor: *English History 1914–45* (Oxford University Press 1965).

Hugh Thomas: *John Strachey* (Eyre Methuen 1973).

———: *Armed Truce – The Beginnings of the Cold War 1945–6* (Hamish Hamilton 1986).

Nikolai Tolstoy: *Stalin's Secret War* (Cape 1981).

Hugh Trevor-Roper: *The Philby Affair* (William Kimber 1968).

Jay Tuck: *High-Tech Espionage* (Sidgwick & Jackson 1986).

Robert E. Tucker: *The Soviet Political Mind* (Allen & Unwin 1972).

James L. Tyson: *Target America* (Chicago 1981).

Richard H. Ullman: *Anglo-Soviet Relations 1917–21* (3 vols) (Princeton 1961–72).

Edward van der Roehr: *The Shadow Network* (Robert Hale 1983).

Nigel West: *MI5* (The Bodley Head 1981).

———: *A Matter of Trust – MI5 1945–72* (Weidenfeld & Nicolson 1982).

———: *MI6* (Weidenfeld & Nicolson 1983).

———: *Molehunt* (Weidenfeld & Nicolson 1987).

Robert Chadwell Williams: *Klaus Fuchs, Atom Spy* (Harvard 1987).

Charles A. Willoughby: *Sorge: Soviet Master Spy* (William Kimber 1952).

Thiery Wolton: *Le KGB en France* (Paris 1986).

Peter Wright: *Spycatcher* (Viking Penguin edition, New York 1987)

Index

218